Classes on Modern Poets and the Art of Poetry

CLASSES ON MODERN POETS AND THE ART OF POETRY

JAMES DICKEY

EDITED BY DONALD J. GREINER

FOREWORD BY PAT CONROY

University of South Carolina Press

Text © 2004 The Estate of James Dickey
Editorial matter © 2004 University of South Carolina

Published in Columbia, South Carolina, by the
University of South Carolina Press

Manufactured in the United States of America

08 07 06 05 04   5 4 3 2 1

Library of Congress Cataloging-in-Publication Data

Dickey, James.
    Classes on modern poets and the art of poetry / James Dickey ; edited
by Donald J. Greiner ; foreword by Pat Conroy.
       p. cm.
    Includes bibliographical references and index.
    ISBN 1-57003-528-8 (alk. paper)
    1. American poetry—20th century—History and criticism. 2. English
poetry—20th century—History and criticism. 3. American poetry—
19th century—History and criticism. 4. English poetry—19th
century—History and criticism. 5. Poetics. 6. Poetry. I. Greiner,
Donald J. II. Title.
PS323.D53 2004
811'.509—dc22

                                                          2003020813

A list of permissions appears at the back of this volume and constitutes an
extension of this copyright page.

Frontispiece: James Dickey teaching during his first year at the University of
South Carolina, 1969. *Courtesy of University Publications, University of South
Carolina*

"I was a good teacher . . . not because I was especially conscientious, but because I loved what I was doing."
—James Dickey to James Wright, 6 August 1959

Contents

Contents

ILLUSTRATIONS

Foreword

In the spring of 1969, I was sitting on the porch swing of a small house at 505 Port Republic Street in Beaufort, South Carolina. The azaleas were at their peak, and I admired their profligate beauty as I sat there wondering how I would go about turning myself into a writer of both substance and worth. I had yet to publish a single word, and I had already been out of the Citadel for two full years. Though I was trying to complete at least one poem a day, I still could not make a sentence do what I commanded it to do or sound the way I wanted it to sound. I returned to a houseful of mediocre poetry each night. Everything I wrote was stillborn, inessential, bloated. I was the only one in the world who believed I was a writer, and I was looking for a sign.

Inside the house, my friend Tim Belk finished his tutorial for the day by putting a flourish on Mozart's 21st Concerto, second movement. Tim taught literature at the local branch of the University of South Carolina and was appalled at my complete lack of knowledge of classical music. He was leading me by the nose through the greatest symphonies and concertos ever written. He also had the most refined taste of any reader I had ever met. Once, Tim had brought me a copy of Walker Percy's *The Moviegoer* on this same porch in the year it came out. Later, when I admitted I had never heard of Flannery O'Connor, he made me sit and finish "A Good Man Is Hard to Find" during a summer rain. He demanded that I read Willie Morris's wonderful memoir, *North Toward Home,* because he thought I would discover an invaluable map about how a southern boy goes about living a life that will bring him across the mighty Hudson River into the great publishing houses of Manhattan.

But on this day, Tim Belk delivered me a book that was beyond a sign or mere marvel; this time Tim handed me a book that would change my life. It was James Dickey's *Poems, 1957–67,* and Tim opened it to a poem called "The Lifeguard."

"I think this is the guy you're after," Tim said.

And I began to read.

In a stable of boats I lie still,
From all sleeping children hidden.

When I finished the poem, Tim called from the house, "Next, read 'The Performance.'" I read about Donald Armstrong doing handstands to defy the Japanese captors who would soon decapitate him and a fellow prisoner of war. "The Leap" came next, and I learned of the suicide of Jane McNaughton Hill who hurled herself in despair off an office building, causing the poet to remember a day in a dancing class when he watched the pretty, athletic Jane McNaughton leap up to touch a streamer that decorated the hall. When my own brother, Tom Conroy, threw himself off a fourteen-story building in Columbia in 1994, I turned to Dickey's poem for the great comfort it offered many years after it was written.

Tim Belk had been right; this was the guy I was after. Tim had just attended a poetry reading that James Dickey had given in Savannah, and he declared that Dickey was the most passionate, mesmerizing reader of his own poems he had ever encountered. With Dickey, Tim felt he was in the presence of a real artist who inhabited every single word he wrote or spoke; although ever the aesthete, Tim said that Dickey's poetry could not touch the work of the magisterial T. S. Eliot

I disagreed that day and have held fast to that disagreement for all of my writing life. Give me two volumes of T. S. Eliot's collected works, then throw in five copies of Ezra Pound's cantos. Tempt me with Wallace Stevens and throw in Theodore Roethke for pocket change. Add Elizabeth Bishop or Marianne Moore, and I begin to waver because I revere those women and their bodies of work. Still, I stand my ground and remain immovable in my resolve to hold on to my volume of James Dickey's *Poems, 1957–67,* and would not trade his work for a baker's dozen of all the luminous poets I have just listed. I do not mean to cast doubt on their greatness but to illustrate the force of Dickey's poetry on me. I felt an accordance and collision of my spirit. His words were meticulous, possessed, bee-stung, and sunshot with all the heart and mystery that could be coaxed from the dark caverns of language. His poems had a great immediacy for me, as though he had written them by dipping a pen in his own bloodstream and scrawled them across my face. I had discovered the poet of my life, the one whose work I would hold up to the light—this was greatness as I defined it. I would never write another word in my entire life without asking myself, "Is this as good as James Dickey's work? Can this language I have just put on paper compare to the best of Dickey?" No, came the answer every single time, but I have been trying to achieve the level of Dickey every time I have sat down to write since Tim Belk handed me those fabulous poems over thirty years ago. Not since I had first encountered the high passes of Thomas Wolfe's prose when I was sixteen had I reacted to another writer's art with such joyful completion. His words sated me, called out my name, and granted me entry into a country of language where delicacy could haunt fire and where great cruelty could shelter itself behind the lilies and the Queen Anne's lace of a stunted garden. Though Thomas Wolfe could sometimes lose himself in the cloud cover and stammerings, Dickey's language was diamond-hard, exact, and breathtakingly pure. When James Dickey was good, one would not choose to alter a single word. He had a gift for precision that left you bedazzled but not exhausted. I found him in May on Tim Belk's porch on Port Republic Street, and James Dickey was carry-on luggage for me the rest of my life. By the time of his death, I think I had read every word Dickey had ever written in his legendary, controversial, and transcendent lifetime.

In 1970, the superintendent of schools in Beaufort County fired me from my teaching job on Daufuskie Island for "gross neglect of duty, conduct unbecoming a professional educator, AWOL, and insubordination." I began writing the book that would appear in 1972 as *The Water Is Wide*. Again, I fought against a prose style that seemed inadequate for the task at hand. I lacked mastery, vividness, and my style seemed pedestrian when I wanted it soaring at a fever pitch. Dickey's volume of poetry rested in a place of honor on my desk, and I would open it up when I wanted to know how English could sound in the hands of a real writer. I turned to his poetry for inspiration, and I kept hoping that if I read him deeply enough I could steal the fire that Dickey brought to the task of composing sentences that shimmered with both jewel and mystery.

When I finished the first version of *The Water Is Wide,* I wrote Mr. Dickey, praising his poetry with all the earnestness of a natural-born sycophant, and asking if I could audit his two courses in the fall of 1971. He wrote me back that he was delighted I found pleasure in his work, that it was fine if I audited his courses, but I would have to get permission from the proper authorities. I framed that letter, and it stands on my bookshelf today, the paper blackening around the edges, but that signature still bold and authoritative.

Twice a week I would make the two-and-a-half hour trip to Columbia in my yellow '68 Volkswagen convertible to sit in the classroom of James Dickey. As his student for one semester, I studied Mr. Dickey with a cold eye and a scrutiny that bordered on obsession. I tried to coax out the secrets of how a great writer moves and acts and postures as he is let loose in the classroom to face those hungry regiments of students eager to learn the passwords that will carry them to fame and cachet—the illustriousness that candor, awe, and genius bestow on so very few. When he entered a room, James Dickey took possession of it, mastered its corners and shadows, adjusted the spotlight to himself, and then he drew the class into himself with an all-encompassing, feral, yet pretty-eyed gaze. Though I was raised among athletes and fighter pilots, I have never met a man who reveled in the deep pools and wells of manhood as he did. Around campus, it would not have surprised me to see James Dickey urinating on trees and lampposts and sorority houses, marking his territory with the swaggering authority of a full-grown Kalahari lion. He gloried in an unapologetic maleness which was only part of his complete mastery of the classroom environment.

That year, Dickey moved across campus as a force of nature, in the prime of his life and his career, well-known and noticed wherever he appeared with his huge, marvelous hats, his guitars, and his morose entourage that seemed to trail along behind him, grateful for the gift of his shadow. His novel *Deliverance* had come out in 1970 to extravagant reviews, and he had spent the previous summer rubbing shoulders with Burt Reynolds and Jon Voight, two of the leading young actors of their time. Dickey received a credit for the film script, was publishing regularly in the *New Yorker,* and seemed quite content to be the most well-known and public poet around. It was both fascinating and a high honor to be taught by one of the most famous writers of his time.

I found Dickey a mesmerizing, fully engaged teacher, an enchanter who could enter into the depths and reveries of any poem and bring back its ores and fluids and essences dripping from his hands, eager to share the wonders he had discovered. When he read another poet's work, he threw himself into it with a completion and generosity that surprised me. As an intellectual, Dickey seemed to have read every poet of importance who had published in any of the world's languages. Not only had he read them, they had become part of the great, voracious engine he employed when he faced a class that had gathered to learn why poetry was one of the most important things in the world. I watched his complete immersion into the spirit of teaching that is also the great glory of this book. When that insatiable, prowling intelligence of his turned toward art, James Dickey was in a league of his own. No one loved to drift into waters where human beings had never been before or were not meant to go, but that is exactly what he required of his classes with every poem we read together. In his classes, we were fully expected to give ourselves up to poetry with a completeness that was sacred in nature.

Mr. Dickey introduced us to dozens of poets I had never heard of, to poets he both revered and reviled, yet he taught with such passion and open-heartedness that he rarely condescended to any poet whose work he read aloud to the class. His singular voice, deep and southern-fried along the edges, would deliver the most perfect and accurate rendition of that poem in homage to both the art of poetry and the seriousness he brought to the task of teaching. In the four months I was with him, James Dickey changed every single thing I thought about writing and art. This book explains why the changes were necessary.

In the world according to Dickey, the only limitations to art were the blindfolds and restraints we would choose to hobble our own free-flowing imaginations. Yet, to imagine alone was insufficient, for then we had to work in a fever and in night-sweats and all the icy fury that great writing demands from all of us who try to enter its broken, demanding ranks and eerie sodalities with the idea of creation on our minds. He spoke of the egregiousness of the craft of writing, the boldness required by it, the helium lift and cry of storm as the language broke in currents around us. Be afraid of nothing, he would say. Listen to what is real and essential inside yourself. Make yourself ready to embrace the spirit of the unknown and the unknowable. Drive yourself to the limits. Let nothing get in your way. Be open to all things, fully alive, the poet with arms outstretched, ready for anything the world or God would fling your way in the bright abundance of our supple language. James Dickey's swagger and strut and braggadocio were all part of the package, but he could back it up with a body of work that was both spectacular and intimidating to me. When he turned to poetry—others poets', his own, or ours—his voice became incantatory, priest-like with poetry. Dickey built his mansion of art and because of his greatness and sufficiency as a teacher, let us enter with him, and sang to us, like Homer at Troy, the loveliest, most consequential words ever written by the best poets who ever lived.

This book brings those long-ago days back to me, and Don Greiner has done a superb job in assembling the material for this marvelous, illuminatory book. It is the first step in a correction of Dickey's literary career which took a hit, I think, by the appearance of the most malicious biography ever written about an American writer. I think the sheer magnificence and ambition of Dickey's writing will carry the day before this story is over. I know there are hundreds of writers, like me, who think he is one of the best writers who ever lived. I thought it then, when I sat through two classes without ever speaking a word, spellbound by the joy the man took in teaching, and I think it now. He was shot through with words; they spilled out of him, and he would have had it no other way.

In the chilling coda that makes up the last three pages of this essential book, the real James Dickey proffers his final, unassailable, and unanswerable gift to all the students he ever taught. It is his philosophy of teaching and art boiled down to a drop of burning elixir, not a word wasted, not a word too much or less. He is saying goodbye to his students on the last day he would ever teach. He lays down his credo in words that deserve to be carved in stone, and he writes a love song to the poets of the world. James Dickey waits for the last day to do the best teaching of his life. It is not a poem he delivers; he gives his students something better and rarer and deeper: James Dickey gives them the last prayer he ever wrote.

There is a poem James Dickey wrote that I have always loved, yet never have I seen it collected in any anthology. It is called "The Bee," and it recreates the day when Dickey's son, Chris, was stung by a bee, and the boy bolts in pain and shock toward a dangerous California highway. Dickey sprints after his son, feeling slow and awkward, until he calls on his younger self for help in the emergency with the thrilling words: "Old wingback, come to life." Dickey recalls his football days in college where he was shaped and strengthened by coaches who urged him to do more and more. The poet reaches his son just before Chris stumbled out into the traffic, and the panting, older Dickey gives thanks to those rough-hewn men who shouted and cursed him to reach even higher levels of performance. It ends with a line I wish I had written to one of my coaches: "Coach Norton, I am your boy."

But I can write it to one of my teachers out of praise and awe and pride that I was once his student and that he lit me up and took possession of me in every class he taught, and my gratitude toward him and his example and his art leads me to say: "James Dickey, I'm still your boy."

Pat Conroy

ACKNOWLEDGMENTS

Acknowledgments are a pleasure to write. Ward Briggs, Carolina Distinguished Professor of Classics at the University of South Carolina, helped identify references to Latin writers. Both Professor Briggs and Benjamin Franklin V, professor of English at the University of South Carolina, advised me on my introductory essay and gave me the benefit of their long friendships with James Dickey. Patrick Scott, associate librarian for special collections and professor of English at the University of South Carolina, tracked down information about some of Dickey's more arcane references. Gordon Van Ness, professor of English at Longwood College and a Dickey scholar, generously answered my queries. Kate Byrd, reference librarian, Thomas Cooper Library, University of South Carolina, supplied bibliographical information that I could not find; Paul Schultz, special collections cataloger, Thomas Cooper Library, vetted the list of sources. Also at the University of South Carolina, Brian Harmon and Jennifer Reid served as research assistants and saved me hours of time while they confirmed names, dates, and titles; Amber Coker transcribed my notations. My greatest debt is to Matthew J. Bruccoli, Emily Brown Jeffries Professor of English at the University of South Carolina. I am grateful to be on the faculty at the University of South Carolina, an institution that supports serious work.

This book is for Ellen and for Bronwen Dickey.

Donald J. Greiner

Introduction

> I have always believed that teaching is the second greatest occupation
> that the human mind and energy can undertake. . . . the *most* important
> is learning.
>
> —James Dickey, *The Weather of the Valley*

James Dickey (1923–1997) was a major American poet for nearly forty years.
From his student days at Vanderbilt University in the late 1940s to his death at
the University of South Carolina in January 1997, he was committed to the
study of poetry and the challenge of writing it. But he was also always a
teacher. The class sessions gathered in this volume date from a course Dickey
organized at the University of South Carolina for academic year 1971–72. They
constitute a veritable encyclopedia of modern British and American poetry.
How he emerged from his birthplace in the suburbs of Atlanta, Georgia, to
fame as a writer and a professorship at a large university is the story of a man
determined to let poetry shape his life.

After studying civil engineering for only the fall 1942 semester at Clem-
son A&M College, James Dickey joined the U.S. Army Air Corps in Decem-
ber. Although he later exaggerated his war exploits, it would nevertheless be an
understatement to observe that his combat record was distinguished. Dickey
served as a night-fighter radar observer in the Pacific war, was part of the
"island-hopping" campaign against the Japanese, earned five Bronze Stars and
promotion to second lieutenant, and was finally mustered out of the Air Corps
on 1 March 1946.

In summer 1946 he enrolled at Vanderbilt University with the aid of the
G.I. Bill and declared an English major. He was graduated with a B.A. in
English (*magna cum laude,* Phi Beta Kappa) in 1949. He immediately entered
the graduate school at Vanderbilt and earned the M.A. in English in 1950 after
writing a thesis on the poetry of Herman Melville.

Following graduation Dickey began a long two decades that alternated
between the university world and the corporate office. His stateside military
duty during the Korean War interrupted both his life and career from March

1951 to August 1952, but sandwiched around his second tour of Army service were two terms as an instructor of English at Rice Institute (fall 1950, and fall 1952–summer 1954). He continued his teaching career at the University of Florida (September 1955–April 1956), Reed College (January 1963–May 1964), San Fernando Valley State College (September 1964–June 1965), the University of Wisconsin–Milwaukee (summer 1965 and July 1966), and the University of Wisconsin–Madison (February–March 1966). He then found his permanent academic home. In summer 1968 the University of South Carolina named Dickey poet-in-residence and professor of English, a position he held until his death.

For a while in the middle of his peripatetic teaching career, he successfully worked as an advertising copywriter for McCann-Erickson in Atlanta (1956–61), but for Dickey the business world was no more than a means to the end of writing poetry. He was always a poet. Like most fledgling artists, he needed living expenses and time. He got both. Two prestigious fellowships provided the opportunity and the funds. The Sewanee Review Fellowship supported Dickey and his family at Cap d'Antibes on the French Riviera from August 1954 to June 1955, and the Guggenheim Fellowship sent him to Europe and Italy from February to June 1962. While there he wrote many of the poems that would soon propel him to fame.

■   ■   ■

Yet the story of "James Dickey, Great American Poet" begins much earlier than the fellowships, the teaching stints, the business connections, and even the student years at Vanderbilt. The spark that fired Dickey toward poetry was struck in the hell of World War II. An indifferent though certainly acceptable secondary-school student at North Fulton High School (Buckhead, Georgia), from which he was graduated in spring 1941, and at the Darlington School (Rome, Georgia), from which he received a certificate in spring 1942, he did not commit to books, poetry, and learning during his teenage years, unlike other celebrated American poets before him: Robert Frost, T. S. Eliot, Ezra Pound. His adolescence was defined by activities typical of a middle-class boy during the 1930s—football, girls, music, and movies.

World War II changed all that. While training at Fort Myers, Florida, and thus before being shipped to the battle of the Pacific, Dickey sent a letter with a list of books to his mother with instructions to "cash in some of my bonds and get these." Among "these" were *Selected Poems of Conrad Aiken, Poetical Works* by James Thomson, *The Sun Also Rises* and *A Farewell to Arms* by Ernest Hemingway, *An American Tragedy* by Theodore Dreiser, and *Ulysses* by James Joyce

(*Crux* 8). This unexpected letter is postmarked 25 February 1944, and it sets the tone for the correspondence Dickey wrote from stateside bases and Pacific airfields during the remainder of hostilities. No one would have predicted what can only be described as a sea change.

A key letter is the one postmarked 29 June 1944 and mailed from Hammer Field, Fresno, California. Writing to his "Folks," Dickey first disparages an article in *Life* magazine that ranks "my boy Thomas Wolfe" in fifth place among an accounting of "the ten leading novelists of the last two decades." This opinion is an early indication of the judgments and appraisals that he would later develop to impressive effect in the lectures collected here. He then surprisingly adds three sentences that forecast the next fifty-three years of his life:

> When I get out of the Army I'm going someplace where I can really get a good education in letters, whether it be L.S.U., the University of Virginia, Harvard, or Oxford. I am convinced that the only thing I will ever have any interest in as a career is authorship, or something akin to it. Though I have not blossomed out as a John Keats, I *have* shown an infinitesimal scrap of talent and originality in my writing, which is more than I have done in any other line of educational endeavor. (*Crux* 10)

"A good education in letters." The War helped him get it.

Writing to his mother from Hammer Field in a letter postmarked 20 October 1944, Dickey briefly mentions the death of his roommate "last night." He seems much more concerned with a poem he has composed and included with the letter, "written in blank unrhymed verse, in a rather involved metrical pattern, stemming no doubt from several of my favorites (Robert Bridges's 'London Snow' was perhaps the unknowing godfather of this unworthy piece)" (*Crux* 11). The poem is titled "Rain in Darkness," and it stands as a precursor to "a career in authorship, or something akin to it." Bridges is prominently featured in the class sessions that Dickey prepared twenty-seven years later.

By 1945 he and his 418th Night Fighter Squadron had been transferred to the Philippines. In a letter to his parents postmarked 6 February 1945 he asks for "any of" the poet Roy Campbell's books (*Crux* 12). Following the pattern of most of his war letters, he reports what he can of the battles and of his condition, inquires about the family, encloses his own poems, and then requests books.

> Here's a short unrhymed cadence I wrote today on clouds. . . . Have any of my books come in yet? (2 April 1945, Philippines, *Crux* 15)

> Mom, look in my Ernest Dowson book and copy out the poem which ends "Mother of God." (29 May 1945, Philippines, *Crux* 17)

Preparing for war, 1943. *Courtesy of James Dickey Collection, Department of Rare Books & Special Collections, Thomas Cooper Library, University of South Carolina*

Say, Mom, will you do me a favor and start buying a New York Times every Sunday and saving the book review section for me? (16 August 1945, Okinawa, *Crux* 24)

I sure am glad Delmore Schwartz's books came in. I wanted his books more than any, except those by Kenneth Patchen (Hint, hint!). (6 October 1945, Okinawa, *Crux* 25)

These and other letters document the primary reversal in the life of James Dickey. Committed for more than three years to the battles of World War II— "When I get home I'll tell you just how miserable the war was" (8 November 1945, Tokyo, *Crux* 27)—he somehow discovered the life of the mind and the art of poetry. Yet the most remarkable of his war letters is a long epistle to his mother postmarked 19 July? 1945 from Okinawa (*Crux* 20). The letter begins "Please order" and then goes on for six pages with nothing but lists of books he needs. Among the several dozen volumes requested are collections by Mark Van Doren, Allen Tate, W. H. Auden, C. Day Lewis, Richard Aldington, Dylan Thomas, Stephen Spender, Robert Penn Warren, and Randall Jarrell—all important writers who eventually became the focus for many of the expansive commentaries collected in this book. Even while being cited for bravery with five Bronze Stars during the conflict with Japan, James Dickey was already planning, as it were, his syllabus for English 760 at the University of South Carolina.

The G.I. Bill took him to Vanderbilt in 1946. Associated since the 1920s with literary activity in general and with the Fugitive poets in particular, Vanderbilt turned out to be the school where, as Dickey phrased it in the 29 June 1944 correspondence to his parents, he could "really get a good education in letters." Along with the past but still felt presences of formidable poets and critics Robert Penn Warren and Allen Tate, writers Dickey had begun to read while on active duty in the Pacific, Vanderbilt offered daily access to such renowned literary specialists as Donald Davidson, himself a member of the Fugitives.

Now a war veteran/undergraduate, Dickey began forwarding his apprentice poems not to his parents in letters home but to the Vanderbilt student literary magazine, *The Gadfly*. The four poems that he published in *The Gadfly* between 1947 and 1949 marked the start of his literary career. He held onto the poems as evidence of his initiation into what he called the world of "letters," and he later published them in an edition limited to 230 copies and appropriately titled *Veteran Birth: The Gadfly Poems, 1947–1949* (Winston-Salem, N.C.: Palaemon Press, 1978). It is instructive to note that he inscribed my copy of *Veteran Birth* with the following comment: "These first peeps from the chick—a few good peeps—not many." Those "peeps," however, led to his first professional poem, "The Shark at the Window," which he wrote while still a student at Vanderbilt and which *Sewanee Review* accepted for publication in its April–June 1951 issue.

Soon after he left Vanderbilt in 1950 for a teaching appointment at Rice, Dickey began keeping notebooks (now housed at Emory University) in which he jotted down subjects for poems, musings on literary techniques, reactions to books and articles, and, most important, drafts of poems and novels. The entries are rarely dated and follow no particular plan, and they do not extend beyond the middle 1950s, but they constitute an invaluable extension of the war letters that he mailed to his family and in which he articulated his first, passionate commitment to poetry. Although the notebooks may be profitably read for both biographical and artistic reasons, they figure significantly in the present context because they contain germs of the formal commentary he later organized for delivery at the University of South Carolina in 1971–72.

Once again, as he does in the war letters, Dickey compiles lists of writers he wants to read in depth. Such poets as Conrad Aiken, Keith Douglas, Dylan Thomas, Gerard Manley Hopkins, and W. H. Auden are first cited in the letters, then commented on in the notebooks, and finally discussed in thorough and erudite fashion in the lectures. This process of development took an astonishing twenty-seven years, from 1944 to 1971, a testimony to Dickey's serious, lifelong commitment to his art.

A sampling from the notebooks illustrates the musings of a mind.

Yeats: masks and antimasks—self and other. (*Striking In* 15)

If my poetry becomes image-bound, a study of E. A. Robinson should work to generalize and abstract it. (*Striking In* 98)

John Peale Bishop . . . did the most he could with a second-hand instrument played with intelligence and discretion. He is not a great poet. (*Striking In* 71)

Study Emily Dickinson's poems wherein she deals with abstractions (pain, fear, love, etc.) without images and without adjectives. (*Striking In* 86)

To count only the accents in the line and to ignore the number of unaccented syllables (Hopkins). (*Striking In* 142)

The notebooks contain thousands of similar observations. Most found their way into the lectures.

While keeping the notebooks and teaching during the early 1950s, Dickey began placing poems with regularity in such major journals as *Poetry, Sewanee*

Review, and *Kenyon Review.* He then published his first collection, *Into the Stone,* in 1960 as part of Scribners' Poets of Today series, and his career as a renowned American poet was launched. Public recognition in the form of official honors came quickly. A partial list suggests the impact of Dickey's poetry from the late 1950s until his death in 1997:

1959—Vachel Lindsay Prize for eight poems published in *Poetry;*

1966—Melville Cane Award from the Poetry Society of America for *Buckdancer's Choice;*

1966—National Book Award for *Buckdancer's Choice;*

1966–68—Consultant in Poetry at the Library of Congress (the appointment is now called Poet Laureate);

1971—Prix Medicis (France) for *Deliverance;*

1972—induction into the National Institute of Arts and Letters;

1981—Levinson Prize for five *Puella* poems in *Poetry;*

1988—induction into the American Academy of Arts and Letters;

1996—Harriet Monroe Prize for lifetime achievement in poetry.

For nearly forty years Dickey garnered these and other honors, not to mention the broader public recognition he achieved with such high-profile activities as covering the Apollo 11 liftoff for *Life* (1 July 1969), publishing the best-selling *Deliverance* (March 1970), and reading "The Strength of Fields" at the inauguration ceremony for President Jimmy Carter (January 1977).

Through it all—through the awards and the acclaim and the applause—Dickey was first a poet and a teacher. To say that he embellished his own myth with occasional outrageous public behavior and consistently sharp-tongued published opinions is only to remark that he played to the hilt the role of private-artist-as-public-figure, a role earlier perfected by Walt Whitman, Robert Frost, and Ezra Pound, not to mention Ernest Hemingway and Norman Mailer. Dickey was "good copy." The difference is that unlike even Frost, who taught off and on for only part of his career, Dickey was committed to the classroom, as the lectures confirm. Even when he was dying from acute hepatitis and fibrosis of the lungs, James Dickey taught. On 14 January 1997 he met his last seminar and, with the aid of an oxygen tank, lectured on the meaning of poetry. Five days later he died.

■ ■ ■

The transcriptions of these lectures were found after Dickey's death. They may be read profitably along with the letters in *Crux* and the notebooks in *Striking In,* as well as with the several volumes of formal criticism that he published between 1964 and 1983, among them *The Suspect in Poetry* (Madison, Minn.: Sixties Press, 1964); *Babel to Byzantium: Poets and Poetry Now* (New York: Farrar, Straus and Giroux, 1968); *Self-Interviews* (Garden City, N.Y.: Doubleday, 1970); *Sorties* (Garden City, N.Y.: Doubleday, 1971); and *Night Hurdling: Poems, Essays, Conversations, Commencements, and Afterwords* (Bloomfield Hills, Mich., and Columbia, S.C.: Bruccoli Clark, 1983).

When Dickey was not writing poetry, he was writing about poetry—in letters, in notebooks, in essays, in reviews, in lectures—and he did so with as much range and learning as any major American poet in the last half of the twentieth century. The commentary that comprises the class sessions dates from academic year 1971–72. The lectures were planned and delivered soon after he took up full-time residence at the University of South Carolina in 1969 following his official appointment in 1968. These were years of triumph for Dickey, just after his winning the National Book Award in 1966, his appointment to what is known today as Poet Laureate for 1966–68, and his fame as the author of *Deliverance* in 1970.

Despite the spotlight, he treated his professorship seriously. Unlike many writers, painters, and musicians who rely on universities to fill the venerable role once played by the Renaissance patron and who then maneuver to teach as few students and as few classes as possible, Dickey faithfully taught two classes each semester. Except for the normal round of occasional leaves or sabbaticals, he routinely was assigned English 600/601 (Verse Composition), a workshop, and English 760 (Contemporary British and American Poetry), a graduate-level survey.

In academic year 1978–79, the University of South Carolina reconfigured the survey into English 760 (American Poetry Since 1900) and English 761 (Survey of Twentieth-Century British and American Poetry). From then on, Dickey's standard assignment was English 761 and the seminar in verse composition. The latter was a two-semester course that required "consent of instructor." The former was an open-enrollment survey that Dickey often, but not always, designed in unexpected fashion: one term on contemporary American poets, the other on contemporary British poets. The lectures were originally researched and delivered for the one-semester English 760 course, but it is clear from the sheer number and variety of the poets assigned for close reading and discussion that Dickey assumed many students would commit to the survey for two terms. His secretary first taped the class sessions and then transcribed the taped commentary to typescript.

Several of the typescripts feature Dickey's holograph corrections and additions. He used the latter as prompts for ad-libbed asides on the topic at hand, as when, for example, he added a holograph comment to the discussion of Emily Dickinson: "Whicher on scenery here." He refers to the critic George Frisbie Whicher's scholarship on Dickinson and the town of Amherst, Massachusetts, where she lived. Similarly, in his penetrating analysis of Gerard Manley Hopkins, Dickey appends the holograph prompt, "Quote myself on 'Wreck of the Deutschland' here." The reference is to an essay on "The Wreck of the Deutschland" that he wrote in 1966 and later used as an introduction to a special edition of twelve hundred copies of Hopkins's poem (Boston: David Godine, 1971). The point is that he lightly revised several of the transcriptions of the taped commentary, thereby indirectly indicating that the editor of the typescripts should proceed with an equally light hand.

■ ■ ■

Throughout the lectures, Dickey's confidence in his students sets the tone. As he remarks in the discussion on Hopkins: "And if there's any justification for a class like this, it's that it's a class for people who do some serious thinking about poetry." There is no question that Dickey "seriously thought." Although educated at Vanderbilt, a university associated with the then-prevailing New Criticism, he was never an advocate of that theoretical position. Articulated in the 1920s, and dominant in literary discourse well into the 1960s, New Criticism posited that a work of art—a poem—was a self-contained whole to be read, debated, and understood apart from the artist's biography, historical and cultural context, or intention. Meaning is determined solely from the words on the page. Among the primary framers of New Criticism were Allen Tate, Robert Penn Warren, and John Crowe Ransom, the very poets associated with either Vanderbilt or the Fugitives, and who in turn played a major role in shaping Dickey's thinking about the theory and practice of poetry. Yet, as these lectures illustrate, Dickey was not a New Critic. In class after class, his method is consistent. He normally begins with an overview of the life of the poet under discussion, a tactic that New Criticism would dismiss as irrelevant. Historical context was important to Dickey. He then reads key poems for analysis and subsequent commentary on the poet's theories of composition before concluding the session with recommendations for secondary books and articles to consult—biographies, letters, criticism. His class sessions are not formally constructed presentations. Full of asides, witticisms, and afterthoughts, they suggest not the pontification of a scholar at an academic conference but the confident learning of a practicing poet who happens to enjoy being in the classroom.

Dickey's rationale for repudiating the New Critical approach to poetry and for including the secondary material about the poets is largely personal. James

Dickey was a reader. When he died, his home library had eighteen thousand volumes. For each class meeting, he entered the seminar room carrying a brief-case stuffed with the relevant books for the day—books from his own collection. An aside in the lecture on Thomas Hardy is pertinent here: "Again, like any class of this sort, I don't know how much you want, but I'll just put out what has meant something to me on the subject, and you can take whatever you want to get." An informed commentary on the biographies and criticism that "meant something" to him then followed.

This teaching method does not mean that Dickey was undiscriminating in his choice of secondary materials to offer the students. Of the thousands of books in his personal library, the ones that were certain to generate scornful dismissal were those written by critics who believe their commentary on the poetry is as enduring as the poems that initiated the comments. Note Dickey's irony in the session on Robert Bridges:

> The next stage would be a critic writing on critics of critics, and so on. We've reached that too. . . . As far as the poor poet was concerned, he was only someone who furnished the occasion for a brilliant critic to write something. . . . The critics say to the poet, "What do you know about poetry? I'm the critic. I know a lot more about it than you who merely produce it."

As he jokes in the discussion of Gerard Manley Hopkins, "I could go on and on in this pseudoscholarly way all afternoon; I mean, that ain't hard to do, if you've been to graduate school." His audience was, of course, graduate students. He was nudging them toward the poetry, not the criticism, and he did not hesitate to identify the critics he disliked or recommended. For example, he mentions both Yvor Winters and Randall Jarrell in the lecture on Bridges. Of the former: "I hated him and he hated me . . . he's an excessively bad critic of some importance." Of the latter: "Randall Jarrell is the finest literary critic of my time."

Yet the primary focus of these lectures is the poets and their art. Dickey offers a provocative definition of poetry in the discussion of Alun Lewis: "It's not 'literature'; it's that human communication in depth that the best poetry is." To say that a poet is great is not to praise indiscriminately. "Human communication in depth" can miss the mark. Dickey cautions the audience during the session on William Butler Yeats: "There are small writers that you can like without equivocation or without reservation, but I think there are no great writers that you have no reservation about whether or not you like them." Toward the end of this volume, in the lecture on Dylan Thomas, he identifies two of his choices for greatness: "Of the great original users of the English language, who brought something truly original to the use of English in poetry, the two finest, the most original in the whole canon of English poetry, are Gerard Manley Hopkins and Dylan Thomas. Hopkins and Dylan Thomas. But of the two, the more original is Dylan Thomas."

Original use of the language is one of Dickey's criteria for effective poetry. Another is articulated in his disarmingly simple question about T. E. Hulme: "What is his importance to us?" As his moving reminiscence about reading Walter de la Mare shows, a poet's "importance" to a reader is not always predicated on aesthetic criteria. Personal reactions merit attention. Dickey says of de la Mare: "I would put forward this collection of his called *Come Hither* as the greatest of all Christmas presents. . . . You won't want to give it away." Yet the joy of the recommendation is sharply tempered by an aside in which he recalls his discovery of de la Mare. During a lull in the Pacific battles of World War II, he picked up de la Mare's *Behold, This Dreamer!* "out of the mud and the coral slop on Okinawa. I had never heard of Walter de la Mare. I just wanted something to read. I read every word." Dickey's war reading led to the expansive learning that shaped the two poles of his long career: poetry and teaching.

His comment on A. E. Housman is an indirect illustration not only of his confidence in his learning but also of his willingness to debate ideas. Describing Housman as the "greatest Roman poet who ever wrote in English," he goes on to elaborate: "Housman is in some ways one of the great enigmas of English poetry. . . . He's a tough man to tangle with in print because he knew and they didn't. And he was quite willing to say that they didn't." Dickey also "knew." The class session documents that he has studied Housman's poetry *and* the two little-read lectures that Housman delivered while a professor of Latin studies at the University of London and Cambridge University.

An unusual feature of Dickey's teaching style is the way he liked to announce unexpected and odd juxtapositions when he made reading assignments. The shock of recognition was a jolt to the students designed to disarm them of the notion that poets should be studied chronologically according to the dates of their lives. For example, he discusses "what is of importance to us" in the poetry of Emily Dickinson: "That she was a recluse, that she was frustrated in her love life; that's not the important thing; it's what she made of it." What follows is a stimulating analysis of the writer he calls "a nun of poetry." Yet he thinks nothing of following the long session on Dickinson with a short comment on Kingsley Amis, a British writer better known for his novels than his poetry. Avoiding the numbing regularity of historical chronology, Dickey creates these unforeseen juxtapositions to demonstrate his conviction that poetry is not a roll call of the dead but a living tradition. Thus a typical class might feature the famous Yeats and the obscure Keith Douglas, or the famous Edwin Arlington Robinson and the equally renowned Thomas Hardy.

Dickey's skill at making surprising connections in class and at reading the poems as extensions of the lives of the poets led inevitably to pithy one-liners and memorable asides. Some of these observations are general, as in "Language changes. And the poet's language must change with it." But most of the sharply focused comments refer to specific poets, as if he were leaving the students with a summation they would likely recall long after class.

On Edwin Arlington Robinson: "Probably the most prolific tight-lipped poet that ever lived."

On Robert Bridges: His diction has "a chilly purity."

On Edgar Bowers: "Reading very much of his work is like trying to wade up-stream in cold mineral water."

On Edwin Muir: the locale of his upbringing urged him to "take on this intensity of smallness."

On Archibald MacLeish: "I don't know exactly what I think about Mac-Leish."

On Wilfred Owen: "The poems have an authenticity from his death that they do not have on the page."

On Conrad Aiken: "Aiken is always talking about lovers standing in a garden."

On Allen Tate: "It's a book that, if you were reviewing it, you would talk about how distinguished it was, but you could not say that you loved it."

His perceptive one-liners combine the incisive and the comic, and indicate the tension-free atmosphere of the classes for which he prepared the lectures. Dickey was a funny man. He spiced his learning with humor. Defining the many reasons for admiring Hardy, for instance, he continues, "Hardy was a remarkable poet, and the thing that made him remarkable is that he has no gifts as a poet. So that gives us all hope." He also had an offbeat way of calling a poet's lifework "stuff," as when, commenting on Dickinson, he pauses to wonder, "What do you suppose the stuff would be like?" The humor occasionally extends to instructions for the next class assignment: "So read Bridges, and let's read Housman before we get into the quagmire of Yeats." To his credit, Dickey was not afraid to turn the humor on himself. Commenting on Tennyson's long popularity, he mocks the enormous publicity that *Deliverance* brought him just one year before he gave the lectures: "It's hard for us to imagine a poet being accorded that kind of status now. Tomorrow you might see a poet's name in headlines, but it would be for having written a novel."

Still, one wonders if he missed the self-irony of his piercing comments from time to time. One example will suffice. In 1971–72, Dickey was at the pinnacle of his art and the height of his acclaim. The success of *Deliverance* and the subsequent movie version, however, unfortunately turned him into a public figure in a way that eventually interfered with his dedication to poetry. Although he continued to write brilliant poems for at least the next decade, the number of memorable poems declined. Too often the public figure became a public spectacle. For observers eager to articulate negative judgments, Dickey's questionable behavior and thoughtless pronouncements became more worthy of comment than the poetry. Thus, his discussion of Robert Frost, a great writer who fell into a similar trap, proves instructive: "It's no coincidence that the quality of the poetry fell off as he began to be paid more and more attention to for his public cracker barrel pronouncements about life, death, love, art, poetry, sex, politics, everything." It is as if Dickey were inadvertently predicting his own fate.

Although Dickey won the annual teaching award given by the Department of English at the University of South Carolina in 1987, he was not a demanding instructor. Beyond selecting the various texts, both primary and secondary, for commentary, he rarely prepared his classes in advance. Dickey was a compulsive reader who retained what he read, and thus he relied on memory rather than systematic planning, research, and review of the assigned material. The results were not only a spontaneity that led to lively class sessions but also occasional factual errors. When it came, for example, to some of the place names associated with a poet's career, Dickey's accuracy was variable. Where identified, his errors have been corrected. In addition, because he was particularly interested in providing an overview of a poet's life and themes, he rarely explicated more than a few poems by each writer. The course was not designed to be an exercise in close readings of great poems. The point is not the facts, which he occasionally got wrong, but the values about the individual poets that he brought to the discussions. Dickey was a celebrated poet discussing the modern poetic tradition from the perspective of a practicing writer. What he chose to foreground about the poets is itself valuable. Some students described his course as mesmerizing. Others called it easy. All learned. As he conceded in his letter to James Wright noted earlier, he was a good teacher not because he was "especially conscientious" but because he enjoyed instructing bright readers interested in the art of poetry.

The prevailing tone of these class sessions is joy—joy in the art, in the language, in the poets themselves. T. S. Eliot, Wallace Stevens, Marianne Moore, Elizabeth Bishop, William Carlos Williams, Theodore Roethke, and Robert

Lowell are not included; but more than fifty other poets are—by any count a remarkable number to lecture on in a two-semester class. Dickey is especially memorable on Yeats, Pound, Thomas, Housman, Hopkins, Frost, Robinson, de la Mare, and Bridges; but the following comment, made about a minor poet named William Bell, summarizes the joy he took in his analyses: "But have a look at Bell. It's quite a lot of fun, and when was there ever anything wrong with that?"

■　■　■

Dickey is like most great writers: the stories about him interfere with the story. The myth precedes the man—the heroics in World War II, the skill with the guitar, the expertise with bow and arrow, the publicity at President Carter's inauguration, the media coverage, a novel called *Deliverance*. But the art will outlive the myth—a poem titled "The Performance," which immortalizes his best friend who died in combat during the war; the spellbinding rhythms of the poems in *Drowning with Others;* the National Book Award for *Buckdancer's Choice;* the appointment to the Library of Congress; the success of the verbal risks taken in "The Firebombing" and "Falling"; the cascading language.

The lectures contribute to the unraveling of the art from the myth. They are in every way a testimony to a man engaged with the rigors of poetry. Yet they are also a testimony to a man committed to readers, committed, as it were, to passing it on. Two days before he died, I visited Dickey in the hospital for the last time. Emaciated, weak, and most of all tired, he was nevertheless eager to talk for a bit about poetry. As I held his hand, he repeated the first line of Frost's resonant poem about darkening toward death, "After Apple-Picking." I said the second. We then alternated lines until we came to the end: "Or just some human sleep."

James Dickey was still teaching.

WORKS CITED

Crux: The Letters of James Dickey, ed. Matthew J. Bruccoli and Judith S. Baughman (New York: Knopf, 1999).

Dickey, James. *The Weather of the Valley: Reflections on the Soul and Its Making* (Columbia: University of South Carolina, 1995).

Striking In: The Early Notebooks of James Dickey, ed. Gordon Van Ness (Columbia: University of Missouri Press, 1996).

A Note on the Text

The reader of James Dickey's commentaries on modern British and American poetry should keep in mind the date of their delivery: 1971–72. By 1970, Dickey had been teaching and writing poetry for twenty years. Like any serious thinker about poets and their art, he shaped his judgments according to not only his skills as a reader and writer but also his reaction to the criticism and biographies of the time. Thus, while new critical perspectives and biographical revelations may today suggest different responses to the poets, the lectures confirm that Dickey was a keen observer of the shifting tides of taste and judgment.

A case in point is Robert Frost. Although Frost was a gigantic presence on the American literary scene from the early years of the twentieth century until his death in 1963, little reliable information was known about his life and opinions except what either he or his devoted followers chose to reveal. All that changed in 1964 with the publication of Lawrance Thompson's edition of *Selected Letters of Robert Frost* (New York: Holt, Rinehart and Winston, 1964), a 650-page collection of correspondence that exposed Frost to be not the simple, gray, farmer-sage that he projected in public but a complex mixture of generosity and jealousy, confidence and fear, kindliness and vindictiveness. *Selected Letters* caused an outcry of denial and dismay among Frost's defenders, but the poet's own words condemned him. When Thompson followed *Selected Letters* with the first two volumes of his three-volume biography of Frost, *Robert Frost: The Early Years, 1874–1915* (New York: Holt, Rinehart, and Winston, 1966) and *Robert Frost: The Years of Triumph, 1915–1938* (New York: Holt, Rinehart and Winston, 1970), the making of what some subsequent Frost scholars called "the monster myth" was all but complete. The challenge to Thompson did not take significant shape until the middle 1980s with the publication of William Pritchard's *Frost: A Literary Life Reconsidered* (New York: Oxford University Press, 1984) and Stanley Burnshaw's *Robert Frost Himself* (New York: Braziller, 1986). Burnshaw was a close friend of both Frost and Dickey. The point here is that Dickey's analysis of Frost in 1971–72 was naturally affected by the then-recent appearance of Frost's letters and by Thompson's controversial biographical revelations, and not by the counterarguments advanced in the Pritchard and Burnshaw books long after the lectures were delivered.

The reader should also keep in mind that Dickey was a poet-teacher of eclectic and even occasionally idiosyncratic tastes. Organizing his classes, he assumed the perspective not of scholarship but of sensibility. He used his reading and learning to discuss the poets he liked and the reasons he liked them. His goal was to introduce an audience to "modern poets," not always to "great modern poets." Thus, as noted above, he enjoyed featuring the known and the unknown: Robert Frost and Alun Lewis, or Ezra Pound and Keith Douglas. Such an approach meant that he might discuss poets few listeners would expect to find in the course, but ignore poets many would assume to be highlighted. Personal choices guided his commentary.

Yet it is important to recall that the year 1971–72 was also the general period when Dickey was publishing his most penetrating and comprehensive collections of essays about poets and poetry. His students wanted to hear a renowned poet talk about other writers, and they would have been aware that many of the significant poets Dickey did not include in the class sessions were nevertheless emphasized in the essays. Three examples are relevant. E. E. Cummings is not discussed in the course, but he is featured in *The Suspect in Poetry* (1964). Similarly, William Carlos Williams and Theodore Roethke are not commented on in the lectures, but they are major figures in, respectively, *Babel to Byzantium* (1968) and *Sorties* (1971). Dickey's commentaries and collections of essays complement each other and should be consulted together for the full range of his impressive analysis of the poets who were his contemporaries and of those who shaped his art.

EDITORIAL NOTE

Editing means recovering and preserving the writer's intention. The good editor organizes, clarifies, and emends, always in the service of the author. These lectures were found among James Dickey's papers by Matthew J. Bruccoli, the poet's literary executor. As explained above, they were not originally in written format. They are transcriptions of Dickey's taped oral presentations and thus include the repetitions, digressions, and misstatements to be expected in a public forum lasting two semesters. For most of the class sessions, Dickey spoke from a few notes jotted down both to guide the discussion and to ensure an informal atmosphere. I have preserved his tone while removing irrelevant remarks.

Dickey's secretary taped the commentaries as the poet delivered his opinions and interpretations. She was then instructed to type, not edit, them. Although Dickey later read several of the transcriptions and added a few asides and reminders in holograph, he made little effort to act as his own editor. Happily for the reader, he thereby maintained the spirit of an oral format for class lectures. I have done the same. Mindful, however, that the sessions were originally intended for a listening audience, whereas the present volume is intended for readers, I have supplied bibliographical information about the many books and titles he alluded to in his analyses.

An impressive command of the poetic tradition permitted Dickey to be unusually wide-ranging in the lectures. He often supplemented his comments by reading specific poems aloud to illustrate his points. I have added most of the lines of poetry he read to the listeners in order to confirm the scope of his learning and to recreate the context that shaped his remarks. I have also silently eliminated repetitions and clarified nuances. Since the original tapes have not been located, I have been unable to compare them with the transcription.

CLASSES ON
MODERN POETS AND
THE ART OF POETRY

TRANSLATION AND POETRY

We need to talk about the difference between the poetry of former times and ours. There are lots of ways I can demonstrate what I want to talk about in connection with this, but I think we ought to take two or three different kinds of topics today and talk about them in relation to each other. One of them is the Heroic Age or the Classical Age, the Age of Epic, in comparison and contrast with ours. The other is, if we want to connect—that is, as personal readers, the ancient age, say, with Greece, with Rome, with medieval Italy, where Dante wrote—we have one or two ways in which to make contacts with the poets of that other time and that language. What are the ways that are possible to each of us in assimilating, so to speak, their work, say the work of Sophocles, or Homer, or Euripides, or Seneca? How do you usually study these people in school?

It's very simple. You don't have to make anything very hard out of it. And since most of us don't read classical Greek, or any Greek or any Latin very well, or at all, or French or German or Spanish or anything else, I can't exactly say we're *reduced* to reading them in translation, but more or less it comes down to that. So it might behoove us a little bit to consider what translation is. Since you're going to take courses in these people who speak a different tongue from you and me, we ought to have at least a provisional notion of what goes on in a translation.

Have you ever tried to translate anything yourself? The whole question of translation in the last fifty years has undergone a complete revision, for example. Now it would seem, on the face of it, to translate a literary work, say a poem like the *Iliad,* for example, from one language into another, would entail only a certain very fixed set of considerations.

What would these be? What would you say the commonsensical view of what you try to accomplish in a translation would be?

You'd just try to do it word for word, as nearly as you can. Now bear in mind that we're taking poetry as an example. Bear in mind that you're translating poetry; you're not translating a scientific text or a treatise, or anything like that. You're translating poetry. What are some possible objections to, say, this kind of *literalism* that has always been practiced in translation? It is a real knotty kind of problem, and nobody's ever really solved it. But it is a problem and it does need to be talked about.

All those other factors need to be considered too. In other words, you're not concerned *just* with literalism, because as I say, you have to bear in mind that this is poetry, and poetry is compounded of a lot of other elements besides the denotative or literal meaning of the words employed therein. So there're a lot of other factors that you have to be concerned with as a translator. Since the *Iliad* is the most translated work in world literature, I'll just give you some examples of different approaches to the rendering of the same scene in Homer. You would not believe that they were being translated from the same poet. Why is this? Simply that the translators were going at it from different assumptions. They were attacking it from different positions from each other. One wants to do this, one wants to do that, one wants to do the other thing. One wants to be literal; one wants to employ the verse form that he himself is best at—not that *Homer's* best at, but that *he's* best at; the other wants to throw out the book and do it a completely different way in a modern idiom, in a more or less twentieth-century colloquial idiom. These are really very important considerations. But one of the things that is more or less coming to the forefront in translation and translation theory is that it doesn't matter how literal you are or how true to the letter of the law or even the spirit of the original you are; if you don't come up with a good poem in the language that you're translating into, you have more or less failed in what you should be doing. Because you should be trying to get the essence of the poetry over from one language to another, and not just a literal transcription.

I don't know how much contemporary poetry you've read, but can you think of the man more than any other—he's an American—who's responsible for this notion of the translation as the attempt to get as good an English poem, say, as the original was in Chinese or Greek? Do you have any idea who that might be? [Ezra] Pound, that's right. Almost the entire theory and practice of translation that we have now is due to Pound's renditions from the Chinese, a language which, in point of fact, he did not even know. He's a great believer in trying to "intuit" the poem and maybe taking some liberties and sometimes taking a great deal of liberties with the text in order to get an original poem in English that he intuits is the equivalent of the original; that is, it carries something mysterious about it that Pound calls "the spirit of the original" rather than the letter. What is it the Bible says, the letter killeth but the spirit giveth life? It's *that* kind of approach to translation which is most prevalent now.

I'll read to you a passage from Book Sixteen of the *Iliad*. This is a translation by a literalist, a fine classical scholar, somebody who does indeed know Greek, and who tries to preserve the letter of the poem, and probably gets something of the spirit too. He's Richmond Lattimore. He's one of the finest classicists we have now. He teaches at Bryn Mawr, and is quite a fine original poet himself. But he knows prosody; he knows Greek; and he's translated the *Iliad* as nearly as he's able to do, which is pretty close to the original hexameters that the original version of the *Iliad* is composed in. Hexameters, you know, long lines, six feet long—I mean six poetic feet—you know, long lines. This is a passage where Achilles is still in his tent refusing to fight, and the whole issue of the war depends on whether or not he's going to come out and fight, but this is before he does. And his buddy Patroclus puts on his armor himself and goes out against the Trojans under Hector. This is an interesting sidelight about the difference between the Age of Epic and ours, if you read the *Iliad* and you get into this story of the kidnapping of Helen by Paris and of the siege by the Greeks under Menelaus and with Achilles as the number one ramrod of the attack—if you read this and you see Hector, who doesn't want to fight, who doesn't think Helen is worth it. He's a good family man, a good citizen, as well as a great warrior; in the eyes of the Greek reader of Homer's epic, superior. Why would they revel in seeing Achilles cut Hector down? Can you imagine? It's so foreign to the way we think. Why? What is it about Achilles that makes him the epic figure and Hector not? I'm not talking about the *tragic* figure. What qualities does Achilles have that give him this stature and don't give it to Hector?

Hector is a man, a man like us, and that's why we sympathize with him. But Achilles is superhuman. He's magnificent, wonderful, *heroic:* Hitler would have understood why Achilles is more exciting. In some ways he was like that himself. But the thing that Greeks would cotton to about Achilles is that he is the undisputed heroic *type.* He is that combination of human form and god-like attribute that anything can be forgiven because he is so absolutely grand. He is so wonderful, so terrific, so beautiful, so fast, so ferocious. What is poor Hector going to do against somebody like *that?* Well, he's defeated. Achilles kills him. He cuts through his tendons and ropes him to the back of his chariot and hauls him around the city walls to show them how their one great hero has been brought low. Humiliating, even disgusting—but the Greeks thought that was what the hero should deserve as his due, to be able to do this to his opponent, to humiliate him and drag him around in the dust. It's much different from our humanitarian ideas of how human beings ought to behave. George Patton, the general, is a figure rather like Achilles, that kind of beyond-good-and-evil type, law-unto-himself. This is a section, as I say, from Book Sixteen when Patroclus puts on Achilles' armor and goes up against Hector. This is the hexameter line as it goes over into English [line uncertain].

That's one of the most exciting things about Homer, because the gods are always intervening and they're always taking these various forms. This time Apollo is coming in and getting around behind Achilles, see, as he's fighting these guys.

Again, a completely different contention in other translations—not literal at all. But it's more or less what they call a "version from Homer," that is, Alexander Pope's poem in heroic couplets based on Homer's poem. But you couldn't call it a translation, of course, because it isn't. It's an original poem by Alexander Pope using his tried-and-true heroic couplet, eighteenth-century diction and technique based on, more or less closely based on, Homer's original.

Now here's the last one I want to put before you. This is by an Englishman named Christopher Logue who does not know one single word of Greek. He's engaged in the project of translating the *Iliad* very much under the Ezra Pound approach of creating an original poem which he calls, oddly enough, the *Iliad*. But it's not in heroic couplets, it's not in hexameters, it's in a very widely and wildly mixed variety of styles. And it's also in colloquial English— a strange kind of approach. Let me read to you the same scene. You can see the difference between Lattimore's and Pope's. Okay, this is when Patroclus fights. Rogue—he's always coming to fights! Not scholarly, this translation, but extremely powerful, vivid, swift-moving, gory, the way Homer is anyway.

EMILY DICKINSON

You can buy this [book] which comes out under the Doubleday-Anchor imprint, *Selected Poems and Letters of Emily Dickinson,* edited by Robert Linscott. This also has a biographical note [JD incorporates passages from Linscott's biographical note in this lecture], which will either serve to turn you off Emily and her weird life and weird personality, or make you fall in love with her.

The facts of her life are these. She was born December 10, 1830, in a New England "where Puritanism was dying and literature was just coming to life." Her father was a very rigid Puritan. He was the town lawyer at Amherst, that is, the city of Amherst, and later became treasurer of the college. Her birthplace was Amherst, a quiet village in the Connecticut Valley of Massachusetts, "nearly a hundred miles from Concord and Cambridge in space"—an Englishman holding forth—"and at least half that number of years in time. Here she lived a life, outwardly uneventful"—and it certainly was; in fact nothing happened at all except what happened in there—"inwardly dedicated to a secret and self-imposed assignment," that of writing a "letter to the world," which is a phrase of hers. Do you remember the rest of that poem? "This is my letter to the world / That never wrote to me"—"that would express, in poems of absolute truth and of the utmost economy, her concepts of life and death, of love and nature, and what Henry James called the 'landscape of the soul.'" That's a particularly apt phrase in relation to her, too, because she had almost no outward experience, only inward. "Unpublished in her lifetime,"—now this is the history of her poetry, all of that poetry, almost eighteen hundred poems— "unknown at her death in 1886," when she was fifty-six—"her poems, by chance and good fortune, reached, at last, the world to which they had been addressed. 'If fame belonged to me,' she had written in 1862, 'I could not escape her; if she did not, the longest day would pass me on the chase, and the approbation of my dog would forsake me.'"

"From her family Emily had love without understanding"—that she did— her family, especially her father, never knew what to make of her at all. He was the "leading lawyer of the village, and, in later life, treasurer of Amherst

College and member of the legislature and of Congress. He dominated the household."—And this is typical of Emily that she would make such a statement which is resonant, but you don't know exactly what is meant. She said of her father, "His heart was pure and terrible." What does that mean? What does "pure" mean in that statement? Could it mean too pure, inhumanly pure? I think something like that is meant. He was an almost fanatical Puritan and terrified Emily her whole life. After his death in 1874 "her gentle, colorless mother lived in his shadow. Austin, the only son, patterned himself on his father but lacked the formidable self-righteousness of the old Puritan." Her sister—to whom she wrote some of her best letters—"crotchety and outspoken, was watchdog and protector of her shy, sensitive, and sometimes rebellious sister. The family lived in a brick mansion set in spacious grounds on Amherst's main street, and neither sister ever married." And if you go to Amherst today, the house is still there and you can go through it and see where she made bread. She made all the bread; her father wouldn't eat anybody's bread but hers.

Here you have this family with this autocratic Puritan father and this rather drab mother and a son who is like the father but not as impressive, and these two girls, Lavinia, who was an old-maid type even from the beginning, and Emily, who is an old maid also, even from girlhood, from late girlhood. But a quite different kind of old maid, quite a different old maid from just *any* old maid. She went to school for two years at Amherst and one at the Mount Holyoke Female Seminary, as it was then called. She "settled down to the customary life of a New England village. Many years later a school friend remembered her as 'not beautiful, yet she had great beauties. Her eyes were lovely auburn, soft and warm; her hair lay in rings of the same color all over her head, and her skin and teeth were fine. She had a demure manner which brightened easily into fun where she felt at home, but among strangers she was rather shy, silent, and even deprecating. She was exquisitely neat and careful in her dress, and always had flowers about her.'"—That's kind of nice to think of.—"She was one of the wits of the school, and there were no signs in her life and character of her future recluse."

About this time something happened which has been the conjecture and the despair of every biographer who's ever dealt with her in any way. *Something* happened. It had something to do with someone she cared for—some man. There are four or five conjectural possibilities, but nobody really knows which one it was or whom she wrote these burning, passionate love poems to, full of longing and renunciation. All we know is that it was somebody she met about this time. It could be one of three or four. It would have had to have been one of them, because she didn't know any other men. And so what happens then is the Emily Dickinson story as we know it, as we posterity folk know it. She withdrew; she withdrew from human society, hardly ever even saw members of her family although she wrote letters to them when they were gone. And she became a nun of poetry, completely withdrawn from all human contact. She lived upstairs. It was a very rare day indeed when Emily Dickinson would consent to come downstairs, even. She was the most totally isolated recluse, I suppose, who has ever written remarkable poetry.

What do you suppose the stuff would be like? Well, the thing is, you don't know that without seeing it. I mean, you could ask for a conjecture about what kind of poetry a person like this would write, but if you haven't seen Emily Dickinson's poetry, you would never have thought it would be like that.

This is perhaps what happened. "Into her life during these years came two young men who may have had some slight influence on her career: Leonard Humphrey, principal of Amherst Academy, and Benjamin F. Newton, a law student in her father's office. Both stimulated her interest in books. Newton encouraged her to write. Both died young" and were remembered in the lines "I never lost as much but twice, / And that was in the sod; / Twice have I stood a beggar / Before the door of God!" "Reticence was a Dickinson characteristic," as it is a well-known New England characteristic. "And most of what we know or surmise about Emily's emotional life comes by inference from her poems and letters. Sometime during her twenties she began seriously to write poetry; just when cannot be known because her early poems were destroyed, or are unidentifiable as such. By 1858 she was copying her poems in ink and gathering them together in little packets"—see, already very old-maidish— "loosely bound by thread. In that year she appears to have written fifty-two poems." In 1862—now this is right in the middle of the Civil War—those total three hundred fifty-six in one year. Of course they're short, all of them are very short, but that's still an awful lot. In 1865, the number had fallen off to about eighty-five, and from there averaged about twenty a year. "The fuse that touched off the creative explosion of the early 1860's appears to have been a Philadelphia clergyman: Charles Wadsworth, forty-one years old, a husband and a father when Emily met him in May, 1855, while on her way home from a visit to her father in Washington. Correspondence must have followed since drafts of three letters to him—letters pathetically eager and pleading, in which the writer calls herself 'Daisy' and the recipient 'Master'—were found among Emily Dickinson's papers after her death."

As a woman, she thought of herself in regard to any male friend she had— and God knows, she didn't have many, just a few acquaintances—but if she committed herself to a person emotionally, not maybe being in love with more than one or maybe two of them, she was a woman who had such an absolute subservience to the man that it's absolutely ludicrous, in these days of women's lib, to see the way she wrote her letters to these people. "May I be your pupil; will you teach me; will you be my master, my preceptor?" and so on in this humble and self-effacing way. She conceived the male-female relationship as many of the New England women of her time did of being one of absolute subservience of the woman, and, as she keeps saying, as a master-slave relationship. That's kind of hard for us to take, but she felt this way unquestioningly, as her letters show. Some of them are very compassionate, also very funny. But evidently Wadsworth, this forty-one-year-old married clergyman, is the most likely candidate for her affection, the person who was more or less responsible for her withdrawal as she saw it. She was so strait-laced, that is, in the conventional way, that some commentators, among them Richard Chase, who is one of the better ones, have conjectured that she would rather withdraw from the world than have a breath of scandal that she might entertain a passion for a married man. Nobody will never know.

"Whether Wadsworth responded to, or was alarmed by, the intensity of the emotion he inspired, as evidenced by these drafts and by certain of her poems, cannot be determined, since his letters were destroyed. But it is known that he called on her in 1860, while visiting a friend in nearby Northampton. And it is conjectured that sometime during the following year he told her that soon he would have 'left the land,' having accepted a call to a church in San Francisco. The shock of separation may account for the prodigious output of 1862." Emily says, "I had a terror since September, that I could tell to none, and so I sing, as the boy does by the burying ground, because I am afraid." And this is the loss to which the last two lines of the poem quoted above must refer: "Angels, twice descending, / Reimbursed my store. / Burglar, banker, father, / I am poor once more!"

Her biographer—and this is an extremely good book, too, George Whicher's book called *This Was a Poet*—says, "Her dream-palace was suddenly left tenantless." Because she of all poets that I know anything about, among a trade where introspection and self-examination are really *the* trade, the stock-in-trade, there have been none who were more introspective, or more withdrawn, or more solitary, or more alone with their own imaginary world than Emily Dickinson. She saw so few men, that I would say—I don't know whether this is true or not—that her attachments to one, say one that she liked, or just that she happened to know, were such, that coupled with her slavish kind of admiration of people, or men, would have been enough to make the person an absolutely godlike figure to her. "In that same year Emily Dickinson seems to have considered, for the first time, the possibility of publication, for she sent four poems to Thomas Wentworth Higginson, a rising young man of letters, with a note asking him to 'say if my verse is alive.'" He was an editor of the *Atlantic Monthly* at the time. "The correspondence and interview that followed so illuminate Emily Dickinson, both as poet and as person," that Higginson's essay is reprinted in the Linscott book. I'll read to you a quote in a minute about where he first meets her, because Higginson is an editor, and he gets these weird kinds of letters from this person somewhere in the middle of the town of Amherst. And he knows that this is an extraordinary kind of personality, but he'd never met her or ever read anything that she's written, and she sends him these poems, that are like nothing that he's ever read. But they got together and they met twice. Let me read a couple more paragraphs to fill the story out.

"If one may think of the first decade of Emily Dickinson's adult life as a period of expansion to the creative climax of 1862, then the remaining years marked a gradual retreat. Year by year the area of her interests narrowed," and she became death-obsessed, and it's no accident that the best of Emily Dickinson's poems deal with death in one way or another. It was even more apparent in her later years. But from the time of her withdrawal she dressed always in white, a perpetual bride. But no one saw her. The only people who ever saw her would just be those who happened to glance up at the window and there'd be a face momentarily at the window of her father's house. And she became quite a legend in Amherst. Year by year her interests narrowed; "year by year her indifference to the outer world grew more arctic. Now she dressed only in white; ventured less and less, and finally not at all, from her home, saw fewer friends, and, at last, none."—Now get this—"But with one curious exception. Judge Otis P. Lord of Salem, a widower in his late sixties and an old family friend, visited Amherst often during these years, and it would appear—on the evidence of surviving drafts of fifteen letters written between 1878 and 1883—that she conceived for him a passionate love, and even hoped for marriage."—In his late sixties, you know.—"In these last years Emily Dickinson tended her garden, baked the family's bread, and watched from her window the passing show of village life. To her friends she sent gifts of flowers with gnomic notes and poems which vastly puzzled them. She grew obsessed with death, as her friends departed to"—this is what she thought of as death—"that bareheaded life under the grass." Isn't it terrific? Nobody but Emily Dickinson would have conceived of it in that way. But I don't think I've ever seen a corpse that had a hat on. "That bareheaded life under the grass." "Long before her death she had become an Amherst legend: the woman in white; the eccentric recluse; the half-cracked daughter of Squire Dickinson."

"How closely Emily Dickinson had guarded her writing"—and the fate of her writing is almost as interesting as her own—"from her immediate family is shown by her sister's astonishment at coming upon a locked box filled with poems." They didn't know that was what Sister Emily had been doing up there all that time. "She had already burned"—the sister had—"unread, Emily's correspondence, but these poems, the work of her dear sister, must be given to the world."

"First, she turned to Sue Dickinson, Austin's wife"—her brother's wife— "but the task was difficult and Sue was indolent. Next Lavinia solicited Mabel Loomis Todd, the brilliant young wife of an Amherst astronomy professor. Reluctantly Mrs. Todd consented to undertake the long labor of deciphering the handwriting, copying the poems, and selecting enough for a slim volume." Emily Dickinson's handwriting was almost indecipherable a good deal of the time—she apparently wrote quickly, but she didn't use any punctuation, just these dashes. Sometimes a period or a comma would get in there. Sometimes the dashes were in place of regular punctuation marks, and sometimes they were just thrown in there, for no apparent reason except that she had a further thought on the same subject, and then she'd put down more dashes. It makes it very difficult—that coupled with her handwriting—makes it very difficult to see what she was saying part of the time.

"With the help of Thomas Wentworth Higginson, [Mrs. Todd] finished the task and found a publisher who agreed to bring out the book if the family would pay part of the cost. It appeared in 1890, and was followed by two others and by two volumes of letters. More poems were published in 1914, and again during the twenties, where their place in literature was at last recognized."—This is, say in the 1920s, forty years after she died.—"Finally, in 1950, Harvard University bought all available manuscripts and publishing rights, and has since issued the complete poems and letters, edited by Thomas H. Johnson."

Now, that's really all the biographical information about Emily Dickinson that you need to know, except maybe one last thing, and that is: when Mabel Todd and Lavinia, the sister, and another editor whose expertise they engaged to bring out Emily's poems began to put the poems together, apparently these editors of Emily Dickinson's poems were so mystified that they not only put in normal punctuation, but they actually changed some of the words around, substituted words. Consequently, you will find in the anthologies three or four versions of the same poem. These were not Emily's changes; they were editorial changes in the interest of clarity and understanding interpreted by these people who were good-hearted and industrious, but simply did not understand the way she wrote or what she was trying to say or the way in which she was trying to say it.

So, there we have a very uneventful life. Out of this came three or four different kinds of poems. There are three or four Emily Dickinsons, but they're all so closely related to each other that the good poems and the bad or indifferent poems are very, very similar. There's a question of what makes one good and what makes one bad. [John] Brinnin himself is very, very good on this. Now let me tell you how he sums this up—this is much better than I could do it— the Emily Dickinson who is the most forgettable. And unfortunately, as with many another good poet, the Emily Dickinson that is the most forgettable is the one that is usually remembered. Emily Dickinson is thought of as this kind of writer, you know. But you should have this because it's damn good. I'll start with the worst Emily first because that's the most characteristically anthologized. One thing that Emily Dickinson did that she surely didn't have any notion she would do: she completely revised the notion of what kind of verse is to appear on greeting cards. The greeting card companies took her up almost from the beginning, took up the worst poems. Many, many people tried to imitate this kind of cute effect that she gets, all this familiarity with nature and bees and flowers and in this particular kind of cute and rather tart way. And there's an awful lot of Emily Dickinson that's like that, that's just playfully silly. But even so, it is in her mode, and that's what makes it so distinctive.

Brinnin says, "The final and the least memorable of the several Emily Dickinsons is unfortunately the most widely quoted. This Emily Dickinson is the writer of verse as quaintly flowered and full of jingles as a rack of greeting cards—which many have been imitated from her. She is the coy Emily who holds to an eternally protracted girlhood, whose childish postures have been outgrown, who assumes the histrionical, culturally pious attitudes of her time, and who flirts with all the creatures of a nineteenth-century Disneyland." She is remarkably like that. This is the Emily Dickinson who makes God "a noted clergyman." I guess he is, one of the more noted ones, I would think—"whose maidenish tolerance of drunkenness and other kinds of misbehavior in the big world makes a sophisticated writer writhe with discomfort. In the poems selected for this book, the version of Emily Dickinson's character least represented is the saucy little rebel in God's backyard, who teases words into the shapes of rococo valentines." But again, even her best work, all but the very, very,

very best has got some element of the "saucy little rebel in God's backyard" in it. And there is something decidedly unpleasant in her complacency in taking this attitude. This is one of the reasons that people who don't like Emily Dickinson don't like her, because she has this eternally cute, kind of smirking cuteness about her, about so much of her work, especially the better known work.

That's one thing. The poets have taken her to task because she was so unadventurous as far as form was concerned. I'd say out of 1,775 poems, 1,700, no, I'd say 1,650 of them are written in quatrains. It must have tired her out to sit up there in that attic, that upstairs room, and turn out three or four or more poems in quatrains. Poets like to think that they experiment around, push out a little bit, change the form some. Not her. Every one of them is written in a plain measure, which is—not every one, but the grand majority are—written in hymn measure, the hymns of her day. Can you think of your favorite hymn? Hymns are usually written in four lines and that's essentially what Emily used. She was essentially unadventurous as far as form and experimentation.

What makes Emily Dickinson remarkable is not so much her formal use of the language as her quality of thought that she put into these rather predictable and flimsy forms. That's what makes her distinctive and remarkable. You grasp the general intent of what she means, but the way of phrasing it is so peculiar to her that you're not sure. And the syntax is sometimes either garbled or deliberately changed from the ordinary way that the syntax or the grammar would run. She has a lot of distinct difficulties in her work. And most of her poems are untitled too, so you don't know whether she's writing about this, that, or the other thing, whether when she says "God" she means God, or whether she means the latest bee in the garden she calls God: a lot of strange kind of cross-pollination of images. Anyway, she says, "Title divine is mine! / The Wife without the sign! / Acute Degree conferred on me / Empress of Calvary! . . . 'My Husband' women say, / Stroking the Melody / Is *this* the way?" Now, you could take an awful long time on that poem. I won't do it now, but just give you some of her tone when she's most bitter. She has, really, what passes over from what certainly was a personal bitterness from the loss of or rejection by the people that she deified to such an enormous extent, that it passes over into a kind of theological or metaphysical bitterness which is yet side by side with a completely accepting nature that loves everything and is interested, tremendously interested, in everything that exists. Trees, birds, flowers, all the things that she can see around the house and in the garden. An occasional snake—*that* must have been a big day. But mainly very more homey and homely and domestic things. Things, animals not like you would see in the jungle, but in a garden—bees, hummingbirds. But she manages to make the most astonishing statements about the universe: the *most* astonishing.

The great thing about Emily Dickinson—and if you'll hold this in mind, you'll know pretty much everything you need to know about the way she was and the way she took the world—is this: all of us have a way of taking the world, or relating to it, individual to us; she had this, in an intensified form. She had such an intense, imaginative life. Things that would be small or unnoticed to anyone else took on for her a metaphysical significance that she was able to get down in some simply remarkable poems. You really do feel, not that she was just a "saucy little rebel in God's backyard," but that she *does* open out these homely images—birds, winds, grass. She really *does* find a way to get through those to a much vaster significance that they all form a part of, whether you would want to call it God, or whatever. It is really a remarkable achievement. We talked last week about a poet like Homer, or one like Dante, whose world is *vast* and deals with vast things that anybody would think were vast—wars, fate, the gods as in Homer, or the medieval theology, the whole of God's creation as Dante has it. When you pass from those large worlds, that anybody would know when one encountered them, to Emily Dickinson's microcosmic world, it's traumatic. But what you find out when you read the good poems is that the microcosm opens into a macrocosm, and that there's very little difference, in fact none. And it's a remarkable feat for this relatively modestly educated recluse to have hit on this very distinctive way of doing this. If a neighbor's barn burned, something she could look out her window and see, that wasn't just her neighbor's barn burning to her. That had suggestions of all fires in all places: with the burning of the library in Alexandria, the burning of Rome, the Heraclitean fire that goes through all things and is the animating principle of nature. That's what she saw. Her inward vision was so intense and her concentration in her own peculiar New England way was so alive and so singular that she was able to do these remarkable things, using the utmost economy of means and the most conventional of poetic forms.

Let's read one of the bad ones. This is the childlike and playful one and a paragraph of commentary by a critic named Yvor Winters. Now this is, probably up until people discovered how good Emily Dickinson was, this was the kind of verse with which Emily Dickinson was publicly associated. This is about a train.

"I LIKE TO SEE IT LAP THE MILES"

> I like to see it lap the Miles –
> And lick the Valleys up –

And stop to feed itself at Tanks –
And then – prodigious step

Around a Pile of Mountains –
And supercilious peer
In Shanties – by the sides of Roads –
And then a Quarry pare

To fit its Ribs
And crawl between
Complaining all the while
In horrid – hooting stanza –
Then chase itself down Hill –

And neigh like Boanerges –
Then – punctual as a Star
Stop – docile and omnipotent
At its own stable door –

The commentator has his teeth set completely on edge by that kind of thing. Winters says, "The poem is abominable." There are a few great poems in which this trace of playful silliness is absent, but it's almost always present to some extent in everything of hers. You just have to put up with it to get the stuff in her work that is really absolutely inimitable.

One of the easiest ways to get into Emily Dickinson is the poem on the bottom of page two. First of all, as you should do with all poetry, you must try what she says—what the poet says—against what you think, against what you've felt, or had happen in different experiences, not of hers, but of *yours*. "After great pain, a formal feeling comes." Is that true? What could be truer? It's said so purely, so simply:

"AFTER GREAT PAIN"

After great pain, a formal feeling comes –
The Nerves sit ceremonious, like Tombs –
The stiff Heart questions was it He, that bore,
And Yesterday, or Centuries before?

The Feet, mechanical, go round –
Of Ground, or Air, or Ought –
A Wooden way
Regardless grown,
A Quartz contentment, like a stone –

This is the Hour of Lead –
Remembered, if outlived,

As Freezing persons, recollect the Snow —
First — Chill — then Stupor — then the letting go —

That's all. Thirteen lines. How does this strike you? Not only as to what is said, but the *way* it's said? What has happened here? What do you suppose, knowing Emily's preoccupation with certain human events? What do you suppose this is about? I mean, you don't know what causes the great pain that she's talking about, but what is the greatest pain? What does "ought" mean? The void, perhaps, but I don't know. I'm not sure. A lot of times you can't tell. But there's no mistaking the origin of some of these things, some of these answers, the "Hour of Lead," and then that last metaphor. What the poem is about, actually, is the kind of terrible numbness that sets in, where you don't feel anything. How do people freeze? What do they feel when they freeze to death? They don't feel anything. And, psychologically, how are they supposed to feel? They feel warm: "I'm not going to fight it; I can't." And that's something like you feel after great things.

Notice how wonderfully Emily Dickinson can begin a poem: "There's a certain Slant of light." Very simple.

"THERE'S A CERTAIN SLANT OF LIGHT"

There's a certain Slant of light,
Winter Afternoons —
That oppresses, like the Heft
Of Cathedral Tunes —

Heavenly Hurt, it gives us —
We can find no scar,
But internal difference,
Where the Meanings, are —

None may teach it — Any —
'Tis the Seal Despair —
An imperial affliction
Sent us of the Air —

When it comes, the Landscape listens —
Shadows — hold their breath —
When it goes, 'tis like the Distance
On the look of Death —

And then, what would be the connection in your mind between the slant of light—where is the sun on winter afternoons? And what is the relationship, image-wise, between that, say, and the image of a cathedral? The light comes down in exactly the same way. Why would that be oppressive, though? Can you

Just before the publication of his first book, 1959. *Photograph by Timothy Galfas*

imagine its being oppressive? Yes, very. In some of those huge cathedrals, with that solemn music playing, you feel like you're buried in stone, stained glass.

So let me finish with what I think is her best poem. It's another one of those short ones, and it's also in quatrains, but there's something in this one. It's so powerful and so Dickinsonian that once you have read it, you never get over it again. Its subject is death.

"I heard a Fly buzz"

I heard a Fly buzz – when I died –
The Stillness in the Room
Was like the Stillness in the Air –
Between the Heaves of Storm –

The Eyes around–had wrung them dry –
And Breaths were gathering firm
For that last Onset – when the King
Be witnessed – in the Room –

I willed my Keepsakes – Signed away
What portion of me be
Assignable—and then it was
There interposed a Fly –

With Blue – uncertain stumbling Buzz –
Between the light – and me –
And then the Windows failed – and then
I could not see to see –

I think the most beautiful recounting of a physical sensation—in this case the loss of consciousness and death—is in that next-to-last line: "And then the Windows failed." We would see that image differently from those in Emily Dickinson's day when they used whale oil lamps. It's as though we—if we were dying and were able to tell of it, and the windows ceased to exist, to us, in 1971, it would seem like what?—like the electricity failed. There's a great deal of difference, and yet same—death—same—for us, for her.

Let me run back through what we've got. First of all, if you want all the stuff, all the poetry, this collection's it [the Johnson edition], and it's got all the original punctuation, or anti-punctuation, so you're going to see how Emily really put the words on the page. Then, if you want a selection with most of the really good poems and most of the significant letters, [the Linscott] edition is quite a good one. If you just want to dip into the poetry, but with the help of an excellent introduction, get the Dell paperback. That's really the best introduction to Emily Dickinson I know, plus a very good selection of poems. If you want an extremely good biography, George Whicher, *This Was a Poet;* it's very good, very thorough. It's not easy to write a biography about a person to whom so little happened, but this is really an excellent one. There's a good essay by Conrad Aiken. There's a good edition of the letters with an introduction by Thomas Johnson. There's a very, very good critical biography by Richard Chase, and you can take your choice and read all of them or none of them. But they're there, if you get around to it. And another good essay, mostly about the theology of her relationship to Calvinism, by Allen Tate. He says—one sentence I'll end up with, and this is the thing you should remember about her, not so much that she was a recluse, that she was frustrated in her love life; that's not the important thing; it's what she made of it—Tate says, "All pity for Miss Dickinson's starved life is misdirected. Her life was one of the richest and deepest ever lived on this continent." So it was, but that was because she was Emily Dickinson. But here the poems are; here're almost eighteen hundred poems, passages from the letter to the world she wrote that never wrote to her.

KINGSLEY AMIS

So, let's have a look at a much newer poet, Kingsley Amis. I don't want to go into a lot of Kingsley Amis's background except to say that he is an English writer, and up until, say, twenty or thirty years ago, was unknown not only as a type of English writer but as a type of Englishman. Almost all English writers that we can remember were educated at one of the big colleges like Oxford or Cambridge. So was Amis, but he developed, or came to be associated, with writers who were not themselves associated with the larger schools like Cambridge or Oxford.

Kingsley Amis made his reputation as a teacher and writer working out of one of the provincial universities or colleges—he taught at several of them, what they call "red brick universities." His great success as a writer came with the introduction—and hilarious it is, too—of a new type of Englishman, an Englishman who does *not* want to be a gentleman. English have always fought to be thought of as gentry, when they came from, say, the merchant stock, or even from the working class; but Amis makes a thing—and a very funny thing it is—about a young university professor at, not exactly a provincial, but not one of the larger colleges in England, who is quite frankly just out for a hell of a good time, who doesn't care anything about social stigmas, who drinks and fornicates, and raises hell and commits terrible faux pas in the house of his superiors, like getting drunk and falling asleep while holding a cigarette, and burning up his host's bed. All this, as Huckleberry Finn would say, is told about in his greatest success, a novel called *Lucky Jim*. *Lucky Jim* is funny. It's not as funny to us as it is to the English, who know the things that Amis is lampooning better than we do. They know all the social nuances that he won't be taken in by.

Now as a poet—no, a little bit more about the novelist, Kingsley Amis. He's written about six or seven novels; by far the most famous is *Lucky Jim,* but he's written other comic novels, including science fiction. He's a great science fiction aficionado, and I think his name—he's much more famous in England as a result of *Lucky Jim* than he has been over here until recently, because when

Ian Fleming died, and the James Bond series would have seemed to have died with him, Kingsley Amis is the one who wrote some of the later James Bond books. He was selected by Ian Fleming's estate to be the official continuator. Amis's James Bond books are entertaining, but they're not nearly as exciting. He's too much of an intellectual, I guess. But anyway, he was selected to do this. He's an extremely urbane fellow, who, the last couple of years—I don't think he's there now—was writer in residence at my old school, Vanderbilt. I met him there and had an afternoon talking with him; and he, oddly enough—these comments are all kind of irrelevant, but they might be interesting to you— he's almost the only well-known English writer who supported the American intervention in Vietnam. He has been almost ostracized by his friends for that reason, but he's *very* eloquent on the subject.

Anyway, as a poet, he's a much lesser figure than he is as a novelist. His novels—like *Lucky Jim,* and *That Uncertain Feeling,* which is a good one, and one called *Take a Girl Like You*—are all very good, very witty, very funny. He has a strong, sharp, satirical edge. You see this in his poems as well. There are two books of poems, in case somebody wants to write on Amis, and I wish somebody would. Two books. One, in his characteristically sardonically modest style, is called *A Case of Samples.* What is a case of samples, by the way? And another, with the same kind of laconic attitude, *A Look Round the Estate.* There's not a whole lot of Amis's work, but the characteristic attitude of Amis is, "Look, fellows, we've had romantic poetry and all this hyped-up poo-bah for too long, all of this excessive stuff. Let's don't have this anymore. Let's recognize our limits and recognize what's possible to us as human beings, and all these poets like [Arthur] Rimbaud, and [William] Blake, and [Percy Bysshe] Shelley who are always giving out with impossible and," as Amis would say, "antihuman visions. They're not doing us any good. They're making us look for things and hope for things that are just chimeras. They're figures of the imagination; they're Freudian visceral images; they're not something we can use. Let's tone it down, fellows. When you say, Mr. Blake, when you look at the sun you see a great multitude of the heavenly host singing praises to the Lord, if you saw that, you were daft. Personally, I think you were putting us on. I don't think people see visions like that unless they're nuts, because they're not there to be seen. What we need in our poetry, as well as more particularly in our lives, are things that are suited to us, not wild visions that are excessive, as well as all the political bullshit that you romantic poets put out. Let's cut that out, fellows; we don't need it; we've had too much of it for too long."

This is the effect that his verse gives; a good deal of quite gentle but very sharp satire is about what you're going to get from Amis. I won't read through it, but the typical poem in which this antiromanticism is expressed is the one called, appropriately enough, "Against Romanticism." What he wants is not "wild dragons and the eyes smeared up with garish paint, tickled up with ghosts." No, that's done us in, "the brain raging with prophecy," and all of that. No, we want an escape, "a path leading out of sight and at its other end, a temperate zone. . . ." Let's stay civilized; let's give over all this wild prophetic business, all this vision-seeing. All this is antihuman; we don't need it; we need something that's right for us, that accommodates us, and then we'll be better to each other, when we have knowledge of what we need, *really.*

He's very funny though, and I recommend Amis if you like a poet who doesn't write long poems, and doesn't write many poems, but will always give you something to think about, who has an unfashionable position. We think of the great poets of our time as being visionary poets like Rimbaud and Dylan Thomas. He hates them. He says, "I hate to be impressed with Dylan Thomas. I am, but the more I am, the more I think he's not what we need. I hate him." He's making those wild noises all the time. "We don't need that. We need somebody who's intelligent and civilized," or, as Amis says, "someone to whom thought is not contemptible."

He's a good literary critic; he's a wonderfully funny novelist; and he's a decent—no, I think better than that; that's sounding too short—he's a *good* poet. And if I said I think he's relatively limited, he would take that as a compliment. *Limit* is one of his favorite words. "Recognize this; work with it; don't try to go through it, fly past it. Limit is the best thing we've got going for us, if we know what it is." This is a funny poem of his. One of the things you like instinctively about Amis when you read anything of his is that he's unflappable; he doesn't let anything bother him. If the critics don't like his work, if his politics is unacceptable to the newspapers, if his books of poetry don't sell, it doesn't matter to him. He's really one of the coolest guys there is. You read the biography of someone like Thomas Wolfe, who gets into a suicidal frenzy when he gets a bad review. You like Amis a lot, you know. It doesn't matter to him. He can look with a tolerant eye on all kinds of aberrations that he thinks are human. What he castigates are the excessive and the deliberately cultivated kind of madness that literary people, especially romantic poets, attempt, as I say, to cultivate, and all of what he calls "poetic poo-bah." He wants an intelligent, witty, understandable, lucid poetry, and that's the kind he writes. This is a very funny poem—I think it's funny—about homosexuality in a boys' school. Many boys in England, apparently, have gone to places where this kind of things goes on, but Amis went through, characteristic of him, one of these places where all these fellows were homosexuals, homosexual companions, his schoolmates. It didn't bother him at all. As a matter of fact, Amis himself is a great womanizer. He has a way of going through things like this that would bother some people, but not being bothered by it at all, and looking at it in a kind of gently, tolerant, understanding way: "If these foibles are human, that's the way these people are, and it's not up to me to condemn them or have any opinions, but just to understand them." And that's what this poem is about. It's called "An Ever-Fixed Mark," which is from a sonnet by Shakespeare, "Love is an ever-fixed mark . . ."—I never did like that poem. But anyway, here is the Amis poem.

AN EVER-FIXED MARK

Years ago, at a private school
Run on traditional lines,
One fellow used to perform
Prodigious feats in the dorm;
His quite undevious designs
Found many a willing tool.

On the rugger's field, in the gym,
Buck marked down at his leisure
The likeliest bits of stuff;
The notion, familiar enough,
Of "using somebody for pleasure"
Seemed handy and harmless to him.

But another chap was above
The diversions of such a lout;
Seven years in the place
And he never got to first base
With the kid he followed about:
What interested Ralph was love.

He did the whole thing in style—
Letters three times a week,
Sonnet-sequences, Sunday walks;
Then, during one of their talks,
The youngster caressed his cheek,
And that made it all worth while.

These days, for a quid pro quo,
Ralph's chum is all for romance;
Buck's playmates, family men,
Eye a Boy Scout now and then.
Sex stops when you pull up your pants,
Love never lets you go.

That's the very quiet, tolerant, witty Amis tone, very understanding. He knows what he is; he knows who he is. Kingsley Amis, *A Case of Samples* and that poem from *A Look Round the Estate*.

THOMAS HARDY

We're here to talk about Thomas Hardy. Did you read Hardy? Hardy was a remarkable poet, and the thing that made him remarkable is that he has no gifts as a poet. So that gives us all hope. Hardy was a product of nineteenth-century determinism and materialism. Let me ask you something. Let me throw it back to you. Do you have theories about the universe? Do you? What is it, really? What is the universe? What's it about? I'd really like to know. I've been living in the world for about fifty years. I'd really like to know what it's about. I'd like to know why I'm here. Wouldn't you? What does it amount to? What's it about? Hardy had theories, theories about what the universe is. You know what he thought? Just what you think—that there is no reason for it to be. There's *no* reason. It's just a chance calculation of atoms. It's just chance. There's nothing here. We're lucky to be here, but it doesn't matter. Hardy would say that it's just blind chance. Your life doesn't matter; the universe doesn't matter; it's just a matter of luck.

Hardy had two sides: he had a philosophical side, and he had ideas about the universe. About determinism, naturalism: he thought none of it mattered. Those are not the greater part of Hardy. Hardy also loved people, and he could *not* reconcile his philosophical ideas about the universe with his great love and compassion. But you know the typical Hardy feel? You talk about the "feel" of a poet. You know what the Hardy feel would be? It would be this: "I can't do anything for you, but I know how it is." That's the Hardy feel. "I can't help you. Nobody's ever been able to help anybody, but I can understand and empathize. I know what it's like for you. It's been like that for many another. I can't help you, but I know what you're going through." Ever felt like that?

Let me tell you about some books on Hardy, some books and some other things. Hardy wrote an epic work on the Napoleonic wars called *The Dynasts*. It's almost impossible to read, but it has some beautiful, beautiful things in it. What he purports to show in *The Dynasts* is an enormous panorama about the Napoleonic wars, attempting to show that there was never any reason for any of it. There was *no* reason for it. It happened, but it was simply a product of chance. There was no purpose in it; there was no reason for it to exist; and there was no outcome. There are many strong parallels with events that have happened since that time. This just happens to be in connection with the Napoleonic wars. It was simply a matter of chance; it was useless, *useless*. *The Dynasts* is full of magnificent writing, but the distance is too great. Hardy is too far from the actual action. He has gods and spirits commenting on the action, saying how useless it is, but he doesn't get in close enough to the people for you to care whether it's useless or not. Anyway, it's a long, long verse drama called *The Dynasts,* and it's got some real good stuff.

You know what's good about this? You know what's good about *The Dynasts*? It's not the interplay between people; the thing that's good about it is the stage directions. If you take an enormous drama like the Napoleonic wars, how would you do it? This can't be played on stage. It cannot possibly be played on a stage. It's too big. But what he does is to say deliberately, "I'm going to write a play that can never be played; I'm going to write a metaphysical play." And if you don't limit yourself to the stage, what can you then do? If you don't ever expect it to be played, you can do anything you want to. You're not trying to write a Broadway hit. If you want to write a metaphysical drama, you can do it any way you like. That is, you can take the godlike view. You can say the meta-sky opens, and Europe is disclosed as a prone and emaciated figure. The interesting thing about this is that you could not do this on the stage, but where could you do it? In the *films*! The meta-sky opens—can't you see a filmmaker doing that? Europe is disclosed as a prone and emaciated figure, the Alps shaping it like a backbone, and the branching mountain chains like ribs, the peninsula plateau of Spain forming a head. Broad and limp the lowlands stretch across the north of France to Russia like a gray-green garment, hemmed by the Ural mountains and the glistening Arctic Ocean. You see the whole thing, the whole continent of Europe like a body. The point of view then slips downward, through space, and draws near to the surface of the perturbed countries, where the peoples, distressed by events which they did not cause, are seen writhing, crawling, heaving, and vibrating in their various cities and nationalities. So, the stage directions for *The Dynasts* are terrific, and I wanted to give you this in case you ever wanted to read it. It's a long, long piece of work. But in its way, it's fascinating, unplayable, but fascinating. Hardy is a writer who has three or four different dimensions. He's enthralled—he's in thrall of an idea of determinism as it happened in late nineteenth-century philosophy, and as in the case of many writers, that there's nothing except blind chance. That's what controls us. That's what makes the world. Blind chance, the calculation of atoms, the random coupling of atoms.

He has philosophical poems; he has poems in which he sets his ideas forth about materialism; but those are not the great Hardy poems. The great Hardy poems are those in which Hardy himself goes against this system. These are poems that have to do with people. Have you read *Tess of the d'Urbervilles?* Where he says that the president of the immortals has had his sport with Tess; he's had all he's going to with her, and has killed her? The best of Hardy has to do with things that go *against* the philosophical system that he has espoused. They have to do with individual human troubles. He's absolutely wonderful. Have you had a pet that died? Tell me about it. That is the typical and great Hardy subject, the bereavement over something, say like a dog or a cat, that there's no explanation as to why it should be like this.

Let me give you some good books on Hardy, and then we'll go through this marvelous poem of his called, "Last Words to a Dumb Friend." What does that mean? If you can, get the connotations of the word "dumb" in Hardy. We'll go through that in a minute, but let me give you some good books on Hardy. Hardy's a wonderful prose writer. He's pedestrian, he's slow, but he's real deep. He's very deep. Again, as in any class of this sort, I don't know how much you want, but I'll just put out what has meant something to me on the subject, and you can take whatever you want to get. There's a very good selected writings of Thomas Hardy in the Fawcett series, *Stories, Poems, and Essays.* But let me introduce you to a really good series by the Grove Press, whom you do, or maybe you don't, associate with nothing but pornographical stuff. This is the Evergreen Pilot Books. And this is a book on Hardy by a man with the improbable but delightful name of George Wing. If you want to read Hardy's novels, there's a very good guide by Lord David Cecil. Now, the thing about [Hardy] that I would reiterate, and it should have something to do with your own thinking: there is a dichotomy between what one figures as an absolute system if one is an artist, and what one actually does feel, what actually moves one. There's no more perfect example of that in all literature than Hardy. Hardy believed in determinism, and he espoused determinism, the nothingness, the void; but his best work, his greatest work, has to do with us, with people.

Let's read through what he has in this collection. One of the interesting things about Hardy—I'm fascinated with him. He's a great man; he's like your father. He's like the kind of father you want, or I'd want. One of the interesting things I tell to young poets in the writing class, if you ever want to experiment in verse, to invent forms, then you should go to this enormous eight-hundred-page volume, because Hardy is an infinite experimenter. There are forms in Hardy that you'll never find anywhere else. Form was a thing with him. It's funny about his career. I'll just give you a real brief rundown of it. He started as a poet and then began to write novels. He quit writing poetry in his twenties and then didn't write any more of it until he was sixty-five. He wrote a novel, *Far from the Madding Crowd*. But he didn't write any more poetry until he was sixty or sixty-five, yet he always wanted to be thought of as a poet. And he had no precedent for what was going to be in *this* collection. Somebody said his work was so wide and diverse they didn't see how he chose things for his collections, and he said he just went to the drawer and took something out. But for young poets it's an interesting and instructive lesson to go to the collected poems of Hardy and look at the kind of thing this clumsy guy does—this clumsy, awkward guy does. It's interesting to see how he does it. I mean, you really could not get anything any worse conceived than some of the things that he does. And yet the great poems wouldn't be great unless he had taken those kinds of chances. It's really strange. He's like somebody said of Balzac: he had genius but no talent. He passed into the stage of being great without ever going through that of being good.

This is a typical Hardy kind of thing. It's full of his clumsiness; it's full of his philosophy; but it's also full of him. Was anybody particularly taken with anything in this? Because it is clumsy and it's terribly awkward, but there is something in it, at least for me; there's something in this that's not easy to forget. That's the Hardyesque moment.

Let me read to you this thing about a cat. Again, it's awkward. But I tell you, my dog ran off about six months ago, and I couldn't think of anything but the lines of Hardy. And it's hell he did it like that. You don't know why, but somehow or other it works out. He's a very good rhymer, a very good metrical worker. It's awkward, but somehow it works. He's imperfect, but he's got this terrific, compassionate feeling about existence. "Tad was never mourned as you / Purrer of the spotless hue." Isn't that awful: "Plumy tail and wistful gaze / While you humored our queer ways. / Or how shrill your morning call / Up the stairs and through the hall / Foot suspend in its fall. / How expectant you would stand / Arched to meet the stroking hand. / Till your way you chose to wend / Yonder to your tragic end. / Never another pet for me. / Let your place all vacant be. / Better a blankness day by day / Than a companion torn away." Now that's the exact opposite from Tennyson, who says it's better to have loved and lost than never loved at all. "Better bid his memory fade. / Better blot each mark he made. Selfishly escape distress / By contrived forgetfulness. . . . That you moulder where you played." So, that's what you call a poet named Thomas Hardy. As I say, there's a big collected poems, there's *The Dynasts,* there's the Irving Howe selected stories, poems, and essays, and the Fawcett paperback. And there's quite a long essay, this would be the one I would start with, by Mark Van

Doren, in a book of his called *The Happy Critic*. If you ever want to use any of this for papers for graduate school or undergraduate school; but no, that's not the main thing. The main thing's not to do it for graduate school, but to do it for *you,* if it interests you.

Let's do "Nature's Questioning." This is the ultimate Hardy poem.

NATURE'S QUESTIONING

When I look forth at dawning, pool,
    Field, flock, and lonely tree,
    All seem to gaze at me
Like chastened children sitting silent in a school;

    Their faces dulled, constrained, and worn,
    As though the master's ways
    Through the long teaching days
Had cowed them till their early zest was overborne.

    Upon them stirs in lippings mere
    (As if once clear in call,
    But now scarce breathed at all)—
"We wonder, ever wonder, why we find us here!

    "Has some Vast Imbecility,
    Mighty to build and blend,
    But impotent to tend,
Framed us in jest, and left us now to hazardry?

    "Or come we of an Automaton
    Unconscious of our pains? . . .
    Or are we live remains
Of Godhead dying downwards, brain and eye now gone?

    "Or is it that some high Plan betides,
    As yet not understood,
    Of Evil stormed by Good,
We the Forlorn Hope over which Achievement strides?"

    Thus things around. No answerer I. . . .
    Meanwhile the winds, and rains,
    And Earth's old glooms and pains
Are still the same, and Life and Death are neighbours nigh.

And this again is in one of his curious forms; you don't know why he did it this way.

Now, let's have a brief look at "A Cathedral Facade at Midnight," which is often anthologized.

A CATHEDRAL FACADE AT MIDNIGHT

Along the sculptures of the western wall
    I watched the moonlight creeping:
It moved as if it hardly moved at all,
    Inch by inch thinly peeping
Round on the pious figures of freestone, brought
And poised there when the Universe was wrought
To serve its centre, Earth, in mankind's thought.

The lunar look skimmed scantly toe, breast, arm,
    Then edged on slowly, slightly,
To shoulder, hand, face; till each austere form
    Was blanched its whole length brightly
Of prophet, king, queen, cardinal in state,
That dead men's tools had striven to simulate;

And the stiff images stood irradiate.
A frail moan from the martyred saints there set
    Mid others of the erection
Against the breeze, seemed sighings of regret
    At the ancient faith's rejection
Under the sure, unhasting, steady stress
Of Reason's movement, making meaningless
The coded creeds of old-time godliness.

Again, Hardy—though he was a master of form, he was a temporary master of form. He wrote well some of the time; most of the time he misappropriated form. But when it worked, it worked fine. As a working writer and a poet I can attest to that.

He was raised to be an engineer and an architect, and he began as a poet— now I don't mean to make any kind of personal parallels—very much like a guy who was working in an office and wrote poetry and had a few things published as a young fellow, and then began to write novels. He was a hard worker, a hardworking writer. He began to read philosophy and he wrote novels, and they're good, very beautiful. But he began to get bad reviews, very bad reviews. And he wrote a novel called *Jude the Obscure*. It's very good. It's slow, but good, but deep. But the law attacked his novel, *Jude the Obscure*. The newspapers called it "Jude the Obscene." He said, "The reception that I received from *Jude the Obscure* cured me of any further interest in writing novels."

So, Thomas Hardy, a couple of things to sum up: he was a guy who wrote novels and poetry and read philosophy, who believed he knew what it's all about—who knew the secret, all right, the secret of the universe which was simply that there's not any secret; it's nothing; it's all a chance, an accident, a mistake—but whose fine talent went against that. In other words, he could not say, he could not look at a woman who had an illegitimate baby in her belly and say, "It's too bad, honey; but it doesn't mean anything, anyway." That's not Thomas Hardy, because his heart went out to her. It went out to her in her human predicament. And that's where you get the great Hardy poems, the infinite compassion. I said so earlier, and I'll say it again, the essential Hardy "feel." He says, "I can't do anything for you, honey, but I know what it's like for you. I know what you're going through. I sure do."

WILLIAM BELL

Let me tell you a little bit about William Bell. This here's William Bell. What's he look like; what does he look like to you? Know what he looks like to me? He looks like one of these overintellectualized English Oxford types who knows a lot more than you. Let me tell you a little bit about him. I'm fascinated with him. He was killed in a mountain-climbing accident on the Matterhorn in 1928. There is a very short reminiscence of William Bell that you might be interested in. The thing that I like about him is that he's good, and he's good in a way in which you would not think it possible to be good, in the era that we're writing poetry in now, because he's extremely old-fashioned, old-fangled. He writes mythology, which is supposed to be passé. Let me just read a couple of paragraphs about William Bell. Has anybody ever done any mountain climbing? What does it feel like? Does it scare you to death? I tried to use some of this in *Deliverance,* some of William Bell's stuff, because he had a great premonition of his own demise. He's an interesting fellow. He died at twenty-four, and the thing that makes him interesting is his tremendous commitment to his personal conception of the craft of verse. He would not give the time of day to somebody who was a romantic poet, because he conceived of himself as a classical poet. He's an odd combination of a classical poet in a very unfashionable vein: invented forms. Very unlike Hardy because Bell is smooth where Hardy is clumsy. At the age of twenty-four he was quite a good craftsman. He had that extreme, remote kind of icy, pure classicism. That was one thing, and the other thing was a devotion to danger. What is that going to produce if you have that particular mix? I don't know. All I can say is it produces poetry like William Bell writes. Most of his books—well, there's only one, actually; he had a couple of tiny little pamphlet things, seven volumes, published.

You really don't get a good sense of Bell's talent, his "thing," in these selections. He was a great experimentalist; he liked to play around with words; he worked on his poems almost incessantly. I taught "The Young Man's Song," and some kid was so taken with it that he set it to music. He was, as I say, a fanatical formalist. He knew French poetry; he knew Italian poetry. But have a look at Bell. It's quite a lot of fun, and when was there ever anything wrong with that?

GERARD MANLEY HOPKINS

You know who Rupert Brooke is? Anybody ever heard of him? He's an English poet. He was the golden-haired boy of the period in English poetry just preceding Ezra Pound and T. S. Eliot. He died in the early part of World War I. Rupert Brooke was the fair-haired boy of English poetry, and everything he said was taken up by the press; everything he said was paid a lot of attention to, and there were many eulogies after he died of a fever, actually an infection, down in the islands of Greece. And he seemed to be, as one of his commentators said, "part of the youth of the world." His work doesn't read so well anymore; it seems old-fangled to us now. But you have to remember that Rupert Brooke was an image, and in some way had a connection between the war hysteria of World War I and poetry. That's the important thing to remember about him.

Now this is the commentary on him. This is where Hopkins is hard to get into, but this is the way I want to get into him. This is from the diary of a guy dying of multiple sclerosis just after Rupert Brooke died, well, a couple of years after Rupert Brooke died. This is by a man who called himself W. N. P. Barbellion; his book is named *A Last Diary*. He made journal entries, and then he eventually died at the age of about thirty. But his journals are fascinating, fascinating. The nice thing about them is that they are so careful, so good-humored, so funny, and so intelligent. Barbellion was a biologist, self-educated. By the way, do you know what a ctenophore is? I'll read it to you, cause you need to know this. "Any of a large group of sea animals with a pair of long stringing tentacles and an oval, transparent jelly-like body bearing eight rows of comb-like plates that aid in swimming." Does that catch you up on ctenophores? Barbellion says of Rupert Brooke in his entry of June 1, 1919, "Rupert Brooke said the brightest thing in the world was a leaf with the sun shining on it. God pity his ignorance. The brightest thing in the world is a ctenophore in a glass jar standing in the sun. This is a bit of a secret, for nobody knows about it, save only the naturalists. I had a new sponge the other day, and it smelled of the sea until I had soaked it. But what a vista that smell opened up!" Now *that* attitude

33

is the attitude of Gerald Manley Hopkins, who was not a professional, or self-taught, or whatever kind of naturalist, but was what you could call God's naturalist. If you *knew* what the brightest thing in the world was, as against the sentimental way that Rupert Brooke *thought* he knew it was the sun shining on a leaf; if you *knew* it was a ctenophore in a glass jar, then God was thereby praised by your knowledge, your observation: that's why it's there, and that's why you're there. And if God wanted you to know it, what does it behoove you to do? Right—to go out there and look for it, to look for it, and find it, and look at it, and into it, open up to it. Because the universe to Hopkins was a universe of signs, a universe of correspondences, a universe in which these things are given to us by God to see and to experience and to know. But they will not be known until we get out there in the natural world and become, as he spent his whole life becoming, an inspired, God-induced naturalist; an accurate and personal *reader of the world*.

GOD'S GRANDEUR

The world is charged with the grandeur of God.
  It will flame out, like shining from shook foil;
  It gathers to a greatness, like the ooze of oil
Crushed. Why do men then now not reck his rod?
Generations have trod, have trod, have trod;
  And all is seared with trade; bleared, smeared with toil;
  And wears man's smudge and shares man's smell: the soil
Is bare now, nor can foot feel, being shod.
And for all this, nature is never spent;
  There lives the dearest freshness deep down things;
And though the last lights off the black West went
  Oh, morning, at the brown brink eastward, springs—
Because the Holy Ghost over the bent
  World broods with warm breast and with ah! bright wings.

First, I want to drop some names on you. I'd like to give you something where you can find out about Hopkins and read him. *A Hopkins Reader* is a good start, and maybe if you don't dig him, and maybe if you do, there's an awful lot of Hopkins in this. This is *A Hopkins Reader* by Oxford University Press. This has most of the major poems, the really good ones, a selection of the letters, which are the most remarkable literary criticism of the nineteenth century, some of the notebooks, which are indispensable for your understanding of Hopkins, and the way his mind worked, and even some of his musical compositions. I'll just put this in parenthetically. Hopkins was a great believer in submitting himself to a discipline for which he had no particular talent. Do you think that's a waste of time, or do you think certain things could be learned by that? Well, he never believed he had it in him to be a composer, but he loved music. So he thought it would be better for him to find out something about it so that he could enjoy music from the inside, whether he could write it or compose song lyrics or anything like that, which he did. I've never heard any of his compositions played. I wish I could hear them played. But he believed in this participatory thing. Do you think it's better to know something about it, or just stand outside and contemplate it? Now, I can't do any ballet. I love the ballet, but I can't do anything. But, I think I would love it more if I tried to do a little bit myself.

Hopkins was a kind of "star of Balliol"—a precocious Oxford undergraduate, very, very precocious, and then he underwent a religious conversion. Nobody knows exactly *why* he did. But he was converted to Catholicism by Cardinal Newman, which is a familiar name to everybody, and entered into the most difficult of all orders of the Catholic church, the Jesuits. He became a teacher: the Society of Jesus is a teaching order. I'll just give you a brief rundown on what happened to him. He had written some poems of very high promise, as an undergraduate, but on entering the Jesuit order, he destroyed them all; he spoke of them as frivolity. No Catholic ever tried harder to fulfill his mission than Father Hopkins. He didn't write. He gave up poetry. He gave up most of the things he cared the most about to try to become a Catholic priest, an effective teacher. He was unsuccessful. His students did not take to him. He was too original and strange to be effective in a classroom, and he died at the age of forty-four without feeling that he had fulfilled his mission as a priest. However, there was one incident that happened to him when he was in Wales. He loved Wales, and there was, as I remember, a kind of a competition for religious poetry. The head of the school where he was studying theology came to him and said that he had heard that Hopkins had written verse, and asked if he would like to make the school look good by writing something. Hopkins, with his fanatical fervor, just pitched into the project, and all these years that he had been thinking about poetry—and nobody ever thought of it to better effect than Hopkins, thinking about prosody, about imagery, all of his observations from nature—coalesced into this wild, mad poem that he wrote called "The Wreck of the Deutschland," which was about the death of five Anglican nuns exiled by the Falk Laws. And the poem becomes a terrifying contemplation of death and salvation.

Gerard Manley Hopkins was a combination of two extremely important qualities for writers, and he's a combination of them in ways that other people before him were not combinations of them. He was an extremely fine scholar with a very, very good analytical mind. Well, really *three* things—a very good analytical mind; he was well-read in philosophy, and especially in theoretical works of literature, learned works on prosody: how English meter works. That part of his being a Jesuit is well established. He was a very great scholar, a fine scholar. Now, the second thing was that he was very original-minded. That is, Hopkins was set in his premise to take nothing for granted about literal things, material things, objects, but also theoretical things, theories about prosody, theories about poetry, theories about poetic imagery. He read works on them, he was conversant with them, but he would not accept anything that he had not tested for himself. He was extremely pigheaded, which sometimes is good, and sometimes not. In his case it was very good. These two things—he was a very good scholar, a very thorough scholar; second, he was very original-minded. The third is that he believed wholeheartedly in the natural world. And he believed that everything in the natural world, like the ctenophore in the glass jar of Barbellion, is put there for us by God to see, for anyone who wants to take the trouble to look at it. When we look at it, when we perceive that thing, the sunlight on the leaf (he would even have admitted Rupert Brooke's observation), when we see that, we see the fish, we see the stone, we see the wind blow, we see the constellations. Those things are full of what he called *voltage*. What runs through them is the voltage of God; they are charged with meaning, with significance, "God's Grandeur" again. And they all go together to show us what there is, what has been given to us as perceptive beings to see, but we've got to get out there and look. We've got to experience. This was absolutely fundamental to Hopkins, this kind of makeup and this kind of belief. To understand the kind of poetry that Hopkins writes, that's the first thing you have to know, that he had this feeling and it never wavered. He never varied from this notion that the earth and everything on it, down to the slightest detail, is loaded, as he says, *charged* with the grandeur of God. But it requires an effort on your part to come into the presence of the grandeur of God. So the next time, look at the icicle. See what it's really like.

The next thing about him that you have to know is that he was an indefatigable experimentalist in language. He believed that there is a very real and tangible relationship among three things—first, objects and events; second, the person who engages himself to come into their proximity; and the third, God. All through Hopkins you find the relationship among things: stones, the way water runs over rocks at a certain place at a certain time, between stars, between clouds, between things and the person who perceives the things, and God, the maker of *all* things. This is definite in Hopkins, and is pervasive. It's through everything he writes, everything.

The next thing is his belief in what he called "inscapes," in essentials. As I say, he was a fine scholar; one of his favorite scholarly pastimes was reading a scholastic philosopher named John Duns Scotus, who is very difficult to read, but also very rewarding. Scotus had a theory of what he called *haeccietas*—"thingness"—the quality that makes this thing not like that thing. This doctrine of particularity, of individual essence, was fundamental to Hopkins. The fact that the stone was not like the leaf, but this stone is not like that stone—"thisness," particularity. He kept a journal for about six years in which there are hundreds and hundreds of these observations, of how things look, how they feel, how he senses them to be in a particular time and a particular place. This is wedded to an extremely individual language gift, very largely developed by him alone, so that consequently when you read Hopkins, you feel that you've never read anybody like him. He's not like anybody you've ever read before. He's so strange; he's so weird; but he's also so good that I myself would make the observation—and I haven't read all the English poets, by any means—but I would say, as a working poet and somebody who has learned so much not only from his practice, but from his example, I would say that Gerard Manley Hopkins is one of the two most original poets in the English language. I don't know of more than a couple that would even stand a chance of being compared to him in this respect. Dylan Thomas is one of them, and John Donne. Again, Shakespeare is a product of Elizabethanism and Elizabethan drama; Wordsworth is very derivative from Milton. I could go on and on in this pseudoscholarly way all afternoon; I mean, that ain't hard to do, if you've been to graduate school. But the *real* originals are very, very rare, and I would say that Hopkins and Dylan Thomas and Donne are the most original, the most inexplicable, the strangest of them all; and of these, I would say that the strangest of those three—Dylan Thomas, John Donne, and Gerard Manley Hopkins—that the strangest and the most original and the best is Hopkins.

Now, wedded to this business of thisness is a curious kind of self-invented language to articulate in *his* particular way this closely observed thing. Hopkins was very original in his theories of poetic practice, and especially in his theory of the poetic line and how it functions. He says in one of his letters that people have misunderstood the way English works across the page. We have been done in by the old iambic pentameter scholarly rules. English can be written in a poetic line far different from anything you have been told you can do. Hopkins says throw that out: we're going to write a kind of poetry in which the foot is determined by the accented syllable alone. So we don't count any unaccented syllables. If we're going to talk about unaccented syllables, we'll call them "outriders." That's typical of him: who else but him would have said *that*? So, he developed this curious jerky kind of poetic rhythm. It's quick and very jerky and very intense, and it goes fast. This is the kind of thing you associate with Hopkins and that every poet since his time has plundered his poems for, to try to get a little of that fast, rapid stuff that Hopkins does. But nobody can do it like him. Dylan Thomas robbed him to death. So did John Berryman.

He was also a great one for word-coiningness, for making up new words. This he got from Germany, from the way the German language works, in compound words. He took this over from the German. He made up dozens of new words that wouldn't have existed without him. All the while in this extremely cloistered atmosphere, and this extremely contemplative, Jesuit, Catholic atmosphere as a provincial teacher—a strange atmosphere, a strange environment for a great poet to come from.

What we should do is read a couple of Hopkins's poems. What is good about Hopkins and what is weird about Hopkins are related. First, what is good about him is that he had these qualities. He had this marvelous observational thing; he had this completely new rhythmical thing going for him; he was a great master of form; he was a devout knower and lover of the world, in intimate, personal ways. As Wallace Stevens says somewhere, the greatest poverty is not to live in a physical world. Hopkins would have concurred heartily with that, because he was a very physical person. He had all of these things going for him. What he didn't have going for him was that he had no sense of the personally dramatic. Very few of his poems deal with people. There isn't any of the give and take between human beings that we think of as being essentially dramatic. His poems, as great as they are, and especially as great and original as their technique is, and as great as their details are, there is very little sense of development. They tend to run to a formula: as original as he is—this is a paradox—they tend to run to a formula. They tend to start off with observations of nature in this marvelous Hopkins idiom that only he could do, and then somehow it all comes out to be Jesus. It's not that he evokes Jesus as his savior and the solution of his difficulties, the answer to everything, but you have the feeling that he evokes Jesus as the answer to the resolution of his *poem;* and that's different. That's what's always bothered me, and you can't overlook it in Hopkins; it's there. He has only two moods: one of them is elation and thanksgiving and the other is doubt and self-condemnation. But what you have to remember is that the Hopkins magic is in all of his stuff; whether it's this thing or that thing, one thing or the other, the Hopkins magic is there.

Let's read one that does deal with a person. This is one of the earlier ones, and you don't get the full-strength Hopkins in this one, but you get an inkling of it. This is about a farrier to whom Father Hopkins, very uncertain of his vocation as a Catholic priest, gave extreme unction. This is about something that we all know, the big strong guy who gets hit with some disease, in fact, several of them, and this is the priest talking.

FELIX RANDAL

Felix Randal the farrier, O is he dead then? my duty all ended,
Who have watched his mould of man, big-boned and hardy-handsome
Pining, pining, till time when reason rambled in it and some
Fatal four disorders, fleshed there, all contended?

Sickness broke him. Impatient, he cursed at first, but mended
Being anointed and all; though a heavenlier heart began some
Months earlier, since I had our sweet reprieve and ransom
Tendered to him. Ah well, God rest him all road ever he offended!

This seeing the sick endears them to us, us too it endears.
My tongue had taught thee comfort, touch had quenched thy tears,
Thy tears that touched my heart, child, Felix, poor Felix Randal;

How far from then forethought of, all thy more boisterous years,
When thou at the random grim forge, powerful amidst peers,
Didst fettle for the great grey drayhorse his bright and battering sandal!

One of the details you might notice about this is that it's a sonnet. But there's not anybody who's ever written a sonnet like this, using these effects, using this particular approach to language. Hopkins has done what all true creative people do; he has made the form his own; he has appropriated the sonnet for his own uses. And he has put his theories into it, and put his own creative inventions into it, and written it his way.

There's a question that comes up about these poems, as to whether they matter as much to people who are not religious, or who are not Catholics, for example, as they do to people who are Catholic. It's no mistake that the best commentators on Gerard Manley Hopkins have been priests and Jesuits. There's a question for us, and this is a fundamental question on belief in poetry generally, as to whether the poems, say, of Hopkins, who is so specialized and is so much circumscribed by the Catholic faith, can mean as much to people who are not Catholics as they can to people who are Catholics. Now you tell me, because I've never been able to resolve this. But I defer to no man in my admiration of Hopkins, and when I read Hopkins, I think, well, Jim, you might not be religious, but maybe you ought to be. I've read through Hopkins dozens of times, the notebooks, the letters, the poems, all the memorabilia, biographies, and my conclusion is, if somebody this smart has put this much time in on pondering the problems of faith, the relationship of men to the universe, there's gotta be something in it: maybe everything. If such an extraordinary person as this man has put his life into it, maybe I'd better have a little bit better look: maybe I missed something. I've learned so much from him, why not this too?

Let me read to you the conclusion of W. H. Auden's essay on Hopkins, which is a review, by the way, of quite a good short biography, *Gerard Manley Hopkins,* by Eleanor Ruggles. I don't think you'll ever need to know any more about the life of Hopkins than there is here, although there are several biographies. He fascinates people, and I don't know anyone, except maybe T. S. Eliot, who's been written on more than Hopkins has been written on. All aspects of him, his theories of *haeccietas,* instress, inscape, of prosody, his life, his psychology, his vocation as a priest. He was not a successful priest at all. He tried, but he was just too crazy, too much of a natural. Auden says, "He didn't matter, he had a silly face. . . ." This is the thing about Hopkins you have to know: that there was held in balance all of his life this terrible frantic, fantastic tension that his priesthood held together in him, this enormous sensuality, including the sexual, and this intense dedication to his priesthood, to his religion, to his church, to his order, the Jesuits. So, consequently, in many of the poems, you get marvelous statements of exaltation where he's so shook and so delighted by the grandeur of God, and then you get this terrible depression, too, where he questions himself and what he's doing: "I'm not a good priest, my students laugh at me. I can't write poetry. I've given my life to it. Despite all these theories I can't write poetry. That's the only thing I want to do is write poetry, but it's no good, it's no good."

I don't want to end on that gloomy note. Let's do another one, a very simple early one, when he was just beginning to make a style out of all these different elements, out of his linguistic studies, out of his prosodic studies and experiments, his theories of aesthetics, out of his notions of sprung rhythm, his notions of imagery, his studies of the thisness of things, when the whole business of the Hopkins syndrome was coming together. And you notice how he always marks the stresses, because rhythm, that he experimented with so endlessly, is a very great part of the effect of Hopkins's poetry, this strange kind of jerky, intense rhythm. "Spring and Fall, to a Young Child."

Spring and Fall

to a young child

Márgarét, áre you gríeving
Over Goldengrove unleaving?
Leáves, líke the things of man, you
With your fresh thoughts care for, can you?
Áh! ás the heart grows older

40

It will come to such sights colder
By and by, nor spare a sigh
Though worlds of wanwood leafmeal lie;
And yet you *will* weep and know why.
Now no matter, child, the name:
Sórrow's spríngs áre the same.
Nor mouth had, no nor mind, expressed
What heart heard of, ghost guessed:
It ís the blight man was born for,
It is Margaret you mourn for.

But let me leave you not with gloomy things about wrestling in the night with "my God, my God," but something that's really cheerful, and very funny and very cute, and very Hopkins. As I say, he's a great sensualist. This was a poem, that, even though a priest, this was what created part of the tension between two sides of him. He was on the one hand a priest, and on the other hand extremely sensuous, and world-oriented and thing-oriented and feeling-oriented. So this is a good one. He was working on this at the time of his death and he never finished it. It's about going out in the woods and taking off all your clothes and going in the water. It's cold, and there are other fellows there in one little pool, and you know, you think, "If they can do it.—they look like they're having a lot of fun—I'll go out here in this deserted one, see, and I'll go in and just see what happens." But it's very hard to read. It's called "Epithalamion," or "Marriage Song." I used part of this in *Deliverance*. Not *it*, but part of the idea I got from the poem where Drew says to himself after Lewis goes out of the tent at night—this is not in the novel, but it's in the movie—"Trouble is, Lewis wants to be one with nature, and he can't hack it." Well, this is about somebody who *can* hack it.

EPITHALAMION

Hark, hearer, hear what I do; lend a thought now, make believe
We are leaf-whelmed somewhere with the hood
Of some branchy bunchy bushybowered wood,
Southern dean or Lancashire clough or Devon cleave,
That leans along the loins of hills, where a candycoloured, where a
    gluegold-brown
Marbled river, boisterously beautiful, between
Roots and rocks is danced and dandled, all in froth and waterblowballs,
    down.
We are there, when we hear a shout
That the hanging honeysuck, the dogeared hazels in the cover
Makes dither, makes hover

41

And the riot of a rout
Of, it must be, boys from the town
Bathing: it is summer's sovereign good.

By there comes a listless stranger: beckoned by the noise
He drops towards the river: unseen
Sees the bevy of them, how the boys
With dare and with downdolphinry and bellbright bodies huddling out,
Are earthworld, airworld, waterworld thorough hurled, all by turn and
      turn about.

This garland of their gambols flashes in his breast
Into such a sudden zest
Of summertime joys
That he hies to a pool neighbouring; sees it is the best
There; sweetest, freshest, shadowiest;
Fairyland; silk-beech, scrolled ash, packed sycamore, wild wychelm,
      hornbeam fretty overstood
By. Rafts and rafts of flake leaves light, dealt so, painted on the air,
Hang as still as hawk or hawkmoth, as the stars or as the angels there,
Like the thing that never knew the earth, never off roots
Rose. Here he feasts: lovely all is! Nó more: off with—down he dings
His bleachéd both and woolwoven wear:
Careless these in coloured wisp
All lie tumbled-to; then with loop-locks
Forward falling, forehead frowning, lips crisp
Over fingerteasing task, his twiny boots
Fast he opens, last he off wrings
Till walk the world he can with bare his feet
And come where lies a coffer, burly all of blocks
Built of chancequarriéd, selfquainéd, hoar-huskéd rocks
And the water warbles over into, filleted with glassy grassy quicksilvery
      shivés and shoots
And with heavenfallen freshness down from moorland still brims,
Dark or daylight on and on. Here he will then, here he will the fleet
Flinty kindcold element let break across his limbs
Long. Where we leave him, froliclavish, while he looks about him,
      laughs, swims.

Enough now; since the sacred matter that I mean
I should be wronging longer leaving it to float
Upon this only gambolling and echoing-of-earth note
What is   the delightful dean?
Wedlock. What the water? Spousal love
        to Everard, as I surmise,

Sparkled first in Amy's eyes
                                turns
Father, mother, brothers, sisters, friends
Into fairy trees, wildflowers, woodferns
Rankéd round the bower

So, Gerard Manley Hopkins, one of the great ones, one of the strange ones, and, above all, one of the inexplicable ones. There's a very, very fine edition of the poems which even has all the fragments—and anything that Gerard Manley Hopkins puts his hand on is worth reading, has got something remarkable about it. All of this study, all of this originality has gone into the single phrase, no matter whether it's a fragment, or a letter, or whatever. His letters are as remarkable as the poems. This is *The Poems of Gerard Manley Hopkins,* edited by W. H. Gardner and published by the Oxford University Press. The one volume that I was talking to you about is either going to make a fan of you for life, or will suffice for all your Hopkins needs. Among other things he was a remarkable artist, and this book even gives a selection of his line drawings. He never did any paintings, but he did some line drawings which are reminiscent of no one so much as of Leonardo da Vinci. I would say you could put a Hopkins drawing—there're only about fifteen of them—up against Leonardo's and it would not suffer in the slightest. The volume has a little bit of his music, which he was singularly inept in, but kept persevering with—composition, halftone scales. He just loved to experiment. He was curious. Things interested him. This is *The Hopkins Reader,* edited and with an introduction by John Pick, a Catholic at Marquette University; this is Oxford also. A very good biography by Eleanor Ruggles. I haven't seen this in paperback, but I'm sure it is, since everything else of his is. It's originally published by Norton. There are all kinds of studies. This one has to do with the various facets of his genius, his instress, his sprung rhythm, his philosophy, his Catholicism. This is a series which might interest you, and probably should interest you, published by the British Council, called British Council pamphlets; and this an unusually good one by Geoffrey Grigson, *Gerard Manley Hopkins.* It has kind of a nice ending, which I ought to share with you in just a sentence or two: "Hopkins considered that poetry was unprofessional."

Don't neglect the letters. He has three enormous collections of letters—to Robert Bridges, who was poet laureate, and to Coventry Patmore, who was a very well-recognized poet in those days, and to another cleric named Canon Dixon, another priest who wrote poetry. Those three volumes of Hopkins's letters have a strong claim to being the greatest literary criticism, especially the greatest literary criticism concerning poetry from the standpoint of a writer of poetry, in the nineteenth century. I would prefer them, for example, to the essays of Matthew Arnold, as crazy as I am about *them*. I would still prefer Hopkins. There's quite a good selection of the more important letters in this John Pick volume.

Next time let's do something that I don't really want to do, but it would be instructive to do. Let's read Bridges, who is Hopkins's great confidant. Now, again, I would be giving nothing away as far as the secret life of Gerard Manley Hopkins is concerned when I say that there was probably at least an incipient homosexual relationship between Hopkins and Bridges, at least on Hopkins's part. Bridges was everything that Hopkins was not. Hopkins was an obscure priest, poor, small, rather nondescript. Bridges was a famous English poet, rich, leisurely, handsome. He was a very striking fellow, 6'4" tall, leonine head—all the portrait painters wanted to paint his portrait. And opinion's now swung around to the belief that Bridges was a pompous ass, and that Hopkins wasted his time writing letters to Bridges. Not so; Bridges was a real poet of a completely different persuasion from Hopkins, and that's where the correspondence, the letters of Hopkins to Bridges, become vitally interesting. And they become even more interesting, maybe, because Bridges destroyed his part of the correspondence. For what reasons I don't think anybody will ever know, but one can guess. But Bridges's part of the correspondence is gone. However, it has to be held to Bridges's credit, even though he never understood Hopkins's poetry, and didn't understand why he wrote it the way he did, didn't understand his metrical experiments, didn't understand anything about why Hopkins was doing things as he was doing, Bridges was still sympathetic. We owe the poems of Gerard Manley Hopkins to Robert Bridges, because he was given the manuscripts. He had the poems, and although he didn't understand them, and really didn't approve of most of them, he saw to it that they were brought out. But he himself is the subject I want to talk about next time, so read Bridges.

So read Bridges, and let's read Housman before we get into the quagmire of Yeats. Now, as far as the poets in our paperback are concerned, there's an extremely helpful book you can get. I'm sure the library has it. If you were going to write a book on contemporary American poets and you thought of this title, would you use it? *Alone with America*. Would you use it? Would you consider it? I don't know. But I like it anyway. It's an enormous book on contemporary poets and poetry. Not Eliot and Pound and Wallace Stevens and all the people you study in school, but the new guys, most of whom you probably almost certainly have not heard of. But this Richard Howard, *Alone with America,* is a good way to hear of them. They're very thorough essays and very interesting. He's read all these people, and he has opinions about all of them.

The fellow that I was hoping to read today, Edgar Bowers, is in here. There's an essay on him that's very good.

And I want you to think very seriously about poetry and rules. You know what I mean by rules? What other people have done and what critics tell you that you ought to be doing. Rules. This is not to say that because they are rules they are necessarily bad. No; you can't be narrow-minded. But just think a little bit about rules: rules of diction, prosody, stanza formation, because these are things that have to be thought about if you're going to do any serious thinking about poetry at all. And if there's any justification for a class like this, it's a class for people who do some serious thinking about poetry. All right?

ROBERT BRIDGES

Robert Bridges is not much read anymore. He corresponded with Gerard Manley Hopkins for most of Hopkins's working life as a writer; and he, himself, was in a much quieter way, I wouldn't say as remarkable a poet as Hopkins, but remarkable indeed in his own way. Let me get into him by way of talking about different approaches to the writing of poetry. I don't believe there'll ever be a substitute for the old dichotomy of romanticism and classicism. I'm sure you get a bellyful of that in college. Does anybody want to come up with a definition having to do with this? What is the difference, essentially, between these things? A poet who's ultimately a romantic poet and a poet who's ultimately a classical poet? Anybody got any ideas? What do they tell you in your other classes? There are lots of different definitions; yours would not be any more incompetent than anybody else's. It has to do with the psychological relationship of the poet to his material—subjective, emotional, excessive. How about classical? I would say the big word characterizing classical would be restraint, and the emphasis on form, usually traditional form. That was the kind of poet Bridges was.

I think we can get into him and also get into another poet who followed in his steps, an American West Coast poet who originally comes from Georgia —he was a fellow I knew when I was growing up—Edgar Bowers, who's one of the newer fellows. I think we can get into this better by looking at the opinions of Edgar Bowers's teacher, Yvor Winters, who said that Bridges, contrary to popular opinion, is the greatest modern poet. You're not going to find anybody who says that but Yvor Winters. He makes some very excessive statements.

Let me introduce you to some books that you can use, if you major in English, or even if you're just interested in the subject. This was one that came out while I was in college. My literary education was conducted in the age of criticism when it was much more important to be educated as a literary critic than as a creative writer. I remember the attitude very well at Vanderbilt while I was there. A book like this would come out—which is a book by a critic writing on critics of critics, and so on. We've reached that too, but we're getting back to a little more emphasis on the creative writer in the college, in a class like this, but in my day, we all were critics. Critics of this, and who thought this and who thought that. And who controverted so-and-so's opinion of such-and-such. As far as the poor poet was concerned, he was only someone who furnished the occasion for a brilliant critic to write something. And there's still a good deal of that around colleges, and especially around graduate schools. It's as though you were present at a hog-judging contest and one of the judges walked over to the poor pig and punched him in the side and said, "Huh! What do you know about pork?" The critics say to the poet, "What do you know about poetry? I'm the critic. I know a lot more about it than you who merely produce it." But this was a book that came out at that time, and it's a very serviceable book by a very good critic on other critics. It is called *The Armed Vision* by Stanley Edgar Hyman, who died last year. He has a chapter on Yvor Winters, whose excessive opinions I'm going to use to begin talking about Bridges. Hyman says, "The highest praise in Winters' vocabulary has been reserved for Robert Bridges." Now get this. See if you could ever conceive of anyone having an excessive opinion of a little-known poet as excessive as this. "Bridges' poetry, according to Winters, is superior to that of T. S. Eliot, Hart Crane, William Carlos Williams, Marianne Moore, and practically every other modern poet. . . ." That's the kind of stuff you get from Yvor Winters. Nevertheless, a very influential man in his time—and very influential on American poetry through a small coterie of people who think as he does.

Now, what do we find when we read Bridges? First of all, although he's represented in our book, he's not really very well represented. "Nightingales" and "The Storm Is Over" are typical of Bridges. First of all, what kind of man was he? His correspondence with Hopkins is one of the things by which he's known. That and the fact that he espoused Hopkins's cause although he didn't understand what Hopkins was doing. And he believed in Hopkins, and he edited Hopkins's works after his death and made him available. If it hadn't been for Robert Bridges, there would be no collected poems or anything else of Gerard Manley Hopkins. This is enormously to Bridges's credit, although they argued and disagreed on almost every fundamental point as regards poetry. Bridges was everything that Hopkins was not. Hopkins was a poor, obscure priest. Ugly. He hated to look at himself in the mirror. He was filled with self-contempt his whole life. Bridges was extremely fortunate in his life, where he was born, the way he was born, the fact that he inherited money. He was rich; he was handsome; and he became poet laureate.

Although it's also to his credit that he never wrote official odes or any of those things. He just accepted the position of poet laureate as a kind of sinecure.

Nevertheless, he was a person who was absolutely and entirely devoted to poetry. He looked on the fact that he had inherited money simply as a means to enable him to devote himself wholeheartedly and whole-spiritedly to the cause of the composition of poetic works. And there can seldom have been such complete dedication to poetry than Robert Bridges had.

What you have here is a person, as I say, who's fortunate as to the composition of poetry, the time for it, the environment for it. He lived at Oxford all his life. Or very near there. You have someone fortunate beyond the dreams of avarice, beyond the dreams of almost any other poet. He had everything going for him. Question is,—now this is a human situation, which is a very difficult one—when you have everything going for you, what is the next question? What do you do? You've got the time, you've got the leisure, you've got the inclination, now how do you use it? Bridges didn't have any excuse not to be a great poet if time and money guarantee this. And he had a great devotion to the craft. If all of these could give it to him, he had it. He had everything. He didn't have to do as most poets do, scramble around, a minute here and a minute there, to put a poem together. No, he had all the time he wanted. Now, the thing that makes it interesting about him is what he did with it. He became a master craftsman. Bridges's work seems very old-fangled. It doesn't seem like it was written by anybody that came on into the twentieth century. It seems like it was written by somebody—I mean if you just look at that aspect of it— it seems like it was written by someone around the time of Tennyson or a little bit before, as far as the diction, or most of the diction, is concerned. When somebody picks up a book of poems by Bridges, he sees thee's and thou's, that kind of business, and he thinks, "Jesus, I'm not going to mess with this guy. I mean, he's old hat; look at the way he writes." That would be a bad mistake. What Bridges does, essentially, is to bring to this old-fashioned diction a chilly purity that might not have been possible to him with another kind of diction. As a craftsman of verse forms and of prosody, he is astonishing. His control is absolutely wonderful. But the thing is that he's cold. He doesn't set you on fire. He's too much of a conventional artist. He's too perfect.

And everything is as consciously and purely English as it can possibly be. Now that's also something that you're going to be aware of if you read very much of Bridges. It is in some sense very mild. Some of it is very penetrating, and all of it is beautifully done. What one misses in Bridges is any sense of a drama or power. It's all, as Conrad Aiken says, poetry which is kind of peaceful and skillful and beautiful, and, I wouldn't say this completely, but I would tend to agree with Aiken, when he says, essentially empty. But you can sure learn a lot from it as far as style is concerned because he's got it cold; he knows it.

Now this business of Yvor Winters as an influence, as a teacher of students, and a very, very influential one, too. He was a teacher at Stanford, and was tremendously controversial all his life. His opinions were extremely unpopular with other people. He had almost no truck with the great gods of modern literature, Pound and Eliot and Joyce, Yeats, Cummings; and he had a few people whose causes he espoused and wrote long essays on, as to how great their work was and how they were sane and civilized men in addition to Dylan Thomas, who was a kind of self-indulgent wild man. He hated Yeats; he hated Eliot; he hated Hopkins. He liked the kind of poetry that Bridges writes, and that's the kind that he taught several generations of students to write, and that is the kind that he, himself, wrote. I wrote an essay which brought me a letter from Dr. Winters threatening a libel action. And I thought you might like to hear about half a paragraph of that. Because I hated him and he hated me. And this is one of these kinds of reviews where you kind of bend over backwards to be fair because you know the guy doesn't like you. But this is nevertheless what I chose to say, and what I would stay with. "Regardless of whatever else may be said of him, Yvor Winters is the best example our time has to show of the poet who writes the rules. . . ." Well, my question was this: It's fine to try to achieve a style for a matter of thirty years, but what is going to lead a man to try to achieve *this kind* of style? Winters said that he wanted a style which was completely free of any momentary topical influence—to write a poem that would be good now and would be good at any other time, be good fifty years, one hundred years, two hundred years from now, and would not depend on anything topical. That's all well and good, but what do you think of that as an attitude for a working poet? I mean, there's certainly an opposite possible—that you can try to be so topical and faddy and "with it" that your work, including its diction, is going to be out of style in not only five years, but in one year, or even six months. But as an attitude for a working poet, what do you think of this? What Winters does not seem to realize, and what he taught his students, like Edgar Bowers, to resist, is the notion that language changes. It is inevitable that it changes; it must change. And the poet's language must change with it.

Bridges had the notion that by going old-fangled with the thee's and thou's and looketh's that his language would also be timeless; Winters the same way. But language changes; it's inevitable that it changes. We don't read Shakespeare and glory in his wonderful language because he was a product of the sixteenth century, or any century, or timelessness, but because he was an Elizabethan and he wrote out of *that* idiom, and he used the dynamics and the resources of the language as it was given to him. And this is what poets have to do. You cannot have an artificial restriction such as Winters imposed on himself and avail yourself of the resources of the living language of your time. You cannot do that; it just won't work.

Randall Jarrell is the finest literary critic of my time, and he had a paragraph on this attitude, on Winters and his influence on his students. And one other thing about Winters—I hate to go on and on about him, but you'll encounter him sooner or later and you probably ought to have a preliminary opinion of him because he's an excessively bad critic of some importance. He has influenced an awful lot of young writers, including, as I say, Edgar Bowers. Jarrell said this of him, "This doctrinaire of directness is as noticeable in the beatnik's opposite. . . ."

EDGAR BOWERS

That's what gets us to Edgar Bowers. Edgar Bowers is a very good fellow. He went to Decatur High School while I was at North Fulton in Atlanta, and I never would have expected in a million years that he would be a poet, and he wouldn't have expected the same of me. But I remember him with affection, although I didn't really know him very well. But he's very serious about what he's doing. He went out to Stanford and studied with Winters, and he caught Winters's eye early on because he's a smart boy and a good writer; he writes with form and grace. And he took Winters's doctrines and labored as diligently as it is possible for a poet to labor to do what Winters wanted him to do. Now that the master has gone, he's in the master's chair, and he doesn't write much any more. He never did write much. He was extremely fastidious. Of this kind of writer, of this writing by rules, of this writing by the doctrines of Yvor Winters, he is the best of the guys that do it. It's an unpopular but, in some ways, influential approach. He has two books only, very slim. One of them is called *The Form of Loss* and the other is *The Astronomers,* both published by Allan Swallow—isn't that a wonderful name for a poetry publisher? *The Astronomers,* the second book, is the stronger book, and it's extremely good—as I say, you always have to qualify Bowers's work, and the work of Yvor Winters's other disciples, or *I* always find myself qualifying it in the end as very good of its kind. I don't like the kind, but good it is. If there is any virtue in Winters's approach it is to be found in the work of Edgar Bowers. He's a graceful, kind of quasi-philosophical poet, but reading very much of his work is like trying to wade upstream in cold mineral water. It's so cold and seems to have that rocklike feel to it. There is one poem of his that has moved me, and "moving" is not the word that I would usually use in connection with him. He has a series of twelve poems called "Autumn Shade" in blank verse, in sonnets, in various other received forms of English verse. This is in blank verse and it's the best thing of his I've ever read. It's the only thing of Edgar's that I've ever read that ever really moved me, that I not only admired because it's well done, but *liked,* and *felt.*

AUTUMN SHADE, PART I

The autumn shade is thin. Grey leaves lie faint
Where they will lie, and, where the thick green was,
Light stands up, like a presence, to the sky.
The trees seem merely shadows of its age.
From off the hill, I hear the logging crew,
The furious and indifferent saw, the slow
Response of heavy pine; and I recall
That goddesses have died when their trees died.
Often in summer, drinking from the spring,
I sensed in its cool breath and in its voice
A living form, darker than any shade
And without feature, passionate, yet chill
With lust to fix in ice the buoyant rim—
Ancient of days, the mother of us all.
Now, toward his destined passion there, the strong,
Vivid young man, reluctant, may return
From suffering in his own experience
To lie down in the darkness. In this time,
I stay indoors. I do my work. I sleep.
Each morning, when I wake, I assent to wake.
The shadow of my fist moves on this page,
Though, even now, in the wood, beneath a bank,
Coiled in the leaves and cooling rocks, the snake
Does as it must, and sinks into the cold.

A. E. Housman

What sometimes happens in our book: we don't have a very good or very typical selection of this particular poet in there. That he's in there at all, though, gives us the chance to talk about him, and I think we should do just that.

He has got something in common with just a few other poets, Robert Frost being one of them, and you can name him your other candidate, the identification being that he is a genuinely good poet, though minor, though small. He is a genuine poet who has been enormously popular. I think probably he's the most popular real poet to publish a book in the nineteenth century, not excepting Alfred Tennyson. When Alfred Tennyson used to walk by on the street, mothers would hold their children up so that they could get a glimpse of him. It's hard for us to imagine a poet being accorded that kind of status now. Tomorrow you might see a poet's name in headlines, but it would be for killing his wife, or having written a novel, or something, but it won't be for having written poetry. Tennyson and Housman were best-sellers. I expect Housman's book, *A Shropshire Lad,* by any conservative estimate you would want to make—it was published in 1896—must have sold at least fifty million volumes. And that's a lot of slender volumes. It would be interesting, I believe, for us at this time to look at what he did and why he was the way he was.

First of all, as in the case of Frost, Housman is a good poet who's read by an awful lot of people who don't normally read poetry. What do they read in our day, people who don't normally read poetry? Rod McKuen. Housman is in that category; but unlike Rod McKuen, he is a good poet who is read by hundreds of thousands of people. Two in the nineteenth century I can think of had this kind of popularity. Of course Tennyson was poet laureate; Housman was not. He was a university Latin teacher who wrote occasional verse. The only two I can think of are Housman and *A Shropshire Lad* and *The Rubáiyát of Omar Khayyám* (1859), which is a different kind of book, but with something of the same outlook, oddly enough, melancholy, singing of the uselessness of existence and the fleeting pleasures before we enter into the long night forever. I can give you in connection with these people that we talk about just as much biographical background or as little as you want. It doesn't matter to me. In this case, I would like to give maybe a little more than usual because the psychological instance is so fascinating and because Housman is in some ways one of the great enigmas of English poetry.

Here's the situation with him. He was born in 1859, if I'm not mistaken. He was the oldest of seven children. He was actually not from Shropshire at all, and during his whole long life of seventy-seven years, hardly ever went there. This is a very curious circumstance. His main volume of poetry and all the poems that made him famous were written about Shropshire, but they were written by a man who only saw Shropshire as the western boundary of his particular county. So what would this indicate to you? The Shropshire place names and the geographical details of Shropshire were not well known to Housman. Now what would you say this would indicate about his relationship to Shropshire? That is, he's writing about a place that he's grown up near, but has not seen, except way in the distance. Would that suggest anything to you about an attitude toward Shropshire, which is very beautiful, by the way? Very, very idealistic. What he called the "land of lost contents." The poetry almost inevitably has to partake of one of two emotions—either he would fill it with his own longing and it would have a kind of melancholy, in this case pastoral, situation; or he would look to the future of going there, somewhere he's never been or he never will go or that he wants to go to. As it was, he never really did go there so that he could create a country of the imagination. What happened was this. He was a very precocious boy, a born scholar, and he took all kinds of honors in the early part of his schooling. He was a Latin and a Greek scholar of the most exacting and self-disciplined kind. He went up to Oxford to take a degree in what they called Greats. I won't go into the Oxford hierarchy, but it's an honors curriculum. Housman was such a self-contained and, you might say, self-obsessed and withdrawn person that he was somewhat contemptuous of the reading he was asked to do for the honors program for the Greats course. He knew that he was as good a Latinist, even at his early age, as anybody at Oxford, *anybody,* and almost as good in Greek. And he was disdainful of these long courses in philosophy and all this reading and philosophy that didn't interest him. He was aware from a very early age of what interested him and what did not, and he was disdainful of the reading he was asked to do. All right, he gets up to the Greats examinations and the questions that he hasn't done the reading on, or that he's disdainful of the reading for, or that he just doesn't want to fool with, what does he do? He ignores them. So, the committee had no choice but to refuse him his degree. He was like that. He was adamant; he was one of the most strong-willed literary men who has ever written—he knew what he wanted. But the result of this bullheadedness was that he was dropped from the university, and it cost him ten years. All right: his family was of modest means, and they have these other children. He was the oldest son; he was expected to have been able to send the family a little money. All that's gone. He flunked; as they say at Oxford, he was ploughed. And that doesn't mean he had too much beer, either.

So, he goes to London, and he goes to work as a minor civil servant in the patent office. But, with a man of Housman's tenacity, he knows that he's got it in him to be a great Latin scholar, so what he does is put all his time in, when he's not working in the patent office, on studying. And he studies. He catches scholars out in small scholarly papers. He learns their weaknesses, and he builds their weaknesses up into his strength. And by the time ten years have passed, he has published so much, and attracted so much notice in scholarly circles, that he's given the Latin chair at the University of London. He goes up there. He's also written some little occasional verses, very rigorous, based on Latin models. In fact, he's written some poetry in Latin, which later came out in various places, and was announced to be by authorities, like Gilbert Murray, as being not one whit inferior to Horace, to whom Latin was a native tongue. Through this enormous force of will, he takes this position at the University of London. He's there for fourteen years; he's all the time publishing, and he withdraws more and more into the life of a hermit. He never had much social life. He was a withdrawn, scholarly, almost monastic type of a person, and this becomes more and more pronounced. And he's then given the highest chair the English can give a scholar of his type. By this time, he's the greatest name in his field. He is the greatest Latin textual scholar in the whole history of English scholarship, with the possible exception of Richard Bentley (1662–1742), and, as he himself said, "I've caught Bentley out many times." And he had. Housman didn't make a move or publish a paper unless he had the facts, unless he knew exactly what he was saying. But from then on, from the time he gets the Canaday professorship, he gets this curious attitude toward other scholars. Now this is a very small, limited field; it's the field of the expert in the editing of Latin classic texts. And Housman not only does this—here's a description that'll give it to you better than I can. One was the editing of classic texts from various texts that have come down to us from antiquity. The chief working hypothesis of his time was that the earliest text was the definitive text. Housman flew right in the face of that. He said, this is nothing but an excuse for lazy scholars. Sometimes the later text is the better text, and he had many instances to show why this was so.

He was a brilliant, brilliant scholar, and his greatest brilliance, in addition to his enormous knowledge that took him years and years of assiduous study to acquire, was that he was the only scholar of his time who knew how a poet's mind worked. See, he edited poets. He was able by brilliant insights and strokes of intuition, which have later been verified by texts that have been discovered since he wrote these papers, to be exactly right in not only *most* of the instances, but in *every* instance in which he did this. Anyway, he developed, in addition to his own editing work—I'll tell you about that in a minute, because it's fascinating—he developed an excessively virulent attitude toward other scholars. Now, I don't know or care how much you know or care about classical scholarship or about any scholarship, but if you want to see one scholar get after another one, you ought to read what Housman has to say about these obscure German textual commentators. He writes about them, and is so unduly insulting that there is something embarrassing about it. He went out of his way to be ugly in a particularly elaborate style because he believed that as a scholar he had a duty to stamp out error, to stamp out laziness, to stamp out incompetence, to stamp out ignorance. Because he believed that the text was pure, the best minds had to be brought to bear on the problem of presenting a classic writer as he actually wrote instead of as some scholar thought he probably should have written, or didn't know any better. So, he spent years and years and years smashing down these other scholars in England and mostly in Germany. If you're interested in this, you can read some of the most virulent scholarly prose, or any kind of prose, since Swift in his *Selected Prose*. He's a tough man to tangle with in print, I tell you, because he knew and they didn't. And he was quite willing to say that they didn't. In fact, he was more than willing, and he said it in this particular style that combined a very high degree of scholarly knowledge and a kind of sarcastic, unforgiving attitude, which must have made those poor other scholars shrivel when they read it.

But there is something excessive and even monstrous about this, especially when you consider that Housman himself, who had done a great deal of work editing the texts of a Latin poet named Propertius (c. 49–16 B.C.E.), who is mainly a love poet, had thrown all this out in favor of editing the works of a fifth-rate Latin poet named Manilius (c. first century C.E.), who wrote long, strange poems about astronomy, not about human beings at all, not a love poet. He didn't even write about people,—not that that would guarantee anything one way or the other—but he was just a person that we happened to have had very many works on and who had never been very well edited. So Housman spends about twenty-five years editing the definitive text of Manilius. Now why? Well, I'll tell you why. Because of this extremely introverted iron-willed personality he had at the beginning and developed progressively through the rest of his life, he wanted to edit Manilius because he could have his way completely and nobody could challenge anything he said. He wanted to do the definitive thing; he wanted to be the greatest scholar that Manilius ever had working on him; and he was. And he always will be. Nobody will ever do that again. Why should they? Nobody reads him anyway. So, this is one thing. But the other thing is that he attained by day-to-day work—say from nine to five every day—thirteen volumes, very closely printed. I went and looked them up one time, and, my God, that's a forbidding-looking bunch of tomes. But he worked all this up and edited these things with all this enormous effort in order to achieve this reputation. All right, he achieves it. Nobody is going to gainsay that he's the greatest Latin scholar in Europe, and maybe the greatest that's ever lived in this narrow little field—textual bibliography and commentary. So honors began to flood in. You know what Housman does? Refuses them systematically, one after the other. It's kind of scholarly revenge on a world that rejected him, or wasn't prepared at the outset to take him at his face value. He is a brilliant guy; he's almost inhumanly brilliant in that particular field, and a very good writer on poetry when he wants to be, although he published just a very little bit on poetry generally. He had an interesting introductory lecture. He never made lectures that he was not required by his job to make. Then he would get one up. But there were only two his whole lifetime—one for the University of London and one for Cambridge.

In the first one, there's a curious attitude he takes about knowledge itself. I think it's kind of a justification for his particular position, spending all this time editing something that really doesn't matter to begin with very much. But he takes the position that knowledge itself is valuable and important, and the individual ought to be free to pursue any knowledge, not because it's important or useful, but simply because it's knowledge. It's a position that I don't think very many of us would hold to, but that's the position he takes. It's an interesting essay that, as Huck Finn would say, is told about in here. It's quite a good little book. You could read through it in a couple of hours, and you'd know quite a bit about Housman. A much more important essay, or bit of literary criticism, that he wrote was written while he was at Cambridge and required to make another lecture. It's called "The Name and Nature of Poetry." And this is going to get us over into his own work. I don't mean to imply, although this may be true to some extent, that he was as forbidding a character in his personal life as I make him seem, although forbidding he surely was. He could be social, and he could be unexpectedly kind, such as donating his money to funds and that sort of thing, but he never wanted it to be known. He was the most retired and withdrawn of men, as I say, almost a hermit. But in "The Name and Nature of Poetry," which is certainly worth your reading—

this was sort of Housman's credo as a poet, what he thinks poetry is—you get an unexpectedly accessible Housman. When you read all these diatribes against these textual critics that he's been famous for, for so many years, or had been up until that time, the essay's unexpectedly easygoing, and even charming, and extremely readable. It says, for example—this is a paragraph I like particularly—"Meaning is of the intellect; poetry is not. . . ." There, he's explaining what he thought he was doing and how he went about doing it. He was the greatest Roman poet who ever wrote in English. And there's a great deal to that.

Now, let me give you the books. All the Housman you're ever going to want is in the *Collected Poems*. And how does it happen that this austere, scholarly, monklike Latin scholar writes these poems that are with almost monotonous, but very beautiful regularity, pastoral poems about death, the loss of life, murder, people being hanged, people betraying each other, and the generally, unbelievably vast futility of everything? Why and exactly how did that happen?

There's a very funny parody, which I must read to you, by the way, which Housman read and very gracefully acknowledged. It's by a man named Hugh Kingsmill, and it's written in Housman style, but it's nonetheless still very much a parody.

"WHAT, STILL ALIVE AT TWENTY-TWO"

What, still alive at twenty-two,
A clean, upstanding chap like you?
Sure, if your throat 'tis hard to slit,
Slit your girl's and swing for it.

Like enough, you won't be glad,
When they come to hang you, lad:
But bacon's not the only thing
That's cured by hanging from a string.

So, when the spilt ink of the night
Spreads o'er the blotting-pad of light,
Lads whose job is still to do
Shall whet their knives and think of you.

Housman said of the parody, "It's the best I have seen, and indeed, the only good one."

The paradox here is that his volume, *A Shropshire Lad,* absolutely took England by storm. Everybody had a copy on the coffee table, or tea table, or whatever kind of table they have over there, and everybody read it and talked about it; and Housman said, characteristically, "The greatest favor that my fellow dons here at Cambridge have ever done me was never to speak to me of my poetry." Well, he was maybe too shy, too withdrawn. There's something strange about Housman and his preoccupation with death, also his preoccupation with soldiers. Some of the, not the absolute, best of Housman's poems are about soldiers marching on, to go somewhere to be killed. Let me read to you this one, "Seasons Go By."

SEASONS GO BY

This time of year a twelvemonth past,
  When Fred and I would meet,
We needs must jangle, till at last
  We fought and I was beat.

So then the summer fields about,
  Till rainy days began,
Rose Harland on her Sundays out
  Walked with the better man.

The better man she walks with still,
  Though now 'tis not with Fred:
A lad that lives and has his will
  Is worth a dozen dead.

Fred keeps the house all kinds of weather,
  And clay's the house he keeps;
When Rose and I walk out together
  Stock-still lies Fred and sleeps.

"Is my friend hearty,
  Now I am thin and pine,
And has he found to sleep in
  A better bed than mine?"

Yes, lad, I lie easy,
  I lie as lads would choose;
I cheer a dead man's sweetheart,
  Never ask me whose.

Very often in literary criticism, it's the purpose to compare Hardy and Housman, who both had something of the generic kind of universal world pessimism, and to extol Hardy at Housman's expense, saying that Hardy is profound and very, very human; Housman is too much of a formula poet, his range is too narrow, he's too repetitive, and too popular. And yet I would say in answer to this, I would say that Hardy is indeed a greater poet than Housman. Housman is determinedly small, he *is* repetitive, and he *is* very limited in his means. But, if you will concede that part of the effectiveness of the poet is memorability, the ability to say memorable things in a particularly memorable way, then you've got to go with Housman. I can remember hundreds of his lines, and only a few of Hardy's. The only two poems that I know by heart— of course Housman wrote real short poems, and Hardy didn't always do that— but the only two poems that I know by heart are by Housman, and I will now proceed to recite them. One is an "Epitaph on an Army of Mercenaries," and this has that particular kind of admiration coupled with irony that is typical, very characteristic, of Housman.

EPITAPH ON AN ARMY OF MERCENARIES

These, in the day when heaven was falling,
    The hour when earth's foundations fled,
Followed their mercenary calling
    And took their wages and are dead.
Their shoulders held the sky suspended;
    They stood, and earth's foundations stay;
What God abandoned, these defended,
    And saved the sum of things for pay.

CHARLES CAUSLEY

Now, let's have a real quick look at Causley. He's one of the few poets around who uses the ballad form, or variations on the ballad form, with all the traditional internal rhyming that other people have used at other times, but not modern poets. You wouldn't think it either possible or desirable for a poet to be a balladeer in our time, the time of Ezra Pound and T. S. Eliot. But he's quite good fun, and he's got a rollicking kind of slightly bawdy, masculine sound to him. It's called "Recruiting Drive."

RECRUITING DRIVE

Under the willow the willow
    I heard the butcher-bird sing,
Come out you fine young fellow
    From under your mother's wing.
I'll show you the magic garden
    That hangs in the beamy air,
The way of the lynx and the angry Sphinx
    And the fun of the freezing fair.

Lie down lie down with my daughter
    Beneath the Arabian tree,
Gaze on your face in the water
    Forget the scribbling sea.
Your pillow the nine bright shiners
    Your bed the spilling sand,
But the terrible toy of my lily-white boy
    Is the gun in his innocent hand.

You must take off your clothes for the doctor
    And stand as straight as a pin,
His hands of stone on your white breast-bone
    Where the bullets all go in.
They'll dress you in lawn and linen
    And fill you with Plymouth gin,

O the devil may wear a rose in his hair
   I'll wear my fine doe-skin.

My mother weeps as I leave her
   But I tell her it won't be long,
The murderers wail in Wandsworth Gaol
   But I shoot a more popular song.
Down in the enemy country
   Under the enemy tree
There lies a lad whose heart has gone bad
   Waiting for me, for me.

He says I have no culture
   And that when I've stormed the pass
I shall fall on the farm with a smoking arm
   And ravish his bonny lass.
Under the willow the willow
   Death spreads her dipping wings
And caught in the snare of the bleeding air
   The butcher-bird sings, sings, sings.

This poem doesn't seem to me to be together any too well, but it has some good things in it, and one of the best things in it is the way he uses the driving, slightly, no, more than slightly, singsong kind of line. If you had a favorite in that, which one of those stanzas do you think is the best? Or do you have any particular feeling? There's one that's a favorite of mine in a way that the rest of the poem is not a favorite of mine, and that's the one about the medical examination. That's damn good: "His hands of stone on your white breast-bone / Where the bullets all go in."

The other one is funny as the devil. It's a kind of tongue-in-cheek variation on all the cowboy ballads, streets of Laredo, and all those things that you've ever heard.

COWBOY SONG

I come from Salem County
   Where the silver melons grow,
Where the wheat is sweet as an angel's feet
   And the zithering zephyrs blow.
I walk the blue bone-orchard
   In the apple-blossom snow,
When the teasy bees take their honeyed ease
   And the marmalade moon hangs low.

Charles Causley

My Maw sleeps prone on the prairie
    In a boulder eiderdown,
Where the pickled stars in their little jam-jars
    Hang in a hoop to town.
I haven't seen Paw since a Sunday
    In eighteen seventy-three
When he packed his snap in a bitty mess-trap
    And said he'd be home by tea.

Fled is my fancy sister
    All weeping like the willow,
And dead is my brother I loved like no other
    Who once did share my pillow.
I fly the florid water
    Where run the seven geese round,
O the townsfolk talk to see me walk
    Six inches off the ground.

Across the map of midnight
    I trawl the turning sky,
In my green glass the salt fleets pass
    The moon her fire-float by.
The girls go gay in the valley
    When the boys come down from the farm,
Don't run, my joy, from a poor cowboy,
    I won't do you no harm.

The bread of my twentieth birthday
    I buttered with the sun,
Though I sharpen my eyes with lovers' lies
    I'll never see twenty-one.
Light is my shirt with lilies,
    And lined with lead my hood,
On my face as I pass is a plate of brass,
    And my suit is made of wood.

But the funny thing is that it's written by an Englishman, and he doesn't know American idiom, and it comes out kind of unintentionally funny. It's good, of its kind, but it also uses Englishisms that no American poet who even knew where Laredo was would use.

William Butler Yeats

There are small writers that you can like without equivocation or without reservation, but I think there are no great writers that you have no reservations about whether or not you like them. You're always of a mixed mind about them. It is true that Yeats had some, we would think of as unfortunate, political opinions. I don't want to dwell on those. We'll get to them when we get down to that part of his work and his life. The thing that's interesting about Yeats is that he is atypical of the usual career of a poet, especially a lyric poet, although he wrote plays and some of the best stuff is in his plays. He wrote the plays in verse, most of them. But he is atypical in that we generally tend to think of poets as being at their peak in their twenties, or even earlier, such as a poet like Rimbaud. Yeats went through, in some ways sort of like Picasso, he went through several phases, and he shows a continuous curve of improvement. So the very best poetry he wrote in his whole life was written when he was an old man, which is very, very unusual. Even Hardy does not show the curve of continuous improvement in the same way as Yeats. Hardy is good in some poems, and maybe a great poet, but he does not have the world stature that Yeats does. And it would be interesting, I think, to look at Yeats's career in some detail, for of all the poets in English, he, in our time, is worth close scrutiny more than any other poet is worth it.

First of all, let me tell you what you should read. Macmillan does his publishing, and there is a great big one-volume Yeats *Collected Poems.* This is not definitive; he was a fastidious and indefatigable craftsman. He changed poems of his, substituted words, changed punctuation, line endings and so on all his life. He never was done working on anything that had his name on it; he was incessantly working to make it better. But if you're not that interested in the scholarly pursuit of Yeats and just want the stuff in the final form in which he put it, you can get it all, almost all of it, in this *Collected Poems;* it's quite a nice book. Yeats lived to be an old man; he was seventy-four when he died in 1939, so he had plenty of time to perfect his work and had the will and the tenacity to get in there and work on it all the time. Okay, now that's one for poetry.

There's the *Collected Plays.* But if you have the *Collected Poems* and the *Collected Plays,* that's really all the verse, all the poetry, you're going to want to have in connection with Yeats. The other passes over from the realm of the poetic to that of the scholarly, and whether or not you want to jump that gap is really up to you. There is also an autobiography and the astonishing work that he calls *A Vision,* which puts forth his system, half astrological, half philosophical, and half something that I never saw anywhere else. It's a weird kind of a piece of work, but I won't talk about it yet. But we'll have to talk about it a good deal later.

What I want to talk about today is the notion of Yeats as a man who willed becoming the thing that he did in fact become. I'll show you stage by stage how he did that later on. This was done by the most curious possible means, because Yeats turned his back on everything that we take for granted—scientific materialism, machinery, technology, social advances. He just turned his back on that and went another way. Question is, what was the way? When we started talking in this class the first couple of days, we stressed this business of the fragmentation of modern life and the need for artists, especially, apparently, poets, to create a new kind of myth. The great example of our time, the great example of the mythographer, the myth maker, is Yeats. He set forth a whole personal, universal mystical system, which was anti-scientific. I'm getting a little bit ahead of myself. He was Irish and this gives him, as a writer, as a poet, certain advantages that, say, an American would not have. Can you think of what this might be? What could have been a great advantage to a poet who was born, say, in 1865, in Ireland? I'm not saying advantages generally. I'm saying advantages to a poet. And living among people, not among factory workers. Peasants, sure, but also the people he admired the most—the great landed gentry. These were the people that he admired, and sought out, and cultivated. What else? They still have a mythology there. Not only the leprechaun appropriated by Walt Disney, but ghosts and fairies and symbolical, or what Auden would call sacred places, sacred objects. A legend of kings and queens and great things being done; a realm of consequence, a past of consequence. The great Irish legendary King Cuchulain, for example, that Yeats writes about all the time. There's the question of whether you'd rather believe in him or George Washington. Cuchulain is much better for poetry, at least for Yeats's poetry. In fact, I've never read good poems about George Washington, or Jefferson either. Maybe Lincoln, Whitman's poem. But Yeats had a built-in mythology, and that's where he started. Yeats comes from the west of Ireland, the place where he's buried now, near a place called Sligo. I won't go into the biography now, but I do want to get into it later on, because it not only bears a very close relationship with the poetry and the personality that Yeats was, but it's fascinating in itself.

Let me give you some more things that you might want to read. The best short life and interpretation is by Richard Ellmann, at least the best one that I know. It's very, very readable. There are many, many, many books. The bibliography on Yeats, if I may sound pedantic for a minute or two, would run not only to hundreds but to thousands of items. I haven't read them all, but the works that have been helpful to me, most of the best articles, are in a book called *The Permanence of Yeats*. Again, part of my feeling about this class is to pass on books that I've read, which are interesting to me and might be interesting to you. Tom Priestley, J. B. Priestley's son, was the cutter on my movie of *Deliverance,* and he got his old man to send me this, and I was absolutely fascinated. It's called *Literature and Western Man* by J. B. Priestley. And it's kind of like Bertrand Russell's *History of Western Philosophy.* It's one man's opinion of most of the writers of the Western world from the beginning of the invention of movable type down to our time. He makes no attempt to be impartial. No, no; the great thing about Priestley's book, as the great thing about Bertrand Russell's *History of Western Philosophy,* is that it is so biased. It is one man's opinion of all these people. It's really not literature of Western man: it's Western literature as interpreted by J. B. Priestley, who had read 'em all. And that's kind of a valuable thing. It's very idiosyncratic and very prejudiced and very biased, and very exciting and very good. It makes you want to throw the damn book out the window when he attacks one of the writers who has meant so much to you personally, but in almost every case, there is something to be said for his point of view; and with some, he is, what do they say, right on. He has a very, very good summation of Yeats. Almost everything you would need to know about Yeats in a couple of paragraphs is in this. I concur with almost everything that Priestley says about Yeats, and I thought I would pass this on to you and also let you know where it is. Don't think that it's limited to Yeats. It's got something about everybody in every language, hundreds, all with very idiosyncratic opinions about them. He says things like, "The thing that's wrong with Shakespeare is this. . . ." And "Thomas Wolfe does this well. . . ." He treats them from the standpoint of a working writer who's read all these people, partly because he enjoys reading, and partly because he's using them as tools in his own work.

I don't want to get into the question of symbolism here, although probably we ought to say a little something about it. I can't really dismiss it, but I can deal with it in just a couple of sentences. It was a literary movement—they do these things in France all the time—which took its instigation from a French poet, first from a French poet named Baudelaire, and then was relegated to a kind of private refinement by another one named Mallarmé and was very, very influential on one generation of Anglo-Irish writers, of which Yeats was one. I don't need to go into the tenets of symbolism. I don't think you really need to bother with that except that when you read a book about Yeats, or when you read an article about him, that says he originally started out in the symbolism movement, you can say, yes, I know all about that. Well, you don't, but at least you ought to know that it exists. It's essentially an esthetic doctrine of things standing for each other. Baudelaire's famous sonnet on "Correspondences"; that nature is to be interpreted essentially as a symbolic text, that one thing suggests another thing, that all things are connected with each other by symbolic inference. Well, Yeats put that to a very special kind of use, and used the doctrine of symbolism—he didn't even read French very well, in fact almost none—but he picked up the notion that things suggest or are metaphorical stand-ins for each other, and he put that to use on his own special segment of experience, which was Irish folklore, and there his work began.

We don't live under any such constraint from the church any more. We have gradually moved over, and increasingly done so, into a secular kind of culture. The great exponents of secularism, philosophically, are the people that are now variously called existentialists, who believe that the whole church thing has held men down and kept them from their true impulses and their true selves for many, many thousands of years, and that we finally find ourselves in possession of a terrible freedom, a dreadful freedom, that we may not really want after all. We've always said we do, but do we really?

Now, all those things are in Yeats. He did labor unremittingly at his craft. If there was anything that had to be sacrificed, if it was a question of his art or his family life, or his love life or his political life, or his life as a prose writer or an essayist, everything else had to go. He was, as Priestley says, first, last, and always an artist. Although he was many other things, he was that preeminently. This is the main thing to remember, that the creation not only of Yeats's work as a poet but the creation of the personality and the system of thought that made the later and greater work possible are all the result of a continuous, lifelong act of will. He was originally not such a strong-willed person; he was just another languid young esthete who happened to come from Ireland. He was a creature of the 1890s who hung around with other writers in London, joined poetry clubs—can you imagine anything more dismal? But he happened to be in this particular club with a couple or three writers of extreme excellence, although very narrow. For example, this was a club called The Rhymers' Club, and it met in a place in London where you can still go, if you get over there, down in Soho called the Cheshire Cheese, which is quite a good pub, and you can still see Yeats's cup hanging on the brad or the nail where it was kept. They do these things much more, and less self-consciously, in England than we do over here.

And they would go and read each other's stuff. Have you ever heard of Ernest Dowson, for example? I doubt that many of you have, but two of the most famous phrases in modern American life, in popular culture, come from the lines of Ernest Dowson, and nobody knows where they came from, but I do. "Gone with the wind. . . ." How about, "They are not long, the days of wine and roses . . ."? That's also Ernest Dowson. He was one of the members of The Rhymers' Club.

DONALD DAVIE

Well, let's continue this later on. We've got about five minutes, and I want to talk about Donald Davie, my old buddy. He is another one of the new breed that came into prominence in English literature in the 1950s. Hitherto, as I said in connection with Kingsley Amis, he was unusual as Amis was, and John Wain and Philip Larkin were unusual, in that they were not, as most of the English literary class had been hitherto, products of wealthy families, landed families, or at least upper middle class. Donald Davie was a scholarship boy from the coal grounds of the Midlands, and went to, I believe it was, Oxford, and graduated there but never felt at all at home in the company of the old aristocratic ruling class. Class distinctions in England are different from class distinctions in this country. What are they based on in this country? Money, almost exclusively. Family, maybe yes, if you have it, but if you don't have it, money will make up the difference, and more money. You won't have that in England. Maybe the old aristocratic class system that Yeats so revered in Ireland, for example, is disappearing, or gradually eroding away, but nevertheless, it's been there in England for an awfully long time. I mean, if you don't come from, say, a social class higher than your own over there, and you try to mix and mingle with those on the basis of a scholarship that enables you to go to Oxford, you are very quickly made aware that you—"He isn't really one of us, Reggie."

Well, Donald Davie was a scholarship boy, an extremely precocious one. He's written several extremely good scholarly and critical books. I have mixed feelings about him as a poet. I think he articulates this class embarrassment. It used to be humiliating, but now it's simply embarrassing, as in the poem "The Garden Party." The garden party is a very much English type of an arrangement, and this is a situation where he's invited, and everybody's being terribly liberal by inviting him to the garden party. This is a very much upper-class type of thing. So Donald Davie goes to the garden party, sort of self-consciously, and this is what he thinks of it.

THE GARDEN PARTY

Above a stretch of still unravaged weald
In our Black Country, in a cedar-shade,
I found, shared out in tennis courts, a field
Where children of the local magnates played.

And I grew envious of their moneyed ease
In Scott Fitzgerald's unembarrassed vein.
Let prigs, I thought, fool others as they please,
I only wish I had my time again.

To crown a situation as contrived
As any in "The Beautiful and Damned,"
The phantom of my earliest love arrived;
I shook absurdly as I shook her hand.

As dusk drew in on cultivated cries,
Faces hung pearls upon a cedar-bough;
And gin could blur the glitter of her eyes,
But it's too late to learn to tango now.

My father, of a more submissive school,
Remarks the rich themselves are always sad.
There is that sort of equalizing rule;
But theirs is all the youth we might have had.

Donald Davie. I think he has one relatively comprehensive book, published by my old publisher, Wesleyan. It's called *New and Selected Poems.* I think about all of Donald Davie that you will want to read will be in that. He also has a marvelously fascinating and original book of criticism, if you are of that scholarly kind of mind and these things excite you, as they do me. It's a study of syntax as it works in English verse; it's called *Articulate Energy.* And there's another quite good book on Ezra Pound called *Ezra Pound, Poet and Sculptor.*

MORE YEATS

Somebody in here said something brilliant—the trouble with science is that it's so goddamn boring. But everything we do is determined by it—the clothes you've got on, the room you sit in, the lights coming down with a discreet hum from the ceiling, the clock. Everything we've got on, everything we do, everything we see is determined by that. Yeats was a person who felt that this was not the true human way, that we deserve something better than mere empirical evidence and more products from General Motors. You have to realize this about Yeats: he was not a progressive; he was not a liberal at all; he was profoundly conservative. His eyes turned back to the past rather than toward the future. He didn't care about spaceships or any of that. What he wanted was a profound human community. You look at what the hippies or the commune people want now, and that's exactly what he wanted. Except he wanted it not on a kind of rootless basis, but he wanted it rooted in the life of the locality and the people. Now, if you don't play the science game, you have to play another game. And the game that Yeats played is that of miracles. Have you ever seen a miracle? Neither have I, but we all hunger for them. Why? What do miracles deliver us from? The humdrum of science. We all want them. We'd love to see them.

Let me start out all this business with a recounting of a crazy man, a nice crazy man such as we'd all like to know. His name was Charles Fort (1874–1932). He spent thirty years as a law clerk in New York. But all the time that Charles Fort was serving as a law clerk, he was compiling evidence that the things that are scientifically accountable are gainsaid by certain strange phenomena that science cannot account for, that there is something beyond the scientific ken that is simply unaccountable. Blood falls from the sky; sea monsters arise and all is not as we thought it was. This is all very much in the Yeatsian camp—that things are not, *not,* to be accountable for by science, that there are certain things that happen, there are certain phenomena that exist that there are records of, that we don't have any way to account for. Let me ask you something. Why do we all want to believe in this? I know I do. As we were talking the other day, there's this enormous interest in the occult now, in devil worship. Why? Look at the enormous plethora of science fiction. What is the appeal of that? There seems to be something in people that does not want everything to be answered and does not want all things to be accounted for. This is Charles Fort's thing. He's a law clerk, a lowly individual, but he reads fifty thousand books to amass evidence that what we think is reality is at base very precarious.

But this is the kind of thing that Yeats seized upon. He seized upon this as being something to controvert the world of Newton and even the world of Einstein, that there is a world behind the world of appearances in which things take place that we have no possible way of accounting for. For example, do you understand, or does anybody understand, about the world of instinct and how animals navigate? It's fascinating, because there's no way to account for it. There's no way. Again, I'm not trying to sell Yeats. He's such a great poet that he doesn't need me to sell him. But, he was interested in all these things that could not be accounted for by scientific means. If you put, for example, the wandering albatross or the tern, for example, in a planetarium at the season when birds begin to go south to mate, and you turn the southern constellations to the east in the planetarium, they will fly to the east; if you turn them to the south, they will fly to the south. In other words, these crazy birds are doing celestial navigation. Now, how could they know that? The parent bird could not say that in October of this year the constellation Scorpio is going to be over there, and that's where you've got to go, baby. There's no way they could tell them that.

Yeats was very much hooked into the unknowable, the things that science could not control. Why? As he said, the naive religion of his childhood had been gainsaid by Charles Darwin (1809–1882) and Thomas Huxley (1825–1895). But Yeats was a man of tremendous power of mind. He was, or perhaps we should say he became, a masterful man. And it looked like science was going to be the name of the game, but Yeats was of such power of mind and such power of personality that he was just not going to play it that way. He didn't believe it. So he began to seek out a different possibility, a different possibility for men and their beliefs and their symbols. What he wanted most to do was come on a system of thought which would be supra-scientific, which was different, which would not be, as you say, boring, but was something in which the symbol, the image, and the action would be simultaneous. The imaginative faculty and the reasoning faculty would not be separated from themselves, but would be essentially similar, or even simultaneous. So what happens? How does he get it? He's fifty years old. He's written some charming poems, some fine poems, some nostalgic poems, but he has not got into the central thing that he feels certainly must be there. So what happens? When he's over fifty years old, he marries. He marries a charming young woman, twenty-five years younger then he, but she really doesn't know what it is she's taking on when she marries William Butler Yeats, the Irish poet. She doesn't know what he's like. She knows he's a fascinating, strange man, which he definitely is. He's been milked dry by his unrequited love for Maud Gonne, thirty years' worth. And he doesn't really know how to settle down as a married man. So, they sit around and talk, can you imagine? And she says that she can do automatic writing. You just say anything that comes into your head. So she starts that. It would be better to let Yeats talk about it, because Yeats above all is someone who needs a system. He needs something that explains *everything*. I mean ordinary people are content to go along day to day in the ways in which everybody else goes along, but a powerful mind like Yeats can't dig it, and above all, he doesn't understand it; he's got to have not their system but his system. So that's what happened when his wife began to talk in her sleep. Again, as Huck Finn would say, all this is told about in a book of Yeats's called *A Vision*.

ALL SOULS' NIGHT
Epilogue to "A Vision"

Midnight has come, and the great Christ Church Bell
And many a lesser bell sound through the room;
And it is All Souls' Night,
And two long glasses brimmed with muscatel
Bubble upon the table. A ghost may come;
For it is a ghost's right,
His element is so fine
Being sharpened by his death,
To drink from the wine-breath
While our gross palates drink from the whole wine,

I need some mind that, if the cannon sound
From every quarter of the world, can stay
Wound in mind's pondering
As mummies in the mummy-cloth are wound;
Because I have a marvellous thing to say,
A certain marvellous thing
None but the living mock,
Though not for sober ear;
It may be all that hear
Should laugh and weep an hour upon the clock.

Horton's the first I call. He loved strange thought
And knew that sweet extremity of pride

73

That's called platonic love,
And that to such a pitch of passion wrought
Nothing could bring him, when his lady died,
Anodyne for his love.
Words were but wasted breath;
One dear hope had he:
The inclemency
Of that or the next winter would be death.

Two thoughts were so mixed up I could not tell
Whether of her or God he thought the most,
But think that his mind's eye,
When upward turned, on one sole image fell;
And that a slight companionable ghost,
Wild with divinity,
Had so lit up the whole
Immense miraculous house
The Bible promised us,
It seemed a gold-fish swimming in a bowl.

On Florence Emery I call the next,
Who finding the first wrinkles on a face
Admired and beautiful,
And knowing that the future would be vexed
With 'minished beauty, multiplied commonplace,
Preferred to teach a school
Away from neighbour or friend,
Among dark skins, and there
Permit foul years to wear
Hidden from eyesight to the unnoticed end.

Before that end much had she ravelled out
From a discourse in figurative speech
By some learned Indian
On the soul's journey. How it is whirled about,
Wherever the orbit of the moon can reach,
Until it plunge into the sun;
And there, free and yet fast,
Being both Chance and Choice,
Forget its broken toys
And sink into its own delight at last.

And I call up MacGregor from the grave,
For in my first hard springtime we were friends,
Although of late estranged.
I thought him half a lunatic, half knave,

And told him so, but friendship never ends;
And what if mind seem changed,
And it seem changed with the mind,
When thoughts rise up unbid
On generous things that he did
And I grow half contented to be blind!

He had much industry at setting out,
Much boisterous courage, before loneliness
Had driven him crazed;
For meditations upon unknown thought
Make human intercourse grow less and less; ˙
They are neither paid nor praised.
But he'd object to the host,
The glass because my glass;
A ghost-lover he was
And may have grown more arrogant being a ghost.

But names are nothing. What matter who it be,
So that his elements have grown so fine
The fume of muscatel
Can give his sharpened palate ecstasy
No living man can drink from the whole wine.
I have mummy truths to tell
Whereat the living mock,
Though not for sober ear,
For maybe all that hear
Should laugh and weep an hour upon the clock.

Such thought—such thought have I that hold it tight
Till meditation master all its parts,
Nothing can stay my glance
Until that glance run in the world's despite
To where the damned have howled away their hearts,
And where the blessed dance;
Such thought, that in it bound
I need no other thing,
Wound in mind's wandering
As mummies in the mummy-cloth are wound.

And you know what they said to Yeats through his wife: "No; we have
come to give you metaphysical poetry." Out of this situation came Yeats's sys-
tem. It is the craziest and most fascinating thing that you can possibly imagine.
You must read *A Vision,* because maybe this is what we all want; maybe this is
the thing that we've missed. It's a system that the communicants outlined to

him through his wife in a trance, which has to do with a kind of weird and fascinating mixture of astrology, historical process, psychology, and a prospectus of what happens to the soul when it dies and waits for another reincarnation. Because to Yeats the soul is very different from Christian entities; to Yeats the soul is an entity or degree which periodically inhabits corporeal bodies. That's a powerful, appealing idea, don't you think? What would you like to be?

We'll take this time on Yeats and then the next class, but I cannot do more than barely suggest the infinite fascination of the man's mind. And the things that make it fascinating are two qualities: one is what we would now call so very original-minded. In other words, you have never known anybody in your whole experience who thought as Yeats thought. It is outrageous; it is so crazy. And the thing is that when you read Yeats you think, maybe humanity has missed the track, and this is the right thing that nobody saw but him. And the second is that he does have such an enormously powerful, overpowering verbal imagination so that you think that if these things, this business of reincarnation and transmigration of souls, are not really the case, then they damn well should have been. He is so persuasive and so powerful. So what happened is this, that what these communicants tell him is that all things have to do with the phases of the moon. This is not astrology; it is not the zodiac that you see every day in the paper. Instead of the zodiac, Yeats proposes something that he calls the great wheel in which there are twenty-eight spokes coming out from the center of it, referring to the twenty-eight phases of the moon. And on these twenty-eight spokes, or phases of the great wheel, are three different categories of things. One of these, and the easiest to understand, is the cycle of history. Each age according to the twenty-eight phases has two thousand years. That's the easiest to understand. It's a kind of Spenglerian kind of thing. Have you ever read Oswald Spengler, *The Decline of the West*? Do you know the civilizations of Spengler? This is something that you should know, because it might very well be true and we're living in one of the phases. Spengler's idea was that every culture, the Greek culture, the Roman culture, the American culture, and so on, corresponds to four phases. And this, Yeats himself would approve of, in fact did approve of. He concocted his own system before he read Spengler, but he felt fortified by reading Spengler, who said exactly the same thing in a different way —that each phase of a culture corresponds to one of the seasons, spring, summer, fall, and winter.

What would the winter phase, say of the Roman Empire, correspond to? Just about when they were fixing to pack it in. The summer, of course, is the full flood of the culture. Yeats's twenty-eight phases of the moon had something of the same notion.

But let me get the full thing before you. The three things that the great wheel can show you, first of all, are the periods of history and the periodicity of a specific and singular culture, where we are now, in other words. The second thing that the twenty-eight phases of the moon of the great wheel show is the types of men and the psychology of people who arise at various historical eras. And the third thing that the great wheel allows you to indicate is what happens to the life of a soul after death. That is really the most difficult part of the whole vision system. It's the hardest to understand, and the most mysterious and frenzied part to understand, and also the most characteristically Yeatsian.

What we probably ought to do is see how this works in the poems. As I say, the textbook that we have is the textbook that we do in fact use, not only because it has an awful lot of poets, and good poets, and poets that you ought to be reading, but also because of the notes in relation to the main figures that we have, particularly Yeats, Pound, and Eliot. Otherwise, you would have to go and look it up somewhere else, whereas in this book you have very copious notes—maybe even too copious—in relation to these major figures. Remember when we started, we talked about the modern poet not having a convenient mythology available to him, as Dante had, or even as Milton had. So what happened is that the major figures are like Yeats, who constructs a mythology of his own, curious, fascinating. They have tried to do this. Yeats with his supernaturalism and his table rapping, his seances, the automatic writing of his wife, and all these various ways that are not subject to science. Yeats was profoundly a reactionary. He was the farthest thing possible from a liberal. He did not believe in the middle class. He believed in the peasants, with their prolongation of the folk tradition. He liked them. He didn't want to be one of them, but he liked to sit around in their cottages and listen to the stories they told. He believed in the peasant and the aristocracy. The middle class, no. They had betrayed their imagination; they had betrayed everything that makes man important, that makes him exciting, that makes him meaningful and consequential. He didn't believe in that. He was an aristocrat, and, as far as Yeats is concerned, you just have to get used to that idea. He believed in superiority in the same way that Plato believed in superiority.

But you can see already what's working here, a very strange kind of system, an anti-scientific system of revelation, of something that is revealed beyond empirical, scientific investigation. This is what Yeats wanted, and spent the rest of his life trying to shadow forth this kind of mystical philosophy. Now again, to us, sitting in a classroom in 1971, what does this mean? There can be different turns of mind about what this is. It can be the hopeless vagaries of a crank, and I must say that I feel the very strong import of that. I mean, why should we be involved in astrology and the phases of the moon? After all, the moon is the *moon*! I mean, it's just a dead rock floating out there in the sky. Isn't it? Again, you tell me. It's a dead rock, and the earth's shadow cuts across it and makes it appear this way and that way. I mean, men have been out there. Pete Conrad's been out there. Neil Armstrong's been out there. There's not anything mystical about it; it's just an accident of the universe. That's all it is. And here Yeats comes up with a system that has to do with all kinds of things, with historical reference, with psychological and personality types, with the fate of the soul after death, which all has to do with the twenty-eight phases of the moon, the great wheel. Are we going to swallow that?

What Yeats thought was that the twenty-eight phases of the moon and the great wheel were symbolic interpretations of experience and of history. We cannot, with our pro-scientific basis of action, think that there is anything in that at all. That's just the vagaries of a crank. And yet, what we have to face up to is that these vagaries and this, would you say, kind of crazy notion of existence, should have produced the greatest poetry of the twentieth century, which could not have been written without it. Where does that leave us? Exactly where does that leave us? Maybe we need to go back toward magic. Maybe what we need is more magic and less science. Maybe we are more primitive than we thought. I don't know.

What we want to do is read one Yeats lyric based on this. Just one. This is called "Two Songs from a Play" [the play is *The Resurrection*]. Lean on your notes, because they will tell you a lot about this. According to Yeats, new civilizations are born in the dark of the moon. There has always been something in the human psyche that is either repelled or called on by the dark phases of the moon. According to the system shown forth in *A Vision,* civilization dies in blood. Blood is a big word with Yeats. Christ was a blood sacrifice to Yeats—not a holy man, but a blood sacrifice. And the Virgin that we think of in our Christian lives as being infinitely gentle, infinitely tender—according to the scheme in the vision of Yeats, is bloodthirsty, calling for the downfall of Rome, drowned in blood, by blood. The Roman Empire, and the Greek before them, which practiced Platonic discipline, all drown in a tide of blood, blood sacrifice, irrationality. Phase twenty-eight of the great wheel.

TWO SONGS FROM A PLAY

I

I saw a staring virgin stand
Where holy Dionysus died,
And tear the heart out of his side,

And lay the heart upon her hand
And bear that beating heart away;
And then did all the Muses sing
Of Magnus Annus at the spring,
As though God's death were but a play.

Another Troy must rise and set,
Another lineage feed the crow,
Another Argo's painted prow
Drive to a flashier bauble yet.
The Roman Empire stood appalled:
It dropped the reins of peace and war
When that fierce virgin and her Star
Out of the fabulous darkness called.

II

In pity for man's darkening thought
He walked that room and issued thence
In Galilean turbulence;
The Babylonian starlight brought
A fabulous, formless darkness in;
Odour of blood when Christ was slain
Made all Platonic tolerance vain
And vain all Doric discipline.

Everything that man esteems
Endures a moment or a day.
Love's pleasure drives his love away,
The painter's brush consumes his dreams;
The herald's cry, the soldier's tread
Exhaust his glory and his might:
Whatever flames upon the night
Man's own resinous heart has fed.

Now that's a tone, an accent, that could not have been possible with any other poet or with any other system of thought. That is terrifying and frightening. It brings us back to the age of the caves, when people believed in magic and cantation.

KEITH DOUGLAS

Let's talk about war and a young fellow killed in the war, Keith Douglas. Who was he? What did he do? What was his life like? What was death like?

I've heard it said that he was a bastard, literally, illegitimate. But apparently that wasn't the case. His father did desert the family when Keith Douglas was six years old. And he was very close to his mother, without the usual results of that, very close to his mother, loved her genuinely. She's furnished a number of very moving accounts of his youth, what kind of person he was. He went on with his education as a charity boy. He went to Christ Hospital where Coleridge and Charles Lamb were, for example, and he won all his education through scholarships. He was at Merton College, Oxford, and he enlisted in the service largely because of the riding opportunities it afforded—horseback. He went into the service at the time just before General [Bernard Law] Montgomery's (1887–1976) breakthrough at El Alamein (World War II battle, May–October 1942). He was, as they say in England, kicking his heels at a base camp, and contrived a transfer to a combat unit where he commanded a Crusader tank, which is a medium tank, all the way from El Alamein, where Montgomery broke through General [Erwin] Rommel's (1891–1944) lines, to a place called Wadi Zem Zem, near Cairo, where he was due to be shipped back to England for a short holiday just before the invasion, and three days later he was killed, at the age of twenty-four. So what is it that constrains us, sitting in a classroom in Columbia, South Carolina, in 1971, to read the work of this boy, killed thirty years ago, who went through the desert warfare in a tank, came out of it, and was able to send back a book of poems and a war diary?

Now, the whole works of Keith Douglas are found in these two books. You should get these, or somebody should get these: whoever catches fire with Keith Douglas. He was remarkable. *Collected Poems,* and his war diary, *Alamein to Zem Zem,* which tells you what it's like to fight across North Africa in a tank under those peculiar conditions. It is terrifying, and also very funny, because Keith Douglas is of a very singular kind of temperament. He was a strange, wonderful type of a fellow; both original and super-sensitive; *detached,* above all, for in war detachment is what saves you. Detached, and at the same time super-sensitive, super-observant.

When we think of people who write poems about wars, what kind of personality do we think of? When you think of a war poet, whom do you think about? What would you say he was like? What he behaves like? He hates war; he talks infinitely about pity and about death. We get Wilfred Owen. He grieves for people he knew who had been killed. I know; I've been through all this myself, and I, myself, would be typical in that instance. Keith Douglas is curiosity: "What is it going to be like? I've got to get into a battle to know."

That is Keith Douglas's temperament. He was interested, not as an infinitely compassionate kind of poet-type; he was *interested* in the battle, war, what happens between men, what happens when men are busted apart with their legs blown off, their guts blown out—that was something that was *interesting* to him, even if *he* was the one to whom this happened. This is a singular, poetic kind of temperament, and Keith Douglas had it to a point that almost no one else that I know did have it. Incidentally, we are often told that poets make bad warriors, bad soldiers. Keith Douglas was a superlatively good soldier. Nobody even knew he wrote poetry at all. Almost all his best poems were written on aerograms. And he said when he was preparing for the Normandy invasion— he wrote to his editor in London, who wanted to publish at least one book of Keith Douglas's poems before he was killed, because he was always volunteering for these things—anyway, he says, "I have to correct these proofs fast because of prior military engagements, which might be the end of me." And they were.

He had this extremely detached, kind of laconic, slightly cynical attitude toward tank warfare, the bombings, physical combat. Let me read to you again from *Alamein to Zem Zem* to show you this particular temper of mind, which is extraordinary and very cool. He was thought of as a great officer, younger officer; he was only twenty-four when he was killed in a crack unit. And all the poetry took place in secret and went back to England on aerograms.

Again, that's the kind of temperament Douglas had. He was interested in any and all kinds of experiences, even when it involved his own terrible pain: that's the stuff that the poems are written out of, disinterested observations. The books: *Alamein to Zem Zem* and *Collected Poems*.

What we need to do now is read some of his stuff. A lower-class boy, who, as I say, was a scholarship boy. He was acutely class-conscious, and also rather contemptuous of classes. He knew he was intellectually superior to anybody he was going to find in any of the other classes, and yet when he goes out to El Alamein and to the Libyan and the Tunisian desert, he's still in contact with these aristocratic boys from the upper class who had gone to Oxford *not* on scholarships, but because of family connections, who had town houses and country houses. His characteristic attitude toward them is, you know, "These people are like dinosaurs. They're relics, but there's something kind of charming about them. There's something kind of nice about them. I'm not of that class; I'm from the lower classes, but there's something kind of endearing about these relics, these dodos. They're called aristocrats."

This is about the dichotomy of a person who's more than one thing. Here the German soldier in the gunpit stands against the British tank as a soldier. When you kill him and go through his wallet, you see he's somebody else, too. He's got a lover; he's got a girl. You realize that too late, but it wouldn't have done any good, because he's trying to kill *you*.

All right, let's do "Cairo Jag."

CAIRO JAG

Shall I get drunk or cut myself a piece of cake,
a pasty Syrian with a few words of English
or the Turk who says she is a princess—she dances
apparently by levitation? Or Marcelle, Parisienne
always preoccupied with her dull dead lover:
she has all the photographs and his letters
tied in a bundle and stamped *Décedé* in mauve ink.
All this takes place in a stink of jasmin.

But there are the streets dedicated to sleep
stenches and the sour smells, the sour cries
do not disturb their application to slumber
all day, scattered on the pavement like rags
afflicted with fatalism and hashish. The women
offering their children brown-paper breasts
dry and twisted, elongated like the skull,
Holbein's signature. But this stained white town
is something in accordance with mundane conventions—
Marcelle drops her Gallic airs and tragedy
suddenly shrieks in Arabic about the fare
with the cabman, links herself so
with the somnambulists and legless beggars:
it is all one, all as you have heard.

But by the day's travelling you reach a new world
the vegetation is of iron
dead tanks, gun barrels split like celery
the metal brambles have no flowers or berries

Teaching with guest William Styron, 1974. *Courtesy of University Publications, University of South Carolina*

and there are all sorts of manure, you can imagine
the dead themselves, their boots, clothes and possessions
clinging to the ground, a man with no head
has a packet of chocolate and a souvenir of Tripoli.

See, the thing about the desert war is that these fellows would be fighting all day, bombing, raising hell, machine gunning, and then in the evening they could get off and go into Cairo, and have a jag, and just a few miles away. This was unusual. I was in the Pacific War, and there was nothing like that for us over there, I can tell you. But *they* could. So, this is about *their* situation: *those* soldiers.

I'm sorry I don't have time to talk more about Douglas, because I had an awful lot to say. Read him; he's a fine, irascible, powerful, cynical, imaginative poet who never had more than a little bit of a chance, as he says, because of military engagements that might be the end of him. And they were. But on the page—the pages—Keith Douglas exists: not *still* exists, but exists. And so does the war in the desert, and the brave and good poet that he was.

MORE YEATS

Okay, as I've said so many times before, small people are quite willing to go along with what is, but the big people want to create their own way. Such a person was William Butler Yeats. He had to have a system in which he could dominate. He didn't dig science; he didn't like it, and so he went a way which is anti-science. Again, as I asked you before, is this possible? You tell me. People want witchcraft now, don't they? They want some kind of strange thing. Or do they? You're a member of the youth; I'm not a youth. I wish I were, and, again, I'm glad I'm not. Now, here's Yeats. He wants a controlling system that he knows about and the scientists don't. So he raises this weird, crazy astrological system, and he writes out of it the greatest poetry of his century. Now this is a paradox because if there were any justice running with the poets, it would be that the poets go with the scientists; that they incorporate and metaphysicalize and use as symbolic data the vision of Einstein. The greatest poet of the century turned his back on all of this, and went back into time, conceived through his wife's dream-talk a new vision of existence which was anti-scientific. Now listen, we are caught, you and I, at a kind of crossroads here. Where do we go? And what is the way that people should live on the earth? Do we go with science or magic?

Now, what we need to do, I think, is read a couple of Yeats's poems of the later period because they are founded on this notion of aristocracy, of intellectual superiority, and, above all, on artistic superiority. Listen to this, because it's really good. Have you seen water spiders on the water? How do they do it? This takes the long-legged fly in three phases.

LONG-LEGGED FLY

That civilisation may not sink,
Its great battle lost,
Quiet the dog, tether the pony
To a distant post;
Our master Caesar is in the tent
Where the maps are spread,

85

His eyes fixed upon nothing,
A hand under his head.
Like a long-legged fly upon the stream
His mind moves upon silence.

That the topless towers be burnt
And men recall that face,
Move most gently if move you must
In this lonely place.
She thinks, part woman, three parts a child,
That nobody looks; her feet
Practice a tinker shuffle
Picked up on a street.
Like a long-legged fly upon the stream
Her mind moves upon silence.

That girls at puberty may find
The first Adam in their thought,
Shut the door of the Pope's chapel,
Keep those children out.
There on that scaffolding reclines
Michael Angelo.
With no more sound than the mice make
His hand moves to and fro.
Like a long-legged fly upon the stream
His mind moves upon silence.

What you should also realize about Yeats is that he is not the poet of the system so much as he's the poet of the broad scan of humanity. The system is fascinating; one loves it, cannot get enough of it. You wish he'd done three or four thousand more volumes, because that might give us the secret of it all, of existence, which is what he wanted more than anything else. But the great thing about him is that he saw past the system, and he brought out a plain-speaking human speech that would speak to everybody.

W. S. GRAHAM

Here are his books. You can get the last three, if you get caught up in his crazy kind of stuff. I'll give you the names of the books. You can probably get them from Gotham. Characteristically enigmatic, *Cage without Grievance.* Isn't that great? But you know, that opens up a whole lot of possibilities, don't you think? What does it open up? The next is *The Seven Journeys.* Why seven? Why not six; why not eight? Now, you won't be able to get all these, but Gotham Book Mart might. But they're really crazy, unforgettable poems. He's a real nut. But the three that you will be able to get are *The White Threshold,* and that's a good one. Graham has a kind of Yeatsian progression in that he changed; he invented a language. But the great one of all is *The Nightfishing.* And the one that I got just last fall is *Malcolm Moody's Land,* the last one.

I'll tell you about Jock Graham and me. The first time I ever met him was at a place called Yaddo. Do you know what Yaddo is, where it is? It's an artist colony in Saratoga Springs, New York. It's like the MacDowell Colony. You know, one of these places where artists are invited, composers, musicians, painters, are invited. So I went up there, and you're handed a sheet thing of what you can do and what you can't do. You're supposed to be going out there and working. And they give you a studio and even if you don't have any work to do, you find some. But in the evening after supper everybody congregates in the downstairs study or living room. And the first time I came down there Graham had a cardboard placard, like you get with your shirt back from the laundry, and he had all these words cut out from the newspaper, and he was placing them around in different places. He cut out words just like they were physical entities. So I went up to him and said, "My name's Dickey. Probably you haven't heard of me." And he said, "My name's W. S. Graham." And I said, "What the hell are you doing? What're you doing with all those little words, those little squares of words? And on that cardboard paper?" And you know what he said? He said, "This is the way I get my poetic ideas. I call it a kind of a metaphysical scrabble." So, maybe that's the way it works, and then, again, maybe it isn't. I don't know.

But what he comes up with, what W. S. Graham is trying to do, is to invent a new language based on English. That's what he does. He's got two things going here. He's got his crazy kind of haphazard language, and he also bases part of his poetic tongue on haphazard bits of conversation. Like, I heard a guy in the bar in New York where the tables are all close together, these two businessmen, and one of them was an older fellow. And the other guy was a young salesman. And you know what he said to the younger fellow? He said, "Now listen, Jack, nobody in the company will believe me when I tell 'em this, but in about two years polyethylene foam is going to be the tail that's wagging the dog." You don't know what the context is. W. S. Graham would have taken that up. He doesn't know what the context is; he doesn't *want* to know what the context is. But W. S. Graham collects small random bits of information which are terrific.

So what he writes about: he comes from working-class people, and he refuses to live any other life than the life of a poet. He would not take a job; he would not do any kind of, as you would say, visible constructive work. What he does is farm out his drafts of poems in exchange for remuneration. I've got a stack of them that high which I meant to bring with me, for which I exchanged a case of Jack Daniels with him for Christmas, which is not a bad sort of exchange between poets.

This is one of Graham's poems in which two things combine: love, sending a letter, a metaphysical letter out to somebody, and his crazy kind of manufactured language. What it comes down to is a metaphysical of the words, a belief in the magical potency of language [poem unidentified].

That's W. S. Graham. The books are *Cage without Grievance* and *The Seven Journeys,* which you won't be able to get, but you can read them if you like him. The three that you will be able to get are *The White Threshold;* the greatest book of all, *The Nightfishing;* and then the new one, *Malcolm Moody's Land.*

EDWIN ARLINGTON ROBINSON

Edwin Arlington Robinson died in 1935 at the age of sixty-five. He was the most honored American poet during his life. It's an extremely curious circumstance as to how this happened to come about because, of all the famous misery of American poets during their early years, there could hardly have been a more miserable childhood and young manhood and middle age than Robinson had. I'll give you a very brief history.

First of all, he was a down-easterner from Maine, a very reticent, taciturn, closed-mouthed person; and, in his case, added to these traits, a pathological shyness, where it was actually a physical effort for him to confront another human being and hold a conversation. He was born in a little town in Maine called Head Tide. His father was a merchant banker, and was affluent for a good part of Robinson's childhood. They moved when Robinson was a young child to a larger town, a logging town, called Gardiner, Maine, and there he grew up. They had for a while no financial worries. He had two brothers, Dean and Herman. Dean was kind of the favorite, the good-looking one. Both were older brothers and were both very promising, Herman as a businessman and Dean as a doctor. Then things began to go badly. The father lost his money, and Dean, who had become a doctor, began taking his own drugs, partly because of the difficulties of being a general practitioner during the terrible winter conditions up there, partly because of guilt at not being able to get to people on time. He became a narcotic addict. Herman lost all the money he had made as a land speculator in midwestern land deals, and he also was ruined.

Edwin had no abilities of any kind. He told his biographer, Chard Powers Smith, quite literally on his deathbed, "I could never have done *any*thing but write poetry." He tried various things. He was not a precocious child. He was quite average in high school, although he worked hard. His father believed that he should take practical subjects, business administration and so on, and that this poetry business that so fascinated the boy was something that would just pass off and that he should better have a solid commercial education. So that's the kind he got, up through high school. His mother said, when he was about fifteen or sixteen, "I'm not worried about Dean and Herman, but I don't know *what* will happen to Edwin." Edwin was off by himself writing poetry, scribbling poetry that nobody understood. The only acquaintances that he had around the town of Gardiner were intellectuals, poor eccentrics, and he also had a certain acquaintanceship with the dockside bums, the drunkards. But he talked to them; he already felt that he had a certain affinity, a certain kinship, with them, and this stayed with him for the rest of his life. He was, from the beginning—partly because of his own nature, partly because of his own situation, partly as a result of the way he was thought of around the town of Gardiner—he had a lifelong obsession with failure, with all kinds of human failure—failures of love, failures of business, failures in philosophy, just failures in life, the failures, for example, who are failures underneath an apparent success. Of his most famous anthology pieces, the one you know is "Richard Cory." You know that one, don't you? We'll read it to give you a kind of a flavor. This is a famous piece, which is probably pretty good to start off with.

RICHARD CORY

Whenever Richard Cory went down town,
We people on the pavement looked at him:
He was a gentleman from sole to crown,
Clean favored, and imperially slim.

And he was always quietly arrayed,
And he was always human when he talked;
But still he fluttered pulses when he said,
"Good-morning," and he glittered when he walked.

And he was rich—yes, richer than a king—
And admirably schooled in every grace:
In fine, we thought that he was everything
To make us wish that we were in his place.

So on we worked, and waited for the light,
And went without the meat, and cursed the bread;
And Richard Cory, one calm summer night,
Went home and put a bullet through his head.

"Richard Cory" is the beginning of the typical Robinson attitude. He's an odd poet in some ways. He's a little bit like [Edgar Lee] Masters, although he writes almost exclusively about people. But he's a far, far greater poet than Masters, and it would be interesting to see what it is that makes him greater. First of all, he has a style of his own, and Masters just doesn't. I mean, Masters has a kind of semijournalistic style that makes its point despite the fact that it is so styleless. Robinson has an easily identifiable style; you can always tell one of his poems. The style is very tight, dry, slightly comic, slightly ironical most of the time, very compassionate, usually; but with the sense always that nobody could do anything for you, the person he's writing about, the *dramatic persona*. "I understand how it must be for you in your situation, you poor bastard. I can't do anything for you, but I can tell about it. Fate is the only agency that can do anything, and it's ruled against you": this is the Robinson climate. People in situations for which there is no help. The poet that he resembles most, I would say, is Hardy, and then to some extent [Robert] Browning.

Robinson's works are of two kinds: they're very short, like "Richard Cory," or they are *enormously* long. As prolific as Hardy was, Robinson's *Collected Poems* would make at least two of Hardy's. I'll show you. This is it: Robinson's *Collected Poems,* fifteen hundred pages of very small type. You could use it for a doorstop. Feel the weight of this thing. You couldn't read all that. I bet not even Robinson scholars have read all that, especially with his style, which sometimes runs to such an intolerable amount of backing and filling and ought and maybe and might and possibly and so on, because he is a poet of *contingency.* He realizes, or I think he does, that you can't have certainty. Hardy's poems are very humane, but with all kinds of cosmic overtones about the Spinner of the Years, and the Fates, and Circumstance, and that sort of thing. Robinson's are not really preoccupied with drawing any conclusions about the nature of the universe except in just a few places. Hardy essentially is preoccupied; Robinson isn't. Robinson is quite willing to say that it's all such a mystery, that it isn't any use in even trying to believe you're going to be certain about the causes of these things. He says, "Look, I'll show you what happened to this fellow, and you can draw your own conclusions from it."

I don't think you would ever want to read through the *Collected Poems.* There's just too blasted much stuff. Nobody, not even Shakespeare, could write a book of fifteen hundred pages of closely printed *good* poetry. And, consequently, there's an awful lot of deadwood in Robinson. This is one of the reasons that he's not very much read today. So what a very fine scholar, Morton Zabel, and I undertook to do about eight years ago was to bring out a smaller work. So I read all of Robinson, and so did he, and we wrote back and forth and put in and took out and changed around, and I think all the Robinson you would ever want to read, and maybe even more than you would ever want to read, is in this book. Unless you just become a Robinson addict, as a rare few do, occasionally, because he's not a poet that you love; he's one you're shaken up by, that you're impressed by, that you've got to acknowledge, but it's very hard to *love* Robinson. He's too taciturn; he's too distant in some ways. He's too tight-lipped. He's probably the most *prolific* tight-lipped poet that ever lived. This, again, is a paradox that he himself would have appreciated. But he is very much worth reading in some things. He's one of the great lyric poets. He's got more psychological depth than almost any other American lyric poet. He knows people, especially failures, who wanted the wrong things out of life. The general conclusion underlined in the poems is that there wasn't anything that would have been right for them. Just as there's not anything that's really right for any of us, completely. There are just things that are wronger than other things. And his people always choose those. Because this, too, Robinson would say, is part of the way people are made up, generally. Robinson was given to strange statements in his letters. For example, "The world is a hell of a place, but the universe is a fine thing."

The family breaks up and he gets—because Herman had saved up some money to send his younger brother to college—he gets two years in college, which were the happiest two years of his life. He went to Harvard, but because he was not able to make social contact with anybody at all, he quits after two years. He goes back to Gardiner. His brother Dean is dying. His brother Herman has come back from the West bankrupt. His father's dead, and his mother is losing her grip on reality. But she's got enough money to keep them fed, and here he is, a grown man, about twenty-three years old, and he's got nothing. He thinks of himself as the greatest of all his failures. He can't get a job; he tries to work in a drugstore. He's fired. He just doesn't have any competence. He tries to teach school; he tries to write novels, poems. Nobody will publish his poems, and he's absolutely at the end of his possibilities and eaten up with guilt over his crushing inferiority complex because of these circumstances. For the first ten years after he published his first poem—he published a poem on Edgar Allan Poe, a sonnet, and was paid seven dollars for it, and the little inferior magazine that bought it, called *The Globe,* didn't publish it for twelve years. That was typical Robinson luck. Seven dollars was all Robinson had earned by the time he had reached his twenty-seventh year. And he'd been writing steadily the whole time—French forms, anything that he thought might work for him. He worked like the proverbial hound on those things, because that was all he had to do. There wasn't anything else he could do, and he wasn't at all sure he could do that. So, frightened or not, he faced the world with the only thing he could do, his supposed talent, but the world didn't want it. He papered one whole wall in his mother's house with rejection slips, a whole *wall!*

People say they paper their walls with rejection slips; he really *did.* And he got together with friends, and they subsidized a private printing of a volume called *The Torrent and the Night Before.* And some of his most famous anthology pieces were in that first little book. On the strength of that and a few newspaper reviews, he got together another book and called it *The Town Down the River*. And this got some reviews. He just couldn't live in his mother's house and take her money any more, so he had a tiny inheritance from his father that he'd been saving, just a couple of hundred dollars. He took off and went to New York, and *that's* where the real nightmare started.

It was bad enough in his family and in the little provincial down-east Maine town of Gardiner, but in New York he was one of the millions of anonymous newcomers, job-seekers, opportunists, and drifting hopefuls. But there was not any job he could do. He was peculiarly helpless all his life and had to be taken care of by people. He had no social graces and was unprepossessing, though not actually ugly; he just looked like any clerk or high school biology teacher. He made little impression on the people he met, couldn't talk to them because of his pathological shyness. He looked like countless other undistinguished people. He might have been a bookkeeper, a bank clerk— couldn't talk. He had to drink himself into a conversation. And this is the reason he became one of the most monumental drinkers in the whole spectacular history of American poetic drinking, because he actually could not hold a conversation, much less go to a party or anything like that, without liquor. But he was living in Bohemia; he lived in the literary district of the day because all he could ever conceivably be able to do had to do with books and poetry. He did have a few friends, but he was a man who lived *among* men rather than *with* men, always a strange, secretive, shadowy sort of figure. You'd just see him go by, wouldn't dare speak to him, might drive him berserk.

About this time, in the low period of his life, he began to see that the strength of his poetry was going to lie in some kind of psychological portraiture, not, say, in writing about nature. He was nearsighted; he couldn't even see very far. But he could see another human being, in the proximity that we usually are in to other human beings. He was acutely aware of the problems of other people, especially those of the failures of various kinds. He brought out a third book called *Captain Craig*. He was thirty-three, and still the only money he had ever earned from writing was the seven dollars for the sonnet on Poe, published in an indifferent magazine.

The reviews of *Captain Craig* were all right, though, surprisingly. They were not enthusiastic, but they were grudgingly admiring. They talked about how obscure and difficult he was and the other things that you usually have said about books of poems. But, he was sustained enough to go on with it. He was discouraged, but he was not defeated. He had the will of Satan, and also the desperation of Satan when he was thrown out of heaven. There was nothing else he could do but write. There was nothing else Robinson could do in New York, in the shabby bohemian part of it he lived in. There was nothing else Satan could do but live in hell, after he got thrown out. Robinson just barely managed to hang on. But what he did was to go to the saloons—a glass of whiskey cost a dime in those days, the last part of the nineteenth century—and when he paid his dime for the glass of whiskey, he could live on the free lunch. So he'd just go from one bar to another, this scholarly fellow with these steel-rimmed glasses. And they would take up collections for him; he was so helpless, so utterly without any means of support, but he managed to hang on. He'd have his bar lunch and his glass of whiskey, and he'd go back to his shabby hotel room where he lived during that time—lived in one after the other—and write poetry, and write, and write, and write, all day, all day. Friends would help him occasionally, and he was humiliated to accept this money, but he did accept it. And once in a while he'd meet important people in the literary world, because he'd published three books of poems, not too badly reviewed. But he had to refuse invitations to their clubs on the rare occasions when they were offered to him, because he felt his clothes were too shabby. He'd move from one dingy rooming house to another. He said to a friend of his, "The first duty of a man is to like beans. I wish you could get into some other kind of slavery, but don't, for heaven's sake, get into my sort unless you have a bean vineyard in your own name."

So finally he couldn't even afford the whiskey, and without buying the whiskey he couldn't get to eat the bar lunch, so he was reduced to having a stale roll for lunch and a glass of beer in the evening. This went on for a number of years. He couldn't pay his rent. He finally got a job in the New York subway. They were building it at this time. He got a job as a time-checker, keeping track of the men's time and the number of wheelbarrows excavated. He's working ten hours a day for twenty cents per hour, and he says at this time, "I was a tragedy in the beginning and it is hardly probable that I can be anything else. What manner of cave I select for retirement is of no real importance. Sometimes I feel that I ought to go and drown myself at cherishing the thought of succeeding at anything, but then I get over it." So what happened is that he got over it largely by drinking. And he got into drinking more and more and got to depend on it so much psychologically that he became one of the great classic alcoholic American writers. And it's strange, because the rest of them fancy themselves roaring boys, like Dylan Thomas or Hart Crane, but Robinson was a withdrawn scholarly type of a person, the farthest possible type of person from Dylan Thomas.

Every evening, when he emerged from his hole in the ground, he made the rounds of the saloons before going to bed, and he got to know in these places all the bums and derelicts, the failures, the would-bes, the has-beens, and so on, out of which he made his most memorable poetry. There used to be a program on Sunday morning at un-prime time called *Camera Three*. Anybody remember that? Anyway, they occasionally had a dramatization of poets. They had a nice one on Yeats, but the best one I ever saw was on Robinson, because they had the scenes in a shabby bar, and all the people around were Miniver Cheevy, all of Robinson's characters, and each would tell his story, which would be reading the poem that Robinson wrote about him, and it was really effective, with these derelicts around. It was strangely touching.

He began, though, to find his true style after all this groping and all this agony and starvation. He began to find that strange kind of flat, ironical, image-less, psychological style that we now can identify instantly with him whenever we see it. If you have a chance—it's a nice poem, one of the real good ones—read the one called "Mr. Flood's Party," about the old guy going out on the hill-side above the New England town with a jug and having a party by himself and talking to himself as though he were his own guest. He doesn't know anybody in the town anymore. He's pretty close to the end, but he goes up on the hill under the moon. There's a beautiful psychological touch after he's drunk about half the jug: he says, "here we stand, under two moons." He sings "Auld Lang Syne." It's a typical type of pathetic, very moving, compassionate Robinson poem, one of the really good ones.

MR. FLOOD'S PARTY

Old Eben Flood, climbing alone one night
Over the hill between the town below
And the forsaken upland hermitage
That held as much as he should ever know
On earth again of home, paused warily.
The road was his with not a native near;
And Eben, having leisure, said aloud,
For no man else in Tilbury Town to hear:

"Well, Mr. Flood, we have the harvest moon
Again, and we may not have many more;
The bird is on the wing, the poet says,
And you and I have said it here before.
Drink to the bird." He raised up to the light
The jug that he had gone so far to fill,

And answered huskily: "Well, Mr. Flood,
Since you propose it, I believe I will."

Alone, as if enduring to the end
A valiant armor of scarred hopes outworn,
He stood there in the middle of the road
Like Roland's ghost winding a silent horn.
Below him, in the town among the trees,
Where friends of other days had honored him,
A phantom salutation of the dead
Rang thinly till old Eben's eyes were dim.

Then, as a mother lays her sleeping child
Down tenderly, fearing it may awake,
He set the jug down slowly at his feet
With trembling care, knowing that most things break;
And only when assured that on firm earth
It stood, as the uncertain lives of men
Assuredly did not, he paced away,
And with his hand extended paused again:

"Well, Mr. Flood, we have not met like this
In a long time; and many a change has come
To both of us, I fear, since last it was
We had a drop together. Welcome home!"
Convivially returning with himself,
Again he raised the jug up to the light;
And with an acquiescent quaver said:
"Well, Mr. Flood, if you insist, I might.

"Only a very little, Mr. Flood—
For auld lang syne. No more, sir; that will do."
So, for the time, apparently it did,
And Eben evidently thought so too;
For soon amid the silver loneliness
Of night he lifted up his voice and sang,
Secure, with only two moons listening,
Until the whole harmonious landscape rang—

"For auld lang syne." The weary throat gave out;
The last word wavered; and the song was done.
He raised again the jug regretfully
And shook his head, and was again alone.
There was not much that was ahead of him,
And there was nothing in the town below—

Where strangers would have shut the many doors
That many friends had opened long ago.

But then, again, as in everything he did in trying to work in the world, the great world of affairs and men, he was fired from the subway job. So, he was out of a job and penniless again. But he always had this wry humor and distance about himself. He confessed that he envied men who ran peanut stands, or swallowed swords for a living, but he added that he knew if he were running a peanut stand he'd burn more peanuts than he sold and that if he were swallowing swords, he wouldn't learn to enjoy the process any more than he had the subway.

But then, some extraordinary thing happened. It's the only thing of its kind that's ever happened to an American poet. He was just barely living; he was down to about 135 pounds, and he was a real tall guy, about 6'2" or 6'3". A fourteen-year-old at the Groton School was looking through the library for something "different" to read. He found, or was helped to find, a book of poems called *The Children of the Night*. The boy was so fascinated by it that he ordered a few copies from the publisher and sent one to his father. His father happened to be president of the United States, Theodore Roosevelt. And *he* was just as much taken with it as his son was, so he wrote to Robinson and invited him to Washington. Robinson had no clothes suitable for a call at the White House, and so, characteristically, he refused. But Roosevelt was very sympathetic to him, and offered him a government job in Mexico or Montreal. When Robinson intimated that he would like to stay in this country, preferably in New York, Roosevelt saw to it that he was installed as a special agent in the Customs House, with a yearly salary of two thousand dollars, kind of a sinecure. Roosevelt wrote to him, "I want you to understand that I want you to put poetry first and your work in the Custom House second." All the struggle this guy's had, all the humiliation, to get that from the *president*. Robinson's reaction was characteristic; he says, "Now I can not only write poetry, but own two pairs of shoes at the same time."

But he never forgot what he owed to Roosevelt. There're some letters at the Library of Congress—I used to look at them when I was consultant there—where he speaks as warmly of and to Roosevelt and to Roosevelt's son, Kermit, as he ever did to anyone in any of his writings. He was really very, very grateful, but he was not one to gush about it. But he's as open and warm here as he ever is anywhere. He writes to Kermit, "I don't like to think where I would be now but for your astonishing father. He fished me out of hell by the hair of the head."

So now, though he certainly was not well off, he was well off compared to what he had been for all these years in the bohemian slums of New York. Because of his extraordinary energy and writing so much, he was able to get out about eight or ten books, and he was by this time a very solid figure in the United States literary scene. A great deal of attention was being paid to him. The people at the MacDowell Colony in New Hampshire sent him an invitation to come live there free during the spring and summer months. He thought, with characteristic reticence, that he might go and see if he liked it, might go for a couple of weeks. But he was so charmed and enchanted by it that he ended up going for thirty years. He became kind of the presiding spirit of the MacDowell Colony; he was the hidden "great man" around there. Writers, artists, who came there would be very grateful to be introduced to him. He came to be a legendary figure there. All the time he was there, characteristically, he was writing and writing and writing all these poems, hundreds of them.

Now, as to the direction he took in his later years, it was both fortunate for him and unfortunate for literature. Robinson's great forte is the psychological lyric in a very short form, either the quatrain or the sonnet or some other very strictly measured form. He was eminently a classical poet. Free verse and these kinds of sprawling poems that people wrote then and are writing a good deal of now made him feel scattered and broken-up. He felt that his gift was pulled together by a strict form like the sonnet or the quatrain, or especially by blank verse. His narrative imagination was not really very strong. He didn't have the storytelling ability especially well, or didn't have a specially distinct form of it. And yet, he began to conceive of these long Arthurian poems, about Camelot, about Arthur and Mordred, and Gawain and Lancelot and Guinevere and some of these figures. Superficially, these would be something like Tennyson's poems, *Idylls of the King*. But about the only thing that they share with Tennyson's poems is the same subject, because the orientation is completely different. Compared to Robinson's stark, disturbing narratives full of the collapsing of old empires and the passing away of magicians, and murders and betrayals, and the psychological motivations for these, Tennyson's *Idylls of the King* just look like Victorian tea-table stories for ladies. Robinson's are very deeply disturbing poems; nevertheless, they are too long and, for narrative poems, surprisingly little happens in them.

The reason for this is twofold. First of all, as I said, Robinson does not have a very strong narrative gift. His gift is the psychological portraiture, for things dealing with people, and *not* in an extended form. The second reason is that because of the psychological bias and the psychological emphasis, Robinson spends too much time on the endless examination of each character's motivation.

It's *endlessly* introspective. And when you read a poem of three, four hundred pages that is nothing but self-torment and decision making about how one is going to act, and why one acted as one did and not another way, which might have been better, and might not have, maybe, then you begin to get restless. It's just too long. Nevertheless, one of these Arthurian poems, *Tristram,* suddenly, for some reason, was taken up by the Literary Guild, distributed, and became a best-seller. In fact, it was on the top of the best-seller list for about six or eight months, and it made Robinson a fortune. It's the last time a serious book of poems has done this, and *Tristram* did in fact finally release him from the financial dilemma that had been plaguing him all his life. He won the Pulitzer Prize for that, and he won it two other times. He won it three times. In the latter part of his life he was the most honored American poet we've ever had, with the exception of Robert Frost, who was a very close friend of his and a very great admirer of his, and was much indebted to Robinson. Robinson was older, of course.

So, that's the life. That's essentially what happened to Robinson. It was an eventless life except for the early family life and the tragedy there, and the New York horror. The latter, more serene days were up in New Hampshire—protected, honored, cared for by everybody, but still very withdrawn, very shy. He never married, and there's some speculation as to whether he was celibate all his life. He very well could have been. I personally don't think so, but the sexual encounters that this agonizingly shy person had must have been very few and far between, if indeed they existed at all.

But what he wrote and how he wrote it are what make him important for us, as forbidding as the bulk of his work is. We think of poetry as coming from a very rich kind of sensibility, sensually rich like Keats or like Gerard Manley Hopkins, for example. Robinson is not like that. His poetry is very, very bleak, almost imageless. Someone complained of Robinson's poetic line that it had too much iron in it and not enough gold. That's very apt. It is very metallic, hard, cold, in the way that Hopkins and Keats are not. Robinson's personality and his sympathy with these poor wrecks that he writes about were anything but cold, and yet the verse itself, if not exactly stiff, as it sometimes is, does not have the characteristics that we normally have come to associate with a lot of brilliant language, like Hopkins or Dylan Thomas. No; Robinson had very much a middle-man style. He didn't write like a god, as Dylan Thomas tried to. He wrote like a man.

I'll show you the books that you can read on him in a minute, but there's a very good comment on him in this book that I reviewed for the *New York Times* where it says in the end, "He chose the middle style, not because he could not fly high. . . . his Wordsworthian conviction that the poet was only a man like other men, but, in a particular way, more so." The "more so" is what counts. And with Robinson, as with Masters, you do feel, and a great deal more with Robinson than with Masters, this interest in people. He does share the ability to make you think, when you read a Robinson poem, as with some of the Masters poems, "*This* is what goes on." You not only believe this happened or didn't happen, but that it is not isolated, that this kind of thing goes on all the time.

This poem is called "Reuben Bright."

REUBEN BRIGHT

Because he was a butcher and thereby
Did earn an honest living (and did right),
I would not have you think that Reuben Bright
Was any more a brute than you or I;
For when they told him that his wife must die,
He stared at them, and shook with grief and fright,
And cried like a great baby half that night,
And made the women cry to see him cry.

And after she was dead, and he had paid
The singers and the sexton and the rest,
He packed a lot of things that she had made
Most mournfully away in an old chest
Of hers, and put some chopped-up cedar boughs
In with them, and tore down the slaughter-house.

He didn't want to have anything more to do with death; no more. There was a kind of funny thing that happened when the poem was first anthologized. Some proofreader or printer's devil misread the last line and put in a preposition that didn't belong, so that it read, "In an old chest / Of hers and put some chopped-up cedar boughs / In with them, and tore down *to* the slaughter-house." You could hardly have a more abrupt change in the meaning of a poem with two letters of the alphabet.

What you like about Robinson, or come to like—and I'm very devoted to him—is that he sees the essences of people that other people don't see, and that the person that he's writing about would be the last to see. He sees the peculiarities that distinguish them, rather than what *they* think distinguishes them. He's really a poet of *psychological essences.* There's one that's not really distinguished; it's somewhere in the middle range of effectiveness. It's not one of the real good ones, but it's not one of the unsuccessful ones. But it's one of the typical Robinson poems, called "Calverly's." Calverly's is evidently a bar that had been closed down. There used to be big parties and they'd get together and they were all buddies, and now it's not there anymore and there're just these two left. This is a very Hardyesque poem, although you would never take it for Hardy, but the attitude is like Hardy's. It's the *ubi sunt* theme: where are they now?

CALVERLY'S

We go no more to Calverly's,
From there the lights are few and low;
And who are there to see by them,
Or what they see, we do not know.
Poor strangers of another tongue
May now creep in from anywhere,
And we, forgotten, be no more
Than twilight on a ruin there.

We two, the remnant. All the rest
Are cold and quiet. You nor I,
Nor fiddle now, nor flagon-lid,
May ring them back from where they lie.
No fame delays oblivion
For them, but something yet survives:
A record written fair, could we
But read the book of scattered lives.

There'll be a page for Leffingwell,
And one for Lingard, the Moon-calf;
And who knows what for Clavering,
Who died because he couldn't laugh?
Who knows or cares? No sign is here,
No face, no voice, no memory;
No Lingard with his eerie joy,
No Clavering, no Calverly.

We cannot have them here with us
To say where their light lives are gone,
Or if they be of other stuff
Than are the moons of Ilion.
So, be their place of one estate
With ashes, echoes, and old wars,—
Or ever we be of the night,
Or we be lost among the stars.

Here you get into that typical Robinson thing, that roll-call, and the way he characterizes those that were here, those that are gone.

Lying to Robinson was not as reprehensible as it is to us. It was just one of the stratagems that some people adopt to stand off a fate which is just too difficult to be lived. As T. S. Eliot said somewhere, humankind cannot bear too much reality. To Robinson, who had it so tough, he thought that anything that anybody did that was not harmful to another person, anything that he did in defense of his own psyche, his own ego, his own spirit, was all right. Anything that you could do for yourself was better than what human life was doing for you or to you. In one poem ["Uncle Ananias"] about an old man telling lies to little boys, he says, "All summer long we loved him for the same / Perennial inspiration of his lies." There's a very peculiar kind of tenderness in Robinson that you just won't find anywhere else. His favorite words, which occur in almost every poem, are "may," or "may not," or "might have," or "could have." These are all things that happen after the fact. Someone's lost his talent, or never developed a talent; someone's lost his money; someone's failed in a human relationship. Robinson always brings in that conjectural possibility. Well, you can't ever know how it might have been. But, we can speculate, because that's all we can do. It might have been all right under other circumstances, but when you read Robinson, you don't feel that it would; it never would have been any different. The place would have been different, the people would have been different, but it would have ended the same as it did, or worse.

My favorite poem of his, or one of them anyway, is one called "Veteran Sirens," about prostitutes, old prostitutes. He saw a lot of these on his saloon rounds in New York and other places. It's a poem about the heartbreakingness of women who depend on their physical attractiveness when they no longer have it, and they still have to go on with the trade, because there's nothing else for them to do. They can't marry now; at least it's very unlikely, and they have to go on with thicker and thicker makeup, pretending harder and harder each year that men still find them attractive and will pay for their bodies. This is called "Veteran Sirens": Ninon de Lenclos (1620–1705), a famous and rich courtesan who continued to be desirable well into old age.

VETERAN SIRENS

The ghost of Ninon would be sorry now
To laugh at them, were she to see them here,
So brave and so alert for learning how
To fence with reason for another year.

Age offers a far comelier diadem
Than theirs; but anguish has no eye for grace,
When time's malicious mercy cautions them
To think a while of number and of space.

The burning hope, the worn expectancy,
The martyred humor, and the maimed allure,

Cry out for time to end his levity,
And age to soften its investiture;

But they, though others fade and are still fair,
Defy their fairness and are unsubdued;
Although they suffer, they may not forswear
The patient ardor of the unpursued.

Poor flesh, to fight the calendar so long;
Poor vanity, so quaint and yet so brave;
Poor folly, so deceived and yet so strong,
So far from Ninon and so near the grave.

Here again, Robinson's stark, solid, straightforward kind of writing. One sees it, and one sees what he felt about these particular "sirens."

Well, I don't think we'll get to anybody but Robinson today, but the books are these: you can get my edition, which is really a Macmillan edition, and my book and introduction in Collier books. There's a very good short life, critical biography, by Louis O. Coxe, published by Pegasus Press. There's the great champion of Robinson as a major American poet by our old friend Yvor Winters. It's the best book by Yvor Winters I've ever read. He's really in sympathy with Robinson, and he's rarely in sympathy with any other writer. Winters is a very good scholar, when he wants to be, and he'll give you the facts, but he'll also give you very strongly his own opinions as to why Robinson is great, and why he's so infinitely greater than Frost. This is strictly a minority opinion, but Winters was ever one for the minority opinions. So this is a good one; I don't know whether it's in paper or not—*Edwin Arlington Robinson,* by Yvor Winters, put out by New Directions. There's quite a good long biography by a man named Herman Hagedorn, but the latest one, with a lot more biographical material, is the one by Chard Powers Smith, who knew Robinson while he was holding forth at the MacDowell Colony, knew him for a number of years, and had probably as many face-to-face conversations with him as anybody had, including the very last of all with Robinson, one on his deathbed. There's a charming reminiscence in a book called *Exiles and Fabrications* by another New Englander named Winfield Townley Scott, who was a college boy when Robinson was an old man and who has a delightful reminiscence of going to see Robinson for a few afternoons in the MacDowell Colony. Robinson was such a recluse that it was accorded among all the literati, the aspiring poets, as an absolute accomplishment to be introduced to him. And there was one woman who was so enamored of his Arthurian poems that she sneaked into his room while he was having lunch, and someone was making up the bed in there, and this woman said, "I just want to touch his bed." Embarrassed him to death! Strangely enough, though an awful lot was written about him at the height of his fame, most of this is unavailable now, except, as I say, these books by Louis Coxe and Yvor Winters and the biography by Chard Powers Smith, plus Robinson's own works. The rest you'd have to look up at the libraries, but there was a great deal of it when he was at the height of his fame, during the middle and late 1920s and early 1930s. But if you read Winters and Louis Coxe, and just maybe the biography by Smith, you'll have plenty of background, to write, or do anything you wanted to do with Robinson.

Let's finish off with his two or three best ones. That poem about Ben Jonson entertaining Shakespeare and kind of trying to sum him up is very short considering the length of a great many of Robinson's blank verse poems. It'll give you some kind of idea of the long-windedness that Robinson does achieve in his longer things. But the great poems are the psychological and interpersonal lyrics, lyrics dealing either with a single person or the interaction between, say, two people here. Now, I want somebody to tell me when we finish what the story is here, because sometimes you know something horrible is happening to these people, but I'm not even sure, after all these years, that even *I* know what the situation is. So, see if you can figure it out. "Eros Turannos": Love, the tyrant.

EROS TURANNOS

She fears him, and will always ask
  What fated her to choose him;
She meets in his engaging mask
  All reasons to refuse him;
But what she meets and what she fears
Are less than are the downward years,
Drawn slowly to the foamless weirs
  Of age, were she to lose him.

Between a blurred sagacity
  That once had power to sound him,
And Love, that will not let him be
  The Judas that she found him,
Her pride assuages her almost,
As if it were alone the cost.—
He sees that he will not be lost,
  And waits and looks around him.

A sense of ocean and old trees
  Envelops and allures him;
Tradition, touching all he sees,

Beguiles and reassures him;
And all her doubts of what he says
Are dimmed with what she knows of days—
Till even prejudice delays
    And fades, and she secures him.

The falling leaf inaugurates
    The reign of her confusion;
The pounding wave reverberates
    The dirge of her illusion;
And home, where passion lived and died,
Becomes a place where she can hide,
While all the town and harbor side
    Vibrate with her seclusion.

We tell you, tapping on our brows,
    The story as it should be,—
As if the story of a house
    Were told, or ever could be;
We'll have no kindly veil between
Her visions and those we have seen,—
As if we guessed what hers have been,
    Or what they are or would be.

Meanwhile we do no harm; for they
    That with a god have striven,
Not hearing much of what we say,
    Take what the god has given;
Though like waves breaking it may be,
Or like a changed familiar tree,
Or like a stairway to the sea
    Where down the blind are driven.

Now, what is the situation here between this man and woman? These are peo-
ple who live in this harborside town, New England town, it must be, and they
once loved each other. They married when they were younger, "where passion
lived and died." Something has killed that off. What is he like? What do the
lines mean, "And Love, that will not let him be / The Judas that she found
him"? Why is he a Judas? Now these people once loved each other in this
house, and they're staying together, although the situation has really turned
her into a recluse. What is *his* attitude? I always think of this as a relatively
well-connected woman, and the guy as a fellow who was maybe a charming
younger man, but who maybe didn't have anything much to him, who's living
off her money. "He sees that he will not be lost." Other women maybe would

kick him out, but she doesn't want to kick him out. She *can't* kick him out. Why? She doesn't want to be alone. Even if he's a Judas, she'd rather have him than *nothing.* And what is *his* attitude? Tradition is with him. Tradition is not going to let her kick him out. Tradition is going to guarantee that she put up with him, because she's maybe from one of these old straitlaced families that frown on divorce, and she won't let him be talked about or looked down on. So he looks around him and he knows that he's got it made, Jack. I mean, if he's discreet about it, he can do whatever he wants to do. She's so afraid of being abandoned and being alone that she'll overlook some of this. And maybe a lot more than she should; maybe more than other women would. And it's turned her into a crank, kind of like Emily Dickinson, a recluse. Who is "we," by the way? "We tell you, tapping on our brows, the story as it should be." The people in the town. They look at this house where something very strange is going on, but the people there stay indoors so much, or at least the woman does, that they have to speculate, whisper, gossip. They don't really *know,* as nobody reading Robinson, including the poet, really *knows,* but they think something—it's unusual, unhealthy—is going on there. But the conclusion, Robinson says, is that if you've had what love gives, some years of passion and love and mutual regard and esteem, if you've had *that* part, the good part, you also have to take the rest. No matter how awful it is, you must "take what the god has given," no matter how bad it is. But I think the imagery in the end is startling and pow-erful for Robinson, who very rarely uses imagery. These are three things that you have to take, if you mess around with the god Eros: you've got to go the whole way. Because the woman has taken advantage of him, too, for her own reasons. They're locked into each other and they can't let go, and they'll perish together.

Well, that's all we can do on Robinson. He's not for all people and all tastes, but he's there.

Walter de la Mare

His life is not especially interesting as some lives of writers are, say, like Byron, or Dylan Thomas, or any of the ones you are accustomed to reading biographies about. His life was essentially an inward life, outwardly uneventful. He took no spectacular trips; he had nothing spectacular happen to him. He lived to be an old man. He worked for the first part of his young manhood, up to the age of thirty-five, for the Anglo-American Oil Company. He began to write stories and poems. They caught on, and he had a small following so that at the age of thirty-five or forty he was able to leave his job and earn a living by reviewing and by other literary pursuits, his own books. Always lived frugally. His audience grew, though it was still small at the end of his life, at least small compared to a popular writer, but enough to give him a certain security. I have always liked de la Mare. I can always read him. His output is enormous, fortunately for us who like him, and, as I say, I've always liked him because he's a haunted man. I don't mean haunted in the sense that someone like, say, Edgar Allan Poe could be said to be haunted. I mean haunted, really, by another world, by a world that is just the other side of the world we think of as reality.

It's very difficult to write about this kind of world that is more particularly de la Mare's world. It's no accident that he's the best of all explorers of the world in which the main thing that figures is the interaction with the other world—spirits, ghosts, whatever you want to call them—things that are not what we would call real, but which are nevertheless capable of impinging on our lives in various, mysterious ways. It's no mistake that he's the special chronicler of that kind of experience, and also the greatest writer for children that we've ever had, I think, in English. The greatest writers for children are writers for people other than children as well—say Lewis Carroll, for example, or [Jonathan] Swift, with *Gulliver's Travels,* which is anything but strictly a children's book, though that is generally what it is sold for, oddly enough—none of them seem to have the apprehension of what it really is like to perceive as a child does with the innocent eye that de la Mare has. His first books were children's books. But they were children's books of a very special kind. He published two kinds of children's books: one is the poems and stories that he himself writes for children. The other kind is in the form of an enormous anthology of writings for children, ostensibly. Except that they're not. I suppose the booksellers sell them for children's books, but he is probably the greatest, the most inspired and creative anthologist in the whole English language. An anthology is usually the last refuge of the creative writer. It's invariably hack work. Not so with him. De la Mare's cast of mind was so profoundly creative that a de la Mare anthology is just as much a work of creative art as a work of de la Mare's original poetry. For one thing, the man is enormously well read. There seems to be nothing that he's ever failed to read. I would put forward this collection of his called *Come Hither* as the greatest of all Christmas presents. I would say that it has only one drawback as a Christmas present if you were going to give it to your nephew or your niece. You know what that is? If you look at it, and read in it a little bit, you don't want to give it away. It's that fascinating. It is probably *the* greatest creative anthology for children. *Come Hither:* it's not at all one of these anthologies that has nothing but the usual so-called children's verses in it. It has pieces in it in which de la Mare says in the introduction, "I found that quality which I call the imagination." I have read things from *Come Hither* to dozens of children, including my own, and they can't have enough of it. But, as I say, like all really good things for children, anthologies, poems, whatever, it has a resonance beyond the child's imagination. I don't doubt at all that many people have bought *Come Hither* to give to children and either have decided to keep it for themselves or have bought another copy to give to the originally designated children. It's a fascinating book.

There are two other anthologies particularly germane to what we want to talk about today. In the world of dreams, the world of sleep, the twilit world between either, which is both and neither, de la Mare has his own special kingdom. This is one called *Behold, This Dreamer!,* another one of his vast, creative anthologies about the world of sleep, an enormously learned and utterly fascinating work about dreams, about sleep, about the connection between the two, and the profound difference between sleeping and waking. How one influences the other. You can still see the water stains on this one. I picked this one up out of the mud and the coral slop on Okinawa. I had never heard of Walter de la Mare. I just wanted something to read, and this was the most intact book around. I read every word. I'd never read anything like it in my life, and still haven't. He has about a hundred-page introduction which is both learned and fascinatingly individual and imaginative in its own right. *Behold, This Dreamer!* There was another anthology which came out while I was in college called *Love,* which I don't think is as good, but which is very good too.

A de la Mare anthology is not like anybody else's. It's got so much stuff in there that is odd, quirky, imaginative, and that but for de la Mare you never would have heard about. This is the main thing. But there are also other things that make these anthologies good. I mean, the anthology is conceived as a work of art. All of his enormous learning, all of his strange and special interests, not in the occult, but in the other world. He was not like Yeats; he had no system. Nothing was systematized, because when the other world breaks into this world in a poem or a story of de la Mare's it is always random; it's not foreseeable. It's not subject to a system as Yeats's system. It's something that's completely unexpected, and there's always an element of mystery as to why it happened as it did. So these are the three great anthologies: *Come Hither; Behold, This Dreamer!;* and *Love.* All great Christmas presents, but, as I say, if you get into them, you won't want to turn loose of 'em.

So you could say, in a way, that de la Mare came into the mansion or the house of serious poetry through the kindergarten, because his mind remained until his death extremely innocent. It's as though de la Mare's mind had two sides to it which in a strange way mingled. On one side there was this world of timeless innocence, which could understand the child because it was itself so childlike and timeless. On the other side was this mind which comprehended this enormous scholarship and this enormous amount of reading. And so they mixed, this kind of fathomless innocence of de la Mare and this enormous erudition, and you get these strange creative anthologies. And they are not to be missed. In *Behold, This Dreamer!* and the one called *Love,* he has very, very long introductions which are worth the price of the book. If they were published by themselves, they would be remarkable essays on these subjects, on the subjects of sleep and dreams and reverie and the world of love and affection. They're big books, but they're books you never get tired of. I haven't. I've read them again and again since that day on Okinawa.

Let me backtrack a little bit. If you want to read a good essay on de la Mare, if you want to write on him, the best introduction to both the prose and the poetry is the one by Horace Gregory in a book called *The Dying Gladiators.* It's published by Grove Press. If you go into a paperback bookstore and if you can get past the Grove Press dirty books, then they also published *The Dying Gladiators* by Horace Gregory, in which you will find an essay on Walter de la Mare called "The Nocturnal Traveler," which is quite a good title for his particular realm of experience, either twilight or night. Almost nothing ever happens in the daytime for de la Mare. He's always been a writer who was completely of a piece, whose prose—he had two novels, one of them, characteristically, called *Memoirs of a Midget.* Here, let me digress on the *Memoirs of a Midget*

"Barnstorming for poetry," mid-1970s. *Photograph by de Casseres Photography; courtesy of James Dickey Collection, Department of Rare Books & Special Collections, Thomas Cooper Library, University of South Carolina*

a minute. I wouldn't say it's one of my absolute favorite books, but I've read it three or four times over the course of the years. It's about a woman who's a midget. She has trouble handling a candle, for example. But the novel expands, and all these bizarre things happen. But it becomes not only the story of a midget who is forever limited in size in a normal-sized person's world, but it becomes a parable of anybody who's different in any way, whose individuality makes it difficult for the person in a general universe of conformity. Now, it's a terribly poignant and very powerful and imaginative way of projecting that particular dilemma, that of the person who's different in some way, and we all are. This casting the central character as a midget is only a way of pointing this up and making it more apparent and more concrete and more down-to-earth than maybe another way of showing the same thing would have been. It's a special kind of book, but it's full of marvelous things, and things that would never have occurred to anybody but him.

I'll talk about the stories in a minute, but I think I want to talk about the poems and then the stories and then the poems again. That might be the way to do it, because, as I say, he's remarkably of a piece. Everything he wrote partakes of his peculiar sort of otherworldly, ghostly, disturbing quality. The reader must decide, and rather early in the game, whether the poems are childlike or simply childish. The childish in poetry is of course unbearable. But childlike is either whimsical or magical. The only thing that can save it from coyness is authentic spell-casting. And this de la Mare does. And it was apparent from the beginning. I think his first book of poems came out in 1902. But if you bought your child a book of poems, and it had this in it, what would you think? You know what mold is, don't you? It's like down in the basement where it's damp and there're spiders and rats. This is called "John Mouldy."

JOHN MOULDY

I spied John Mouldy in his cellar,
Deep down twenty steps of stone;
In the dusk he sat a-smiling,
    Smiling there alone.

He read no book, he snuffed no candle;
The rats ran in, the rats ran out;
And far and near, the drip of water
    Went whisp'ring about.

The dusk was still, with dew a-falling,
I saw the Dog-star bleak and grim,
I saw a slim brown rat of Norway
    Creep over him.

> I spied John Mouldy in his cellar,
> Deep down twenty steps of stone;
> In the dusk he sat a-smiling,
> Smiling there alone.

I read my child that—scared him to death. And yet you know how children are. Fear is one of the things that de la Mare understood first. I think very few writers before him understood this about writing for children. They like personifications. Maybe it's been understood, but it's never been understood in the same way that de la Mare understood it. And his personifications are not just any personifications. They have a special kind of character. I don't think you'd find John Mouldy in any of the works of Beatrix Potter.

So, to sum up the children's books: it was just natural for him to come up with personifications and situations that would form a new kind of imagery in a child's mind. Children are the hardest to get to as far as imaginative works on the page are concerned. They've got so much imagination of their own, children have, that it's very difficult to mold that to your way. De la Mare didn't want to mold it to his way. He wanted to present things in *their* way that they might have perhaps thought of themselves. There we get John Mouldy sitting down in the cellar with the rats crawling around all over him. And yet, although he's sinister, he's just sitting there smiling in the dark to himself. He's sinister, but there's still something about him. I don't know. I don't know how you feel about John Mouldy. I don't know how *I* feel. It's typical of the way de la Mare affects you. You don't know exactly how to take him. You don't know whether you like him or you're frightened of him or fascinated with him or what. Very ambiguous. De la Mare is the most elusive of writers, and one of the most endlessly fascinating because he never draws any distinct conclusions about anything. He just presents this strange impingement of other worlds on ours. There's nothing unusual about a cellar and there's nothing unusual about mold, but John Mouldy sitting down there with his rats, smiling to himself, is something else. He's got something to smile about that we don't even know. He *likes* those rats. They get on him.

You should know this next poem, because it has an unconscious, funny thing in it that's funny to us but shouldn't be funny. This is about a gardener. Again, notice the unusual personification, which is like nobody else. Old Shellover was, of course, a snail. I don't know who Creep is—a beetle maybe, or perhaps a slug, something that inhabits gardens when the gardeners go to sleep. In the third line there's a word that we put a different connotation on than de la Mare would have done, and it makes the poem kind of temporarily funny to us, and yet such is the strange kind of de la Mare magic of the poem that we forget to snicker.

OLD SHELLOVER

"Come!" said Old Shellover.
"What?" says Creep.
"The horny old Gardener's fast asleep;
The fat cock Thrush
To his nest has gone;
And the dew shines bright
In the rising Moon;
Old Sallie Worm from her hole doth peep:
Come!" said Old Shellover.
"Aye!" said Creep.

Dylan Thomas was quite an admirer of de la Mare, and Dylan Thomas was quite a good literary critic in a knockabout way, and he's talking here about de la Mare's stories, which are very much like the poems. As I say, these are remarkably of a piece. You'd never mistake a de la Mare story for anybody else's. The difference between the stories and the poems is that in the poems there is operating one of the most exquisite ears for cadences that the English language has ever had. Walter de la Mare is a great technical master of a limited sort. I don't mean this as a disparagement. He's a very good lyric poet, but the sensibility and the imagination in the poems, in the children's poems, in the other poems —it's in the stories, too. This is a typical couple of paragraphs from a de la Mare story. This will really give you the de la Marian climate. If you like it, you can't have enough of it. If you don't like it, you just think it's much ado about the kind of supernaturalism that nobody could possibly be interested in. The people in de la Mare stories are always meeting in remote railway stations in the middle of the night waiting for trains. Now, I don't want to make him sound like a conventional writer of ghost stories, and if you're interested in him, I hope you will read some of the stories because they are really distinctive.

In other words, if you want to get this effect of frightening someone as movies obviously try in every possible way to do according to their limited imaginations, if you want to frighten somebody, first of all, if you're good, you make him believe that these events could happen. And if you're a real master of the genre, you not only make him believe that it could happen, but that it could happen to *him*. Then you've got 'em. If they honestly believe that, then you've solved the fundamental artistic problem involved, and that's what [the movie monsters] Rodin and Godzilla, and even Dracula, try to do. The original *Dracula,* the novel, does this to a certain extent because it's all made up of letters and diaries, devices of this sort, to bring in this atmosphere of verisimilitude: letters to people, diaries, documents, and things of that nature. The thing about de la Mare's encroachment on what we call the world of reality is like that because there is not anything in de la Mare's stories that has a mask on or that has long claws or has any of the characteristics of the scare techniques of our time.

One of his two novels is called *The Return,* for example. A man named Arthur Lawford, who is a different, intelligent, sensitive, rather weak man recovering from an illness, goes out into an old English cemetery. His doctors told him to take walks, and he goes out into this cemetery, and he sits down on a sunny afternoon in the cemetery, and begins to read the gravestones, and there's a man who's committed suicide there. And he dozes off and wakes up feeling kind of strange and goes back home to his wife, and she thinks he's acting oddly. What happens is that—it's a short novel, only about two hundred pages —the spirit of this fellow in the tomb is trying to take possession of him. And the whole rest of the novel is the struggle between Arthur Lawford's own soul or spirit trying to cast out this other spirit that's trying to take him over. You'd have to read it to see how subtly it's done. You don't know what's happening for a long time. But this all takes place in a very calm English village countryside sort of an atmosphere, and there are no outward signs of the tension at all. I mean, the appearance doesn't change, but the struggle that's going on in Arthur Lawford's mind and body as this battle for the possession of his body takes place is more violent than the clash of arms between Hector and Achilles on the plains of Troy. And yet nobody knows it's happening. It's a wonderful story. It has the most beautiful love scene in it I've ever read. It has a description of a house in it that I've wanted to live in ever since I've read about it. The only people who understand what's going on with him—his wife doesn't understand, his daughter doesn't understand—are two—a brother and a sister— eccentric people who live in this house by the river. He goes to talk to them, and they try to advise him and they don't know what to do either, but they believe that what's happening to Arthur Lawford is happening. It's called *The Return.* That and *Memoirs of a Midget* are the two novels.

Now the poems. You read the poems, and you're struck by a couple of things about them. One of them is that the diction is terribly, terribly oldfangled. You would not be able to tell from reading most of de la Mare's poetry that he did not write in 1855 or 1860. I mean, he never saw fit to change that at all. He uses this old-fashioned diction unashamedly. He never felt any need to become modern. He's always got his own way. And if he seems to us terribly old-fashioned, which he is, then I don't think we should let it go at that. He is in some sense, maybe a minor sense, a very real magician. And the proof of how good Walter de la Mare really is, is in the fact that he can throw out one of the things that we think necessary for a modern poet to be able to do, and that's to sound like modern people. He can just set that aside, throw it out, and spin his own webs and work his own magic in his own ways. That will set a lot of people off. They think, "My God, I can't read anything as old-fangled as this. I'm supposed to be reading Dylan Thomas." But he began in the nineteenth century, and he continued in that idiom until he died. He never saw fit to change. He was very much his own man, never influenced by anybody, except by the main lyric tradition of the English verse as it came down to him. But he never felt any need to experiment. He worked in the old forms, the sonnet, the quatrain. In this way he's very much like Hardy, whom he greatly admired, and who admired him, although Hardy, of course, was a much older man. They are both very, very English poets, and de la Mare's ghosts are very much English ghosts.

They're not American ghosts; they're English ghosts. The countryside, the southern part of England, the sheep, the birds, the flowers, the trees, the grass, the clouds, the rain are all very, very English. It requires in some ways a very special effort on the part of an American to get into a rapport with something which is so un-American as their particular little green island world, rainy world, that has meant so much to so many generations of English writers. But once you've gotten past that—the old-fangledness and the particularly English kind of idiom that they use and the references that they use—there's hardly anything in de la Mare but delight and a disturbing nocturnal kind of otherworld quality, plus a beautiful lyric gift.

There's an awful lot of de la Mare, as you can see in the size of *Collected Poems.* He lived a long life. He worked himself very hard trying to get his visions of ghosts or the spirit world down on the page. He wrote a lot of poems; he wrote—or at least edited, which is almost the same as writing them—and introduced three magnificent anthologies; and he did a certain amount of very perceptive and sensitive literary criticism. And I think probably his reputation is about as sure as any poet of his time. His prose works are not so much read as they might be, but among the people who care for very special kinds of talents, they will always be read. You may think, as some Americans do, that he's not with the world; he's not connected enough with the world that we all live in. He gives a little too much to the world just on the other side of the veil. But if you know his particular magic, and if you know how really good he is at working his spells, the spells that are indigenous to him, then you don't care so much about realism as you thought maybe you did before. His spell is a very strong one, although spun out of very thin, gossamer-like threads.

The most famous anthology piece of de la Mare—it's quite typical of him —there's a great deal of justice in the fact that this is the most famous anthology piece of his—is called "The Listeners."

THE LISTENERS

"Is there anybody there?" said the Traveller,
    Knocking on the moonlit door;
And his horse in the silence champed the grasses
    Of the forest's ferny floor:
And a bird flew up out of the turret,
    Above the Traveller's head:
And he smote upon the door again a second time;
    "Is there anybody there?" he said.
But no one descended to the Traveller;
    No head from the leaf-fringed sill
Leaned over and looked into his grey eyes,
    Where he stood perplexed and still.
But only a host of phantom listeners
    That dwelt in the lone house then
Stood listening in the quiet of the moonlight
    To that voice from the world of men:
Stood thronging the faint moonbeams on the dark stair,
    That goes down to the empty hall,
Hearkening in an air stirred and shaken
    By the lonely Traveller's call.
And he felt in his heart their strangeness,
    Their stillness answering his cry,
While his horse moved, cropping the dark turf,
    'Neath the starred and leafy sky;
For he suddenly smote on the door, even
    Louder, and lifted his head:—
"Tell them I came, and no one answered,
    That I kept my word," he said.
Never the least stir made the listeners,
    Though every word he spake
Fell echoing through the shadowiness of the still house
    From the one man left awake:
Ay, they heard his foot upon the stirrup,
    And the sound of iron on stone,

And how the silence surged softly backward,
When the plunging hoofs were gone.

Who owned that house? The Listeners. But who are they? Are they ghosts or spirits or just moonbeams, or are they people just incapable of saying something to him? It's that very eerily atmospheric thing. You don't know whether there was anybody there or not, or whether it was just some kind of phantom. He never tells you anything.

On Walter de la Mare's seventy-fifth birthday some notable English writers were asked to contribute dedicatory verses and essays, and the last good poem that T. S. Eliot wrote was written for this occasion ["A Tribute to Walter de la Mare." The first two lines read: "The children who explored the brook and found / A desert island with a sandy cove . . ."]. Eliot was a great admirer of the music of de la Mare's verse, the way he wove syllables, vowels, and consonants together in this spell-casting way, and Eliot wrote this, first about children, about de la Mare's connection with children and then about the de la Marian universe generally. Eliot starts out with children who go out and inhabit their own universe. They play like they're pirates. They play like they're explorers; they come out of the woods back of the house and play like it's a jungle full of exotic animals. And then they come in and they tell us a story, just before they go to bed.

So, the books. There are innumerable collections of de la Mare. The one I happen to have is the *Complete Works,* but I don't think you would like to start out with a book of de la Mare's that had that much in it. There're selections of all the writings. There are the complete tales or collected tales, stories and so on, strange as anything you've ever read. There's *Memoirs of a Midget. The Return:* I have it in a small book called *Six Novels of the Supernatural* [edited by Edward Wagenknecht] with five other inferior novels in it. I don't have a copy of *Come Hither,* but you can dip into these enormous, tremendously fascinating anthologies that I do have, or you can get *Come Hither,* too. *Behold, This Dreamer!* and *Love.* And that should do you. The best essay I know is, as I say, in Horace Gregory and *The Dying Gladiators.*

The adverse judgments: of course, they're going to be plenty of those, because someone who's special and as specialized as de la Mare is going to get, especially from American critics, a good deal of it. Randall Jarrell says, "It is easy to complain that de la Mare writes about unreality. . . . The hard hot flesh in the sunlight has nothing to stand for it but vacancy." Jarrell would have de la Mare be more with ordinary experiences and reality than with this dim twilight world, this limbo world between reality and the other world, whatever it is, or whatever it may be. I don't think Jarrell's is the whole story. Americans live in a country which is not haunted, in the sense that England with its enormously long past, its long history, is haunted. We have great impatience with ancestral ghosts, possessions, things of that sort. De la Mare could never have been an American poet, and I don't think Jarrell takes that nearly enough into account. But in his special world he's not only supreme but also about the only inhabitant. He's the only one that can take you across that limbo into the other world and bring you back properly through the twilight. That's the book; that's the man; that's the work.

Michael Hamburger

We'll have a very brief look at Michael Hamburger. Michael Hamburger was born in Germany, spent some time in concentration camps. He's known, more than not, as a critic and translator from the German. However, he's a relatively prolific poet. I think he has five or six collections, and they are distinctive without being really "stoppers." They don't really stop you; they're good, but they're not—I hesitate to use the word competent, because that is kind of pejorative; they are competent, they're better than that—but they're not really outstandingly good. But they're readable, and sometimes they rise above what seems to be a relatively modest level. Did we read the poem of Hamburger's about the pool player? About the artist compared to a snooker player? It's called "A Poet's Progress." I've always liked this. I don't think anybody but a real poet would have thought of this comparison, and the way he works it out is kind of good without being great.

A Poet's Progress

Like snooker balls thrown on the table's faded green,
Rare ivory and weighted with his best ambitions,
At first his words are launched: not certain what they mean,
He loves to see them roll, rebound, assume positions
Which—since not he—some higher power has assigned.
But now the game begins: dead players, living critics
Are watching him—and suddenly one eye goes blind,
The hand that holds the cue shakes like a paralytic's,
Till every thudding, every clinking sound portends
New failure, new defeat. Amazed, he finds that still
It is not he who guides his missiles to their ends
But an unkind geometry that mocks his will.

If he persists, for years he'll practise patiently,
Lock all the doors, learn all the tricks, keep noises out,
Though he may pick a ghost or two for company
Or pierce the room's inhuman silence with a shout.
More often silence wins; then soon the green felt seems

An evil playground, lawless, lost to time, forsaken,
And he a fool caught in the water weeds of dreams
Whom only death or frantic effort can awaken.

At last, a master player, he can face applause,
Looks for a fit opponent, former friends, emerges;
But no one knows him now. He questions his own cause,
And has forgotten why he yielded to those urges,
Took up a wooden cue to strike a coloured ball.
Wise now, he goes on playing; both his house and heart
Unguarded solitudes, hospitable to all
Who can endure the cold intensity of art.

The other one I like is the one about the pregnant woman. There's a lot in there I would object to, and yet the thrust of it I kind of like. This is, I think, very much the way people feel about bringing children into the world: "Here I perpetuate the grief of the world in this child, but here I perpetuate the joy, too. I'm not the source or giver; they're only passing through me."

The best poems of his I know have to do with horses. This is just a very short one, called "Epitaph for a Horseman," where the horse's bones have been buried there and the rider has been carried off. Either the rider wasn't killed or there is the usual refusal to bury the horse and the rider together. The word "jade" means, in the parlance of the English, what we would call a nag.

EPITAPH FOR A HORSEMAN

Let no one mourn his mount, upholstered bone
He rode so cruelly over bog and stone,
Log, fence and ditch in every kind of weather;
Nor glibly hint those two came down together:
A horse fell dead and cast his master down,
But by that fall their union was undone.
A broken jade we found, the rider gone,
Leaving no token but his cold clean gear,
Bit, reins and riding-crop for friends to gather.
None but a beast's remains lie buried here.

A classic composition; nothing stirs.
One little streak of grey that matched the walls
Removed, but in that half-light far too faint
To leave a gap, and soon to be replaced.

This one is called "The Horse's Eye." This is about walking near a fenced-in place for horses near a place where they're building some apartments.

Michael Hamburger

THE HORSE'S EYE

I did not stop today at the five-barred gate,
Did not wait for the old white draught-horse at grass,
Unshod, unharnessed these many years; walked past,
Preoccupied, but something made me look back:
Her head was over the gate, her neck was straight,
But I caught her eye, a wicked, reproachful look
From one small eye slanted in my direction.
What right, I defied the old mare, what right had she
To expect caresses, the grass foolishly plucked
For her hanging lip, her yellow, broken teeth
And her great historical belly? Of course she's a relic,
Curious now as the old white country house
That stood empty and alluring in the wood behind her
Till converted into flats—not as useless as she,
Who will never become a tractor! What farmer would care?
Only some town-bred, animist, anthropomorphic rambler
Or week-end motorist looking for what he's lost.

I walked on; but plainly her glance had spoken to me,
As an old peasant's might in a foreign country,
Communicating neither words nor thought, but the knowledge
Of flesh that has suffered labour in the rain and wind,
Fed, relaxed, enjoyed and opposed every season.
Broken now. Close to death. And how differently broken
From that Cossack mare the clumsiest rider could sit,
All speed and nerve and power that somehow responded
To the faintest twitch of a will less tense than her own!
Wild nature still; her eye no peasant's eye,
But lava under glass, tellurian fire contained.

As for the old white mare, her reproach was just:
Because she was too intelligible I had passed her by,
Because not alien enough, but broken as men are broken,
Because the old white house was converted now,
The wood about to be felled, a tractor chugging
Beyond the hill, and awkwardly she trotted
On legs too thin for her belly bloated with age,
Alone in her meadow, at grass, and close to death.

The last of the books I have, and I believe I'm not mistaken when I say this is
the last of the collections he's put out, is called *Travelling,* and it's by far the best.
I had sort of written Michael Hamburger, if not off, at least written him down
as somebody who was never going to be any better than a certain relatively

skillful competence, readable, a poet who gives you a little something to think about. But he *is* better than that, and *Travelling* is a very powerful piece of work. We'll end up with one from that. This is the title poem, "Travelling."

TRAVELLING

(Part 1)

Mountains, lakes. I have been here before
And on other mountains, wooded
Or rocky, smelling of thyme.
Lakes from whose beds they pulled
The giant catfish, for food,
Larger, deeper lakes that washed up
Dead carp and mussel shells, pearly or pink.
Forests where, after rain,
Salamanders lay, looped the dark moss with gold.
High up, in a glade,
Bells clanged, the cowherd boy
Was carving a pipe.

And I moved on, to learn
One of the million histories,
One weather, one dialect
Of herbs, one habitat
After migration, displacement,
With greedy lore to pounce
On a place and possess it,
With the mind's weapons, words,
While between land and water
Yellow vultures, mewing,
Looped empty air
Once filled with the hundred names
Of the nameless, or swooped
To the rocks, for carrion.

ROBERT FROST

Dickey began his session on Frost by reading from his essay on Frost in Babel to Byzantium *(1968), which is omitted here.*

What does Robert Frost mean to you? Who is he? How did he come to your attention? I'm asking you to be the public. Public with a capital P, because he had a great deal to do with the public. Robert Frost. Well, you want me to tell you, right?

Robert Frost was a nice old New England guy with a lot of cracker-barrel wisdom that the government, somehow or other, saw fit to honor because he read a poem, or something, at the Kennedy inaugural. He has a lot of real sage, witty comments. He's a real man of the soil. Aren't those some of the things you think of when you think of Robert Frost? Or are they? I'm not talking about our intelligentsia's report. I'm talking about the great Public's report. Because T. S. Eliot is only incidentally heard of. If he's heard of by the public, it's only very, very vaguely. I'm not talking about people in universities. But Robert Frost they have heard of. He's bracketed with another wise old cracker-barrel poet with white hair. [Carl] Sandburg. They have nothing more in common than that they both lived to a very great age and they both pronounced sagely and interminably on all kinds of affairs, public, private. But what is it in the American psyche that harks back to some kind of earlier time that makes us revere this kind of a person? And why Robert Frost? Because there has been no more mistaken notion than Frost of what the man was like and what the poetry was about. I mean when John F. Kennedy says, "'And I have promises to keep / And miles to go before I sleep / And miles to go before I sleep.' A poem by Robert Frost, a New Englander like me," everybody thinks, God knows, American poetry isn't dead. Now this is a strange reckoning. Robert Frost is a public figure. He's like somebody who's engraved on Mount Rushmore. He has very engravable features. God knows, he'd look better up there than Teddy Roosevelt. So Robert Frost is very craggy, rugged, very photographic as a person.

The *real* Robert Frost, the Frost who wrote the *really* good poems that the American public has no more notion of reading than nothing, that doesn't even know the existence of, is not the genial, neighborly, fence-mending, apple-picking, hoeing-and-plowing, hay-raking type of person that he would have you believe. No; he's not the healthy embodiment of the pioneer spirit that we take him to be, that he insisted on our taking him to be. No. Of all the haunted artists, from Sophocles to Shakespeare to Dylan Thomas to Hart Crane to Baudelaire, in any language, in any poetic idiom, Robert Frost is the most haunted of all. And his whole life work was an effort to do his thing, to write his own work no matter *what* it cost him or anybody else. Robert Frost— instead of being a genial, kindly old cracker-barrel New England philosopher —was, in point of fact, one of the most horrifyingly egotistical and hardhearted men who ever lived. He drove his mother into an early grave with his egotism. His sister Jenny went into an asylum and died there. He "killed" his wife with his overbearingness. His own son committed suicide. One of his daughters went into some sort of state where nobody can reach you; I don't know what it's called. So, when he was an old man, and his wife was dead, and he asked one of his other children (he had six children), Irma, whether he might not as an old man come to live with her, she said, "No; I do not want you to exercise the influence on my children that you did on myself and Carol and the other children of yours." She turned him out. She wouldn't have anything to do with him.

Now, this is very strangely at variance with the popular image of Robert Frost, who really came closer to being a poet laureate than any poet we've ever had. What is it in the American sentimental soul that takes to something in a figure like Frost? This is a paradox, and it is the interesting thing about him, his relationship to the public. His public is far vaster than any American poet ever had, any American poet of any description. Even sentimental newspaper versifiers never had the public that Robert Frost had. What is it about him or about what the American public believed he was that gave him this enormous public? It's fascinating, because it not only says something about him; it says quite a lot about us. Here you have a man who presents himself, and with certain credentials, as being close to the land. He farms; he builds fences; he cleans out his well; he rakes hay; he picks apples. Now we, in our time, in the last seventy to one hundred years at least, have been going away from the land into the cities, into the urban areas, and, God help us, the suburban areas. What is it about Frost that would appeal to us?

We say we should want the pastoral, and so we say we do. That's really a very large part of it, I think. I mean, we never mended a fence in our life, particularly a stone fence. But we read about him, and he's earnestly talking about mending stone fences, and we think there's something of the land still left. Here's this rugged guy who writes these wonderful poems. So here he is as an old man; he says all these wise things about international politics; he goes and visits Russia. He delivers a poem of his own at the Kennedy inaugural, and we think America has produced a poet who just won't quit. This guy is ninety years old. They don't know what he's talking about, but he must be saying something if the president wanted him up there.

There's an awful lot of that sort of thing in Robert Frost. And the interesting thing about it is that Frost, the *real* poet, is very, very different from the public image. Another interesting thing is that when Frost, so late in life, began to be paid so much attention to, he began to take his public proclamations seriously. And that is bad for a poet to do. The serious stuff should go into the poems. It should not go into the international newswires. It's no coincidence that the quality of the poetry fell off as he began to be paid more and more attention to for his public cracker-barrel pronouncements about life, death, love, art, poetry, sex, politics, everything. He couldn't tire of the sound of his own voice. So you get a lot of blabber. Some of it fairly good blabber, but his stuff just keeps getting worse and worse. But he had a long life. He lived to be eighty-eight years old, and he wrote an awful lot of poetry. And some of it is good, but of a kind which his public adulators would not even understand if they read, and would never seek out anyway.

We always talk about beloved poets. What makes a poet beloved? Grandma Moses is a beloved artist. Who is a beloved composer, that is, one who has any pretensions of being a serious composer? [George] Gershwin. Frost is a beloved poet. John Wayne is a beloved screen actor. It says an awful lot about this country. And so does Robert Frost. Beloved is a term that should always be mistrusted when it's applied to artists, and particularly to poets. Poets are likely to be beloved for only a few of the right reasons and for almost all of the wrong ones: for saying things we want to hear; for furnishing us with an image of ourselves that we enjoy believing in. Here is Lawrance Thompson's *The Early Years*. Now, if you want to read something horrifying about a man who wants to write poetry and have a family, you should read this. There are two big volumes already published: *Robert Frost: The Early Years* and then *Robert Frost: The Years of Triumph*. They make very good reading and point up the difference between what you are told about somebody in a public role and what actually happened. It's all documented and it's all horrifying and tremendously fascinating.

The main thing with him, though, was that poetry was a kind of armor-plate for his ego. If people accepted his poetry, then they were going to have to accept him. And in the end they accepted him and didn't read the poetry.

But you can tell, if you write the stuff, who's good and who isn't. And he's *good,* and tremendously original, and very economical of means. We'll read one or two in a minute and I'll show you what I mean. What my conclusion is, is that at his simplest, his most rhythmical and cryptic, Frost is a remarkable poet. He surely is that. In other words, if you were chopping wood, that chore had some kind of universal significance to Frost. If you were picking apples, this had a general conclusive principle somewhere involved in it, or with it, in some way. This localizing way of getting generalities to reveal themselves, all kinds of large abstractions, like universal design, original sin, love, death, fate: Frost found a way to do this, to make anything that has ever concerned mankind relate to a New England farm. So that if he's chopping wood and he leans the ax against the stump and the ax handle stands up, you know what he says it's like? It's like when the snake stood up for evil in the garden. Which is terrifically good, original. Perhaps it is contrived. Maybe all poetry is to some extent contrived. But you would have to grant him, according to you, the perhaps dubious honor of saying that he's the first, and maybe the only, poet that ever connected those two things. But I would say it was something that gave me enough pause to remember it, and most poetry doesn't.

So that's what happens with all the public appearances and all the public adulation and being the nearest thing we've ever had to a poet laureate—all these things pass away. Nobody remembers that especially, but the poems are still there. And that, ironically enough, is his immortality. Some of them are remarkable and very original. They have this thing, this quality, of making large things small and small things large. And the diction of Frost's poems has got a convincingness of tone that makes it necessary that other poetry be measured by it. Beside Frost's plain-speaking kind of imagination, other poetry seems literary and dandified. When Frost says something, I mean in one of the really good Frost poems, you believe it. As, in a way, you don't believe Dylan Thomas. Dylan Thomas seems intolerably literary. Robert Frost seems to be a man like you and me, only more so, who has found a way to say what we think, if we could think it. Frost says somewhere that a poet is a man speaking to other men if he could. Well, in the best Frost poems, he can.

He laid for himself a very original personality. He's evasive. Frost is evasive. So that when you finish a Frost poem—and the better the poem, the more you have the feeling—it's that "I'm not sure I get it. I'm not sure I understand the implications, but I know that it really shakes me." It's disturbing; it's profoundly disturbing. But the thing that Frost cultivated all his life—two things: one was to be authoritative, and the other was to be evasive, not to be caught, not to be pinned down, but also to exert enormous authority through his presence, his personality. He did not believe in things like the community of man. A community of nations, a kind of great, bursting swelling hymn for common humanity of which he was a part, would have reduced him. It would have taken away from him; and he wasn't having any of that. He wanted to be not only unique but a law unto himself. Imagine you see a butterfly, and its beauty is something you want to capture and take home with you. First of all, can you do that? You catch the butterfly and place it carefully on cardboard under glass, and to your sorrow you haven't caught the butterfly at all. Where once the butterfly had a subtle, vibrant aliveness, the mere act of pinning it down has destroyed it. Frost always wanted that elusive quality for himself and for his poems where you don't know whether you've quite got it or not, but you keep trying for it. And that's what gives the best quality to his poems, that elusive quality. Is this wisdom or is it nonsense? You could spend your whole life trying to make up your mind. You never know. But his letters also are full of the same stuff. Let me read to you this one excerpt from a letter. This is really horrible; horrifying. This is in [27 October] 1917 when he really thinks he's going mad. He's only had a couple of friends in his life, people who would put up with him, but they were absolutely devoted to him. But they were not equals. They were followers. This is to one of them, to Louis Untermeyer, the anthologist. [Specific passage unidentified.]

Now, I don't think any of us have been that far along that particular path, but it was that borderline, between not knowing whether you made that hideous sound yourself or whether it was a factory whistle. Whether it was you or something else. Whether it was some demon or whatever it was. We don't have to contend with that. But he did, his whole life. And when you think of the good gray poet, the massive New England rocky face giving out platitudes about being good neighbors, think of the man whinnying like a horse behind the house, at night. That was what he made his poetry out of, the near madness. The persona, the mask of Robert Frost, the creature he willed himself to be, that he wanted the public to accept, and the hidden, insensitive, nearly insane artist on the New England farm he couldn't be anything like, hacking his poems out hour after hour, driving everybody else to suicide, into the insane asylum. His own wife had a terribly bad heart. This is just one example. This was when he was an old man and his wife was an old woman. He used to go to Florida in the wintertime. They were in Gainesville, Florida, where the University of Florida is, and they had two rooms. His wife wanted their daughter and their ménage on the upper floor, and Frost and herself on the lower floor, because they were old people and she had a bad heart. No, no. That didn't suit Frost. He said, *we'll* go on the upper floor. And you know what his reason was? To make his wife with angina pectoris climb the stairs every day? It disturbed him to hear people's feet overhead. Now that's our boy. He couldn't be bothered with that sort of thing. So, as a result she climbs up the flight of stairs, she falls down, she suffers. He didn't know *that,* of course, but he knew there was a certain risk involved, but it couldn't interfere with his particular egocentric existence.

Now, we'll read a couple of poems. One of them is one of the great love poems, called "To Earthward." But let's read "The Most of It" because Frost is always asking questions. So the guy's sitting out in the woods, asking questions of the universe. What do you want? You want an answer. Well, this is about that kind of a situation.

THE MOST OF IT

He thought he kept the universe alone;
For all the voice in answer he could wake
Was but the mocking echo of his own
From some tree-hidden cliff across the lake.
Some morning from the boulder-broken beach
He would cry out on life, that what it wants
Is not its own love back in copy speech,
But counter-love, original response.
And nothing ever came of what he cried
Unless it was the embodiment that crashed
In the cliff's talus on the other side,
And then in the far distant water splashed,
But after a time allowed for it to swim,
Instead of proving human when it neared
And someone else additional to him,
As a great buck it powerfully appeared,
Pushing the crumpled water up ahead,
And landed pouring like a waterfall,
And stumbled through the rocks with horny tread,
And forced the underbrush—and that was all.

Here you have the typical Frost ambiguity, the elusiveness. Was *that* his answer? And if so, what did it mean? Frost is not going to say. He doesn't know. And this has given some of his most powerful detractors weapons against him, or what they think are weapons against him. Our ubiquitous friend, Yvor Winters of Stanford, says that this is a magnificent poem but embodies all of Frost's faults. The title of Winters's essay is "Robert Frost, or the Spiritual Drifter."

Winters wants a conclusion. He wants to know, what did the deer mean? The buck came swimming across the lake, he has the answer, now what was it? Was it anything? Winters would say, "Come on now, Frost, goddammit, whadayamean?" Frost would say, "Winters, I beat you again."

"To Earthward" is one of the really good love poems.

TO EARTHWARD

Love at the lips was touch
As sweet as I could bear;
And once that seemed too much;
I lived on air

That crossed me from sweet things,
The flow of—was it musk
From hidden grapevine springs
Downhill at dusk?

I had the swirl and ache
From sprays of honeysuckle
That when they're gathered shake
Dew on the knuckle.

I craved strong sweets, but those
Seemed strong when I was young;
The petal of the rose
It was that stung.

Now no joy but lacks salt
That is not dashed with pain
And weariness and fault;
I crave the stain

Of tears, the aftermark
Of almost too much love,
The sweet of bitter bark
And burning clove.

When stiff and sore and scarred
I take away my hand
From leaning on it hard
In grass and sand,

The hurt is not enough:
I long for weight and strength
To feel the earth as rough
To all my length.

When you're young you think it's all a matter of flowers and sweet smells, but real love has to do with pain and coming out of the earth. It's like natural things, as when you lean on the sand and you get a mark on your hand from it. And, as he gets older, he wants the whole thing. He doesn't want it just on his hand. He wants it all over. Because that's the true thing, when you get into it deep with another person, when you have that sort of earthly pain. It's not just the pretty part, the sweet part. That doesn't get you in deep enough.

"After Apple-Picking" I personally consider the best of all of his poems. I'll just read through it and let you draw your own conclusions. It's about work. We've all done that. But here again is this Frost thing about making a local, apparently routine workaday kind of work assume enormous dimensions and have all kinds of meanings that no other poet would have seen in this at all. So thereby Frost sort of enlarges our particular scope of vision. I've never picked apples in my life. The only apples I've ever picked were in this poem. But this is one of the good things about Frost, too, that he can make you feel what it's like to do something you haven't done. How it feels, not only how it looks or how it sounds, but how it feels. And, also, in this particular kind of way of his, the larger significance of it.

AFTER APPLE-PICKING

My long two-pointed ladder's sticking through a tree
Toward heaven still,
And there's a barrel that I didn't fill
Beside it, and there may be two or three
Apples I didn't pick upon some bough.
But I am done with apple-picking now.
Essence of winter sleep is on the night,
The scent of apples: I am drowsing off.
I cannot rub the strangeness from my sight
I got from looking through a pane of glass
I skimmed this morning from the drinking trough
And held against the world of hoary grass.
It melted, and I let it fall and break.
But I was well
Upon my way to sleep before it fell,
And I could tell
What form my dreaming was about to take.
Magnified apples appear and disappear,
Stem end and blossom end,
And every fleck of russet showing clear.
My instep arch not only keeps the ache,
It keeps the pressure of a ladder-round.

I feel the ladder sway as the boughs bend.
And I keep hearing from the cellar bin
The rumbling sound
Of load on load of apples coming in.
For I have too much
Of apple-picking: I am overtired
Of the great harvest I myself desired.
There were ten thousand thousand fruit to touch,
Cherish in hand, lift down, and not let fall.
For all
That struck the earth,
No matter if not bruised or spiked with stubble,
Went surely to the cider-apple heap
As of no worth.
One can see what will trouble
This sleep of mine, whatever sleep it is.
Were he not gone,
The woodchuck could say whether it's like his
Long sleep, as I describe its coming on,
Or just some human sleep.

What will trouble this sleep of his? There are two kinds of apples: the ones that you did drop, and the ones that you didn't drop. It really has something to do with moral responsibility. I won't elucidate that too far, but it has something to do with having the responsibility to get the apples down into the baskets and not letting them drop. And if you do that all day, and if you're extra special careful with all these apples, hundreds of apples, you've got a kind of special feeling when you go to sleep about your responsibility to the apples, the ones that you didn't drop, but there're bound to be a few that you did.

The books are these, and they are all put out by Holt, Rinehart and Winston, everything. There are all kinds of things written on him. There's this big new *Collected Poems* with all eleven books of the poetry, and then there's the two-volume, with the third volume yet to come out, *Robert Frost* by Lawrance Thompson. There's also a book of prose, very small, short book, but very good, startlingly good. The two best critical books I know are *Robert Frost: Constellations of Intention,* by a man named Reuben Brower, and another one called *The Major Themes of Robert Frost* by a man with the unlikely and wonderful name of Radcliffe Squires, published by the University of Michigan Press.

ANTHONY HECHT

He was advised by his psychiatrist to continue writing poetry. He wrote his first book, *A Summoning of Stones,* published in 1953, and the next book, which did not come out until two years ago, won the Pulitzer Prize, and is in all ways a remarkable book, called *The Hard Hours.* I think if you wanted to write on Tony Hecht you would only need the one book, because this is in essence a kind of collected poems. He writes very, very little, but of a very high quality, and it would maybe be interesting to talk about what the quality is.

He is what I would call an "elegant." At the beginning he wrote marvelous poems, usually in complicated stanza forms, about gardens, about ballets, about paintings, and all those things that you would not care too much to write or read about. He's an elegant, an esthete. But during the time of his commitment, he was persuaded, or persuaded himself, to enlarge his themes. He then discovered, as so many American writers have done, his Jewishness, and he wrote powerfully moving poems on concentration camps and the link-up of his own heritage as a Jew to what happened in central Europe in the late 1930s and early 1940s. If you are an American Jewish writer it's easy to write about those things. You figure it's your heritage. You can write about what happened to your kinfolk when there was really no danger to you yourself. But Tony Hecht has managed to make an intense and powerful poetry out of his kinship with martyrs, with his own kin. Let's read the one in our book about the miscarriage. And notice how his formalism makes the poem better than it would be if it were looser. It's a very tight poem called "The Vow." He married an Irish girl; the children were raised in the Jewish faith, and this is an account of his wife's miscarriage and the father's feelings about it.

THE VOW

In the third month, a sudden flow of blood.
The mirth of tabrets ceaseth, and the joy
Also of the harp. The frail image of God
Lay spilled and formless. Neither girl nor boy,
But yet blood of my blood, nearly my child.

Anthony Hecht

All that long day
Her pale face turned to the window's mild
Featureless grey.

And for some nights she whimpered as she dreamed
The dead thing spoke, saying: "Do not recall
Pleasure at my conception. I am redeemed
From pain and sorrow. Mourn rather for all
Who breathlessly issue from the bone gates,
The gates of horn,
For truly it is best of all the fates
Not to be born.

"Mother, a child lay gasping for bare breath
On Christmas Eve when Santa Claus had set
Death in the stocking, and the lights of death
Flamed in the tree. O, if you can, forget
You were the child, turn to my father's lips
Against the time
When his cold hand puts forth its fingertips
Of jointed lime."

Doctors of Science, what is man that he
Should hope to come to a good end? *The best
Is not to have been born.* And could it be
That Jewish diligence and Irish jest
The consent of flesh and a midwinter storm
Had reconciled,
Was yet too bold a mixture to inform
A simple child?

Even as gold is tried, Gentile and Jew.
If that ghost was a girl's, I swear to it:
Your mother shall be far more blessed than you.
And if a boy's, I swear: The flames are lit
That shall refine us; they shall not destroy
A living hair.
Your younger brothers shall confirm in joy
This that I swear.

JOHN MASEFIELD

Masefield, of course, was poet laureate before the present one, C. Day Lewis. He had a very curious kind of life and career. He was, for example, the last English poet to sail before the mast, to sail on clipper ships. He lived to an incredibly old age and died just a couple or three years ago; must have been in his nineties. He had a very odd career for an English poet, or any poet. He did, as a boy, actually run off to sea and was trained as a sailor on the old clipper ships. He lived in New York. He was a bartender and worked at a number of odd jobs and traveled a very great deal. He must be the only English poet of any note, or probably the only English poet at all, who went round the stormy, dangerous passage around Cape Horn in a sailing ship. That was supposed to be the most difficult of all sailing feats, but he was on one of the last sailing ships that did that. He went into journalism around the age of thirty, which would be in the early part of this century; he was born in 1878. And then he gradually through great and astute and assiduous work as a writer built up a reputation as a kind of all-around man of letters. He wrote poetry; he wrote novels; he wrote plays; he wrote literary criticism, some of which is quite good. Around 1912, for example, he wrote a book on Shakespeare which is still readable; very unorthodox, but still readable and a very good introduction to Shakespeare. He served in World War I, and wrote what Ernest Hemingway, of all people, said was the best account of a battle ever written, a book called *Gallipoli,* about one of the more disastrous campaigns of the Crimea, the British against the Turks.

He's quite a good historian, and his two war books, both of them extremely short but very good, are *Gallipoli* and one about the evacuation of Dunkirk in the part of the Second World War called *The Nine Days Wonder.* The evacuation of British troops from Dunkirk, for example, was effected very largely by civilian pleasure craft. So if you had a boat on the east coast of England, you simply got your Chris-Craft, or whatever it was you had, and went over there and picked up some soldiers. Now, all these civilians in all these pleasure craft were bringing back all the soldiers from Dunkirk. And the way

Masefield makes you see the national effort by which this was done makes an extremely fascinating kind of document called *The Nine Days Wonder*. All the British Expeditionary Force was out of Dunkirk in nine days. I think it's the best account that will ever exist.

Nevertheless, Masefield's main thrust as a creative writer was not in the plays (one or two of them had a pretty fair success), not in the literary criticism, not in the novels (he never really quite had a big literary success as a novelist); he's mainly known as a British poet who started out as a kind of champion of what [Fyodor] Dostoyevsky called the insulted and the injured, the coal haulers, the common sailors, the farmers, the small industrialists. He struck a note around the turn of the century in British poetry that, except for him, would not have been there at all. He dealt almost exclusively in the poems that made him famous with subjects that had hitherto been deemed unfit subjects for poetry. Not Tennysonian, not gardens in the rain, not relationships of men to god, but the workaday, dirty, disgusting, frustrating world of the small, exploited British laboring man, whether on the farm or the forecastle of the sailing ship. He is essentially a narrative poet. Can you come up with a kind of provisional definition or distinction between, say, an epic poem and a narrative poem? Of course, an epic is narrative, but does the fact that a poem is narrative make it an epic? Because Masefield did not go for the epic; he went for the straight narrative. What is the difference? The epic deals with the same thing that tragedies deal with—elevated and exalted themes, kings, enormous wars, the adventures of heroes. Masefield is nothing like that. The lives that Masefield writes about are usually small, squalid lives. A lot of excitement is going on, but it's not the excitement of grand people; it's the excitement of brutality, the excitement of things going on in a poverty-stricken atmosphere.

But what made him famous was not so much the themes, although they aroused a very great deal of commentary at the time. What made Masefield famous was the *way* he wrote about these things. The first poem that brought him attention was called "The Everlasting Mercy," about a reprobate named Saul Kane, the dirtiest dog in seven counties. He lived out in the country of England. He raises hell, he wenches, he drinks, he betrays everybody that ever had any belief in him. He steals, he poaches, and in the end he gets religion. And you get the feeling, and Masefield probably would assert this, that he's not saved through any regeneration of heart. He just turns to that as the next thing to do. Masefield is not sentimental about the regeneration of these people; it's just another event to them. But "The Everlasting Mercy" is a very powerful poem, written in what would seem to us an archaic way. But the thing about Masefield's work that made it immensely popular is that it is so accessible. He writes in short-line couplets, almost in jingles, but the narrative moves through all these grim events so fast that you just can't put it down. His next poem, which was even more popular, is the most eminently English poem that has ever been written in the whole history of English literature, because it's about fox hunting. It's called "Reynard the Fox." It's about that particularly English pursuit that Americans try to emulate up in northern Virginia and Maryland, that Oscar Wilde characterized as "the uneatable pursued by the unspeakable." But Masefield's sympathies are on the side of the fox, and the whole thing is told from the standpoint of the pursued fox, where he runs, how he tries to get the dogs off his trail, where he goes next, all these English place-names of these hills and valleys and streams that he goes over. And the poem just goes so fast it's almost like speed-reading.

I can give you more of a feeling of the kind of things that made Masefield famous by reading a parody of it. You can learn an awful lot from parodies about the distinctive features of any particular writer's work. This is a self-parody in which John Masefield is supposed to be rewriting, in his own inimitable style, the Mother Goose rhyme of "Tom, Tom, the Piper's Son." This is "Tom, Tom, the Piper's Son" as it might be written by John Masefield in this kind of knockabout, half-doggerel, easily accessible, public style, which is very, very swift-moving, but doesn't pay a great deal of attention to exactness of rhyming. In other words, Masefield's poems like "The Everlasting Mercy" and "The Widow in the By-street" and "Reynard the Fox" are poems that any man would write if he had a very vivid imagination and a very quick, perceptive eye and wanted to write a rhyming poem but didn't pay a great deal of attention to finesse. And this is a parody of it, which brings out almost all the qualities that I've been talking about. This is called "Mother Goose Up-to-date; John Masefield Relates the Story of Tom, Tom, the Piper's Son."

MOTHER GOOSE UP-TO-DATE
Relates the Story of Tom, Tom, the Piper's Son

Thomas, the vagrant piper's son,
Was fourteen when he took to fun;
He was the sixth of a bewilderin'
Family of eleven children.
Mary, the first of all the lot,
Was married to a drunken sot;
And Clement, second on the list,
Fell off the roof and was never missed.
Susan and little Goldilocks
Were carried off by the chicken-pox;

And Franky went—though I can't recall
Whatever happened to him at all.
Thomas was next—and he's still alive,
The only one of them all to thrive.
The rest just petered out somehow—
At least, nobody hears of them now.

Now Tom, as I said when I'd begun,
Was fourteen when he took to fun.
Wine was the stuff he loved to swim in;
He lied, and fought, and went with women,
He scattered oaths, as one flings bounties,
The dirtiest dog in seven counties.

One morning when the sun was high
And larks were cleaving the blue sky,
Singing as though their hearts would break
With April's keen and happy ache,
Thomas went walking, rather warm,
Beside old Gaffer Hubbard's farm.
He saw that wintry days were over
And bees were out among the clover.
Earth stretched its legs out in the sun;
Now that the spring was well begun,
Heaven itself grew bland and fat.
So Thomas loafed a while and spat,
And thought about his many follies—
Yonder the gang was tipping trollies.
The sight made Tom's red blood run quicker
Than whiskey, beer or any liquor.
"By cripes," he said, "that's what I need;
'Twill make a man of me indeed.
Why should I be a roaring slob
When there's Salvation in a job!"
He started up—when lo, behind him,
As though it sought to maim and blind him,
A savage pig sprang straight against him.
At first Tom kicked and fought and fenced him,
And then he fell. But as they rolled
Tom took a tight and desperate hold
And thought the bloody fight was over.
"Here is one pig that's *not* in clover—
Tonight I'll have you in my cupboard!"
Who should come up but Graffer Hubbard.
"Leggo that pig."

"What for?" says Tom.
"It's mine, you thief! You vagrant scum!"
"It ain't."
            "It is."
                    "Clear out!"
                            "We'll see."
"I'll fix 'ee!"
            "Better let me be."
With that the farmer turned again
And called out half a dozen men.
Up they came running. "Here," said he,
"Here is a pig belongs to me—
But ye can have it all for eating
If ye will give this tramp a beating."
"Hurroo!" they shouted in high feather,
And jumped on Thomas all together.
So the pig was eat, and Tom was beat;
And Tom went roaring down the street!

Like all parodies it's exaggerated, but that gives you a good idea of the thing that made Masefield famous, that consolidated his position as a poet, with all these other works, with the war books, with the criticism, which is, as I say, surprisingly good, with plays, with novels.

He wrote over a hundred books. Can you imagine that? Over a hundred books! And after the death of Robert Bridges, he was appointed poet laureate, and there the sad tale begins to take a downward trend, because no one ever took himself and his duties as the poet laureate more seriously than John Masefield. About the time that he was appointed laureate, he died as a creative writer, so that the whole last part of his life, which was a very long life, was devoted to nothing but official odes and coronation odes and celebrations of the British cricket team's victory over Australia, and that sort of thing. It's very, very sad stuff to read, but the fortunate thing about Masefield is that he did have, at one time at least, a genuine spark as a writer, as a poet. He had this rough, masculine, knockabout style, which is very effective and very enjoyable to read. He had this enormous sympathy with the downtrodden, with the insulted and the injured, with the laboring man. And he acquired, in the course of a very, very long life, quite a good approach to English verse technique. He was a superb writer of anything that concerned action, whether it was a ship rounding Cape Horn or a fox being chased or a prizefight or anything in which there was rapid movement. He is one of the few contemporary poets in England who knows how to write a narrative poem, which is not just a versified novel, which uses the resources of poetry for the purposes of the narrative. There is a long poem of his about the sea, and the sea and the land are his two great themes. And his identification is really with the farmers and the sailors before the mast rather than the high and the mighty. And he has given them a voice that they otherwise would not have without him.

He's preeminently an Englishman. Nobody would ever take him for anything else. When he rolls those English place names across the pages, an American says, "Well, this must mean an awful lot to the English people who go for this sort of thing, but me, I'm from White Path, Georgia, those are my place names; they're not this Malvern Hill and all the places that Masefield obviously loves and reveres." So as an American reader you have to have some reservations about Masefield's poems of the land, because Americans have never loved either the land that the poems are about or the poems that are about this particular English kind of countryside that Masefield delights in writing about. An American could never love that or feel the same way about it as Masefield does. The sea poems are different; the waves don't have those place names, so therefore, I think for me, as an American reader, the poems about the sea, about sailing ships, about rounding the Horn, about life on board ship among the fellows in the forecastle are probably the best thing he did as a poet, and the best one of those poems is called "Dauber." It's about a young fellow who's a painter, and he deliberately ships out on a British clipper ship, a ship of the line, in order to get firsthand information about sailing ships, about how they look at various times of day so that he can paint them. And he's put on the crew just like everybody else and made to go aloft and furl the sails, and he's no good at it, and he becomes the butt of jokes of the crew. But he sticks it out; there's no place that he'd rather be. He loves being there because he gets to see these ships at all times of the day and night, and he senses that he's getting this feeling for sailing ships on the sea, something he needs to do the work of painting them that nobody else has ever done. The story is of his apprenticeship on the ocean with these big rough fellows, and at the end he's sent aloft. They have to go up on the mast and get the sails down with this howling wind and the snow and sleet. But at the end he's sent aloft, and he falls onto the deck and is killed. None of the fellows on board ever understood what he was doing trying to be a sailor anyway; they never understood his mission to paint sailing ships and the life of the sea. And they put him on a table and put an oilcloth over him until they get the burial service ready. They'd never had a burial on that ship before, and they don't know exactly how to go about doing it. But here's this guy, this enigmatic fellow that none of them has ever understood, and this is when they

Signing copies of *God's Images,* 1977. *Courtesy of James Dickey Collection, Department of Rare Books & Special Collections, Thomas Cooper Library, University of South Carolina*

John Masefield

put the ensign—that is, the British flag—over him. And, after the funeral is
over, the ship sails into this port, and there's a beautiful image of this ship com-
ing to rest in the port and the stars coming up and the mountains there around
the harbor.

ROUNDING THE HORN
(from Dauber: A Poem)

Then came the cry of "Call all hands on deck!"
The Dauber knew its meaning; it was come:
Cape Horn, that tramples beauty into wreck,
And crumples steel and smites the strong man dumb.
Down clattered flying kites and staysails; some
Sang out in quick, high calls: the fair-leads skirled,
And from the south-west came the end of the world.

"Lay out!" the Bosun yelled. The Dauber laid
Out on the yard, gripping the yard, and feeling
Sick at the mighty space of air displayed
Below his feet, where mewing birds were wheeling.
A giddy fear was on him; he was reeling.
He bit his lip half through, clutching the jack.
A cold sweat glued the shirt upon his back.

The yard was shaking, for a brace was loose.
He felt that he would fall; he clutched, he bent,
Clammy with natural terror to the shoes
While idiotic promptings came and went.
Snow fluttered on a wind-flaw and was spent;
He saw the water darken. Someone yelled,
"Frap it; don't stay to furl! Hold on!" He held.

Darkness came down—half darkness—in a whirl;
The sky went out, the waters disappeared.
He felt a shocking pressure of blowing hurl
The ship upon her side. The darkness speared
At her with wind; she staggered, she careered;
Then down she lay. The Dauber felt her go,
He saw her yard tilt downwards. Then the snow

Whirled all about—dense, multitudinous, cold—
Mixed with the wind's one devilish thrust and shriek,
Which whiffled out men's tears, defeated, took hold,
Flattening the flying drift against the cheek.
The yards buckled and bent, man could not speak.

The ship lay on her broadside; the wind's sound
Had devilish malice at having got her downed.

How long the gale had blown he could not tell,
Only the world had changed, his life had died.
A moment now was everlasting hell.
Nature an onslaught from the weather side,
A withering rush of death, a frost that cried,
Shrieked, till he withered at the heart; a hail
Plastered his oilskins with an icy mail. . . .

"Up!" yelled the Bosun; "up and clear the wreck!"
The Dauber followed where he led; below
He caught one giddy glimpsing of the deck
Filled with white water, as though heaped with snow.
He saw the streamers of the rigging blow
Straight out like pennons from the splintered mast,
Then, all sense dimmed, all was an icy blast,

Roaring from nether hell and filled with ice,
Roaring and crashing on the jerking stage,
An utter bridle given to utter vice,
Limitless power mad with endless rage
Withering the soul; a minute seemed an age.
He clutched and hacked at ropes, at rags of sail,
Thinking that comfort was a fairy tale

Told long ago—long, long ago—long since
Heard of in other lives—imagined, dreamed—
There where the basest beggar was a prince.
To him in torment where the tempest screamed,
Comfort and warmth and ease no longer seemed
Things that a man could know; soul, body, brain,
Knew nothing but the wind, the cold, the pain.

To get the full effect of Masefield, you have to read through one of these long narratives and see the narrative story build up. He's much better with an accumulative force behind the narrative than he is in isolated passages, although I like that one very much. But it's my impression that you won't get much good said about him these days. He was a big poet when Eliot came along and turned the whole direction of English poetry around. Nevertheless, there are very positive and solid virtues in Masefield.

Let's finish off talking about him by reading this first poem here, "Night on the Downland."

John Masefield

NIGHT ON THE DOWNLAND

Night is on the downland, on the lonely moorland,
On the hills where the wind goes over sheep-bitten turf,
Where the bent grass beats upon the unplowed poorland
And the pine-woods roar like the surf.

Here the Roman lived on the wind-barren lonely,
Dark now and haunted by the moorland fowl;
None comes here now but the peewit only,
And moth-like death in the owl.

Beauty was here on this beetle-droning downland;
The thought of a Caesar in the purple came
From the palace by the Tiber in the Roman townland
To this wind-swept hill with no name.

Lonely Beauty came here and was here in sadness,
Brave as a thought on the frontier of the mind,
In the camp of the wild upon the march of madness,
The bright-eyed Queen of the Blind.

Now where Beauty was are the wind-withered gorses,
Moaning like old men in the hill-wind's blast;
The flying sky is dark with running horses,
And the night is full of the past.

A sense of tradition, of history, was very strong with Masefield, who, in some ways, is the ultimate English, English, English poet. But for myself, I've been reading around in Masefield for close to thirty or forty years, off and on, and not always in connection with classes either, but my predominant impression, if I had to reduce it to one feeling that I have about him, is that his main characteristic is a kind of steady, masculine sadness, melancholy. He's like someone who has stood maybe too many watches on the fore deck, looking out over the sea, had a chance to think too much. I don't know how much early English literature you know; do you know Anglo-Saxon? The closest equivalent to Masefield is the [unknown] poet of "The Seafarer," the melancholy born of long vigils and discomfort and danger and enormous expanses of water, and midnight watches and the kind of melancholy that that kind of life would engender. There's some of this in Melville, in *Moby-Dick,* but the main affinity with Masefield is that earlier and unknown poet that wrote the Anglo-Saxon fragments that have come down to us as "The Seafarer."

As I say, there's a lot of him. I don't know if I can really recommend his book on Shakespeare. It would be only if you were interested in the subject of

Shakespeare and in what Masefield thinks of him and why he thinks so. He's very unorthodox. Or, if you have to take a course in Shakespeare and you want to surprise your teacher because you read Masefield's book on Shakespeare and it wasn't on the reading list and you found out about it all by yourself. I'll let you be the judge.

VACHEL LINDSAY

Why don't we take Vachel Lindsay for a couple of reasons? First of all, because in the first class I taught at the University of South Carolina, Vachel Lindsay's granddaughter was a member of it. She's a very talented writer. Vachel Lindsay's son lives down here on the coast, goes around giving readings of his father's work. Vachel Lindsay is what I would call a village genius, as naive as a child. He came from Springfield, Illinois, and his mother was a kind of a theosophist. The boy was looked on, even from his earliest days, as the people around Springfield said, as being half-cracked, which he definitely was. He had a couple of early notions about poetry, three or four, which are kind of unique and kind of fun. One of them was that poetry is, or should be, like a circus act. It should be what he called the "higher vaudeville." He himself read his poems for a period of ten or twelve years to the largest audiences that have ever been in this country for poetry. Everybody was absolutely wild about him. He used to insist that anybody who came to his poetry readings should show a book of his own collected poems at the door so that they would have the text, because, along side the text were written instructions to the audience who would join in certain passages. He was like a poetical revivalist. And he would turn his readings and his public performances into tent shows, carnivals, which combined about one-half religious fervor and the other half the enthusiasm of the carny barker, carnival barker. But they were supposed to be great fun.

The American public tired of them after a while. After he had made such a success doing this sort of thing he fell from favor, but he had committed his life to going around giving readings. He didn't have any other means of livelihood. His audiences continued to dwindle. He'd been a fad for a while, and the audiences got smaller and smaller and smaller, and finally he didn't have any livelihood from it at all. He was engaged in a tragic love affair with another American poet named Sara Teasdale. What happens to Vachel Lindsay, at the age of fifty-two, after his vogue passed, his vogue of the village genius and the revivalist carnival poet, what happened was that he went back to the house where he was born in Springfield and swallowed a bottle of Lysol and died this hideous, agonizing death by his own hand. It's funny, isn't it, how these ecstatic, ebullient types always end up as suicides or alcoholics or come to some kind of tragic end. I've heard Vachel Lindsay spoken of as a precursor of Dylan Thomas, and in some ways indeed he was. He had the same kind of naive, enthusiastic sense of mission. He was a great public performer. At his height he got the highest prices for public readings of anybody up until the time of Dylan Thomas. He burned out quickly. He was demoralized by his personal life. He felt betrayed by his public. And in the end he had no personal resources to draw on.

But he is what I would characterize as a hell of a lot of fun as a poet. He wrote far too much. He was really completely uncritical of his own work. He didn't know what was good or what was bad. He wrote easily. He wrote in very heavy rhythmical cadences. He wrote poems that are so odd and so crazy and so naive that you wouldn't believe them unless you saw them, but in a few they catch the accent of the American ballyhoo, the carnival, the circus atmosphere, where native types or folks legends are caught up and made, not only larger than life, but into something like a display by P. T. Barnum. But he was completely undiscriminating. For Vachel Lindsay, it didn't make any difference to him whether he mythologized Abraham Lincoln or Johnny Appleseed or Mary Pickford. It was all the same to him. If he got going on one of these figures, they were all just part of his sideshow. So therefore there is an enormous lot of waste and enormous lot of undistinguished stuff, but the best of it is really inimitable.

He was an absolute child, all the way up until the age of fifty-two, when he died. This is his idea, for example, of a Negro minister giving sermons. And Lindsay has this marvelous capacity, which a poet really ought to have, of really throwing himself, in his own way, into the subject. This is Vachel Lindsay's idea put into the mouth of a Negro preacher. This is called "When Peter Jackson Preached in the Old Church." Here's the circus-style Vachel Lindsay.

WHEN PETER JACKSON PREACHED IN THE OLD CHURCH

To be sung to the tune of the old negro spiritual "Every time I feel the spirit moving in my heart I'll pray."

> Peter Jackson was a-preaching
> And the house was still as snow.
> He whispered of repentance
> And the lights were dim and low
> And were almost out
> When he gave the first shout:
> "Arise, arise,
> Cry out your eyes."

And we mourned all our terrible sins away.
Clean, clean away.
Then we marched around, around,
And sang with a wonderful sound:—
"Every time I feel the spirit moving in my heart I'll pray.
Every time I feel the spirit moving in my heart I'll pray."
And we fell by the altar
And fell by the aisle,
And found our Savior
In just a little while,
We all found Jesus at the break of the day,
We all found Jesus at the break of the day.
Blessed Jesus,
Blessed Jesus.

As Randall Jarrell says in one place, you have to be either a genius or naive beyond belief or maybe both, which is kind of what genius is anyway. It has certain elements of naïveté, sort of like Blake. Jarrell says you come across things in Lindsay and you don't believe you see what you saw. What other American poet would ever refer to himself and his lover as "fairy Democrats"? Not homosexual; enchanted. No, I never saw anything like it, either. And you never saw anything like most of Vachel Lindsay. He's a figure that to some people belongs to the *history* of American poetry, particularly popular poetry, rather than to the real literary history, particularly since it's come to be dominated by figures like T. S. Eliot, who was *so* scholastic and *so* academic, and who would have sneered *so* much at Vachel Lindsay. And yet there should be something good said about him, because he had one sure instinct, as naive and innocent as he was, about poetry in general or maybe just about a certain kind of poetry: he saw just what a hell of a lot of fun it could be, and what an atmosphere of play there is in it. And his best poems have that feel to it. I like his style.

GEOFFREY HILL

If you have a taste or think you might develop a taste for poetry that is absolutely unfathomable, read the work of Geoffrey Hill. He sends me all this stuff for some reason or another because I wrote a favorable review and got together with him in England one time. We argued bitterly over poets we liked or disliked. He has a notion that I'm a great American champion of his. I do think he's a remarkable writer, but he's really a complete mystery to me. I can't understand more than a third of what he's saying, despite the best will in the world. But there's something going on in Geoffrey Hill. He has only three books in twenty years. The first one is called, with his characteristic mysteriousness, *For the Unfallen*. And this had come out when I saw him in 1962, and I said, well, this must have to do with the people in war who were not killed, because you see so many poems for "the fallen." No, he said, it doesn't have anything to do with that; it has to do with politics. What politics? And the next, with characteristic mystifying ingenuity, is called *King Log*. And one that is the most mysterious of all I just got week before last from him, asking if I would review it for some of the American journals. And I told him if he would give me a complete gloss on every poem telling me what the hell he's talking about, I might be able to do it. But I certainly couldn't do his rarified intellect justice unless I had some help from him. It's called *Mercian Hymns*. "Mercia" I looked up in the *Encyclopedia Britannica*. It was a kingdom in the west of England in the middle ages. He would know that. I wouldn't know that. Nevertheless, I don't mean to run Geoffrey Hill down, because there is something mysterious working there that I am convinced is remarkable, if you could just get onto what it is.

The trouble with him is he's so full of private references that nobody but him knows what the reference is to. It's like Edith Sitwell, for example, a terribly bad poet. I shouldn't even bracket her in the same sentence with Geoffrey Hill. She refers in one place to someone having "Emily colored" hands. But you don't know what she means unless you know that Edith Sitwell, when she was a child, had a nurse who always wore a certain shade of brown and that's what

"Emily colored" meant to Edith Sitwell. That's what you call a private reference. Geoffrey Hill is full of them. Nevertheless, when he does objectify, he's got some very impressive characteristics. Look at this poem, for example, the one called "Genesis."

GENESIS

1

Against the burly air I strode,
Where the tight ocean heaves its load,
Crying the miracles of God.

And first I brought the sea to bear
Upon the dead weight of the land;
And the waves flourished at my prayer,
The rivers spawned their sand.

And where the streams were salt and full
The tough pig-headed salmon strove,
Curbing the ebb and the tide's pull,
To reach the steady hills above.

2

The second day I stood and saw
The osprey plunge with triggered claw,
Feathering blood along the shore,
To lay the living sinew bare.

And the third day I cried: "Beware
The soft-voiced owl, the ferret's smile,
The hawk's deliberate stoop in air,
Cold eyes, and bodies hooped in steel,
Forever bent upon the kill."

3

And I renounced, on the fourth day,
This fierce and unregenerate clay,

Building as a huge myth for man
The watery Leviathan,

And made the glove-winged albatross
Scour the ashes of the sea
Where Capricorn and Zero cross,
A brooding immortality—
Such as the charmed phoenix has
In the unwithering tree.

4

The phoenix burns as cold as frost;
And, like a legendary ghost,
The phantom-bird goes wild and lost,
Upon a pointless ocean tossed.

So, the fifth day, I turned again
To flesh and blood and the blood's pain.

5

On the sixth day, as I rode
In haste about the works of God,
With spurs I plucked the horse's blood.

By blood we live, the hot, the cold,
To ravage and redeem the world:
There is no bloodless myth will hold.

And by Christ's blood are men made free
Though in close shrouds their bodies lie
Under the rough pelt of the sea;

Though Earth has rolled beneath her weight
The bones that cannot bear the light.

Now this poem is clear as nine-hundred crystals compared to *Mercian Hymns* or *King Log* or any of these poems that he mysteriously calls "of commerce and society," which don't have anything to do with either commerce or society, as near as I can tell. Now this poem is mysterious, too, and it's mysterious in the same way as some of the rest of his work is mysterious. It's mysterious in the same way, but it's not *as* mysterious.

One of the things I like about Geoffrey Hill is that he does not seem to belong to the twentieth century at all. You don't find a single reference in anything of his to an automobile, to a train, to a telephone. Most of them are about kings and kingdoms and obscure religious rites, Druidism. You think, my God, a modern poet must really be self-obsessed to cut his own time, the time in which he lives and moves. What the hell does he think he's doing? Who's going to want to read that stuff? He doesn't care; he's going to do it his way. And that seems to me to be a possible indication that he's got the seeds of some kind of grace as a creative writer.

How is he thought of in England?

The greatest! But nobody can understand him. Since Eliot, that's been a mark of approbation. He wins all the prizes over there. The reviewers are completely mystified, and they say Geoffrey Hill is mighty deep. Maybe he is; I don't know. But he's got something there, some kind of mystified ability, strange and original. Now look at the poem.

First of all, this is about genesis. It's called "Genesis." It's about the creation of the earth. But the most difficult thing in the whole poem for me is, who's speaking? Who is it? It's not God, because he's doing the bidding of God. I've got an idea. This is a typical, private Geoffrey Hill interpretation of some big mythological event—in this case genesis, the creation of the world—who is *I*? An angel, an emissary, someone who creates the world at God's bidding? The key lines are the last two lines in the fourth section, and then the sixth line down from there, "There is no bloodless myth will hold." Does that have any reference to Christianity? Is Christianity a bloodless myth? It's a blood myth, and here, in some inexplicable way, the poem passes over from this business of the predatory animals spilling each other's blood during this half real, half mythological creation of the earth; passes over from that into men and their needs as far as their mythology is concerned. He turns away from abstractions like the phoenix, which is a legendary or classical, mythical creature, to the reality that engendered the Christian culture. And yet even when you say that, you're not sure you have him. You're not sure that something else is not intended here. That's a fascinating poem to me. I love some of the details. I think that "On the sixth day, as I rode / In haste about the works of God, / With spurs I plucked the horse's blood" is absolutely wonderful. I'm sure that's what you do when you use the spurs: you pluck their blood, sort of like a stringed instrument. But again, he's not for all tastes.

Let me read one stanza. He's a Catholic, a fanatical Catholic. This stanza, I won't read the whole thing, is about the crucifixion and about Thomas looking on. This shows you what he can do. This is "Canticle for Good Friday."

CANTICLE FOR GOOD FRIDAY

The cross staggered him. At the cliff-top
Thomas, beneath its burden, stood
While the dulled wood
Spat on the stones each drop
Of deliberate blood.

I won't read the rest of it, because it gets so unfathomable that you wouldn't get anything from it, but the first stanza is full of concrete detail. I don't know of any poet who has gotten that scene for me as deeply and as movingly as that, those five lines. That's exactly what it must have been like. And if it wasn't it should have been.

There's one about graves that's nice. Generally [*For*] *the Unfallen* is an easier book than the other ones. I'll read to you one about a petition to a patron. You know what a patron is. This is called "To the (Supposed) Patron." Writers nowadays—they don't have patrons. This was the great thing in the eighteenth century where you would petition a nobleman to support you while you wrote your works: [John] Dryden, Ben Jonson, and all those were always trying to get themselves patrons. This is Geoffrey Hill's lines to his supposed patron.

To the (Supposed) Patron

Prodigal of loves and barbecues,
Expert in the strangest faunas, at home
He considers the lilies, the rewards.
There is no substitute for a rich man.
At his first entering a new province
With new coin, music, the barest glancing
Of steel or gold suffices. There are many
Tremulous dreams secured under that head.
For his delight and his capacity
To absorb, freshly, the inside-succulence
Of untoughened sacrifice, his bronze agents
Speculate among convertible stones
And drink desert sand. That no mirage
Irritate his mild gaze, the lewd noonday
Is housed in cool places, and fountains
Salt the sparse haze. His flesh is made clean.
For the unfallen—the firstborn, or wise
Councillor—prepared vistas extend
As far as harvest; and idyllic death
Where fish at dawn ignite the powdery lake.

So, as I say, *For the Unfallen, King Log,* and *Mercian Hymns.* That is all there is of Geoffrey Hill, that most mysterious man.

EZRA POUND

There can hardly have been any other human being in the history of human culture who has had such an implicit belief in the value of the arts as Ezra Pound. Like everything else he does, and did, he is fanatical on that point. He is an esthete in the best and worst sense of the word. His other manias came in later, but he began as an esthete, someone who believed that there is nothing that a human being could produce, no new vaccine, no new bridge-building principle, no new plastic, no new anything that's as important as a work of art, music, poetry, sculpture, the novel. This has been his guiding principle from the beginning, and it will be till the end. He influenced other figures—Joyce, Eliot, two of the main ones. He was Yeats's secretary. Yeats submitted his poems to Pound, who was much younger, and Pound said he didn't like them at all, too flowery, too many adjectives. This was when Yeats was trying to change his style from the old 1890s romanticism and the Celtic twilight that had made him famous. He was trying to speak a barer, more stripped, convincing human speech. Pound showed him how to do it.

There is a funny story that Yeats tells. Pound was at that time living in Italy on the northern coast at a place called Rapallo, and Yeats came over there to see him and submitted his work to Pound. Pound was busy and couldn't see him right away, so Yeats sent the packet of poems up by messenger, and in about forty-five minutes the messenger came back down with the poems, and on the outside of the poems was written one word: "putrid, E.P." And after that they got together, and Yeats followed his suggestions, as in Eliot's case, almost completely. There was born from that, at least in large part, the great Yeats plain-speaking later style that made him not a fine minor poet but a world figure. It's absolutely uncanny how right Pound was in the case of the most important figures in literature in the twentieth century in English. He was influential in getting D. H. Lawrence published, and without Ezra Pound, Robert Frost probably would never have been published. It's typical of Robert Frost and his churlish temperament that he should have turned on Pound, and only exerted his influence as poetry consultant to the Library of Congress to get Pound out of St. Elizabeth's madhouse when most of the rest of the influential writers threatened to get Frost himself kicked out of his post unless he did something. So he finally, grudgingly, put in a kind of formal request that Pound be released, and with his help and the help some other people, after thirteen years he was released.

We'll go through the life just very briefly. Now first of all, Ezra Pound's life and his principles—principles of art and the primacy of the artist and the work of art, and his principles of economics and government and the rest of his fanaticisms that he became more and more in the thrall of as he became older and more cranky and crotchety and more unbalanced—all these things are really of a piece with his work. There has rarely been a writer whose ideas and whose life are so inexplicably twined up with his writing. With a writer like Eliot, you very rarely find the man Eliot in the poem. The poem to Eliot is an artifact. Pound would applaud that, except in his own practice it's not an arti-fact; it's a statement of belief, plus being an artifact, most of the time. But mod-ern literature is really impossible to understand without knowing the part that Ezra Pound has played in it, because he has played almost every part that there was to play in the most important formative stages of modern literature, for better or for worse. It might have been worse if Ezra Pound had not existed, or if Ezra Pound's ideas had not been systematized and given a respectable, that is to say, college professorish decor, by T. S. Eliot. T. S. Eliot is the man who made Ezra Pound's wild-man cultural ideas acceptable to college professors, and Eliot himself was very much like a college professor of both the good and the bad kind. But Pound is not like a college professor. In fact, the only teaching job he ever had was a very brief one at Wabash College in Crawfordsville, Indi-ana, from which he was kicked out after a few months, as he says, all accusa-tions save that of being the bohemian type successfully refuted. Actually what happened. . . . Well, I'll just go through his life.

He was born on what was at that time, in 1885, virtually a real frontier in this country. He was born in Hailey, Idaho. [His family] moved to Pennsylva-nia, and he grew up in a little place called Windcove, and went to Hamilton College and the University of Pennsylvania for a while, where he met William Carlos Williams, who became kind of a disciple of his, although Pound was a little bit younger than he was. Then he took this post at Wabash College as pro-fessor of Romance languages and literature. He went out to post a letter one evening, and there was this girl who had been abandoned by a carnival, just left there in Crawfordsville, of all places. And Pound took her in and gave her his bed and slept on the floor, he said, anyway. But he was called in by the author-ities the next day and fired, whereupon he immediately got sick of living in

Signing copies of *Night Hurdling*, 1983. *Courtesy of James Dickey Collection, Department of Rare Books & Special Collections, Thomas Cooper Library, University of South Carolina*

America and attempting to be an artist in what he called this "half savage country," so he left and went to Venice, where he had a book of poems printed at his own expense. He then caught a cattle boat or something to England and decided to crash London literary society. He sent out his book for review; got favorable reviews and, gradually, year after year he began to build up an enormous influence.

He was active everywhere; he was starting magazines; he was consorting with the writers; he was the most active man they'd ever had on the London literary scene. Everybody knew who he was. A lot of people resented him for a bumptious American, but he was so helpful and so strong in the cause of the arts and poetry that he built up a very large following, and among them a lot of influential people, magazine editors. He wrote indefatigably. He wrote pamphlets; he wrote brochures for art shows; he wrote a lot of literary criticism, and all the time he was writing poetry. His influences from the beginning were not really the influence of the world of living men, but the influences of past cultures and the influences of books. He was a demon linguist, not strictly accurate all the time, but it's said that it was possible for Ezra Pound to pick up a language that he had never seen a word of before, in approximately a week, well enough to read it and translate it. And he came to know dozens of languages. He never knew any language very well, but he knew at 'em. He knew something of them. He knew enough of them to work with them in his way, do his kinds of translations, Japanese, Chinese, Persian. But he was a very impatient man. This is one of the threads that runs all the way through Ezra Pound, through everything he ever wrote. You feel about him that he's a victim of a vast impatience, that he will not sit down to think anything through. He's a great master of the snap judgment. Very forceful; he's one of the great forceful personalities in all of literature.

Well, what happens to Pound then, after he makes his mark in London? His own poems are discussed everywhere; he goes through several styles. He's kind of the Picasso of modern poetry because he had so many different styles, any one of which has been the making of a reputation of dozens of lesser artists. But by the time Pound could have consolidated his own position in that style, he, like Picasso, has moved on to something else. Pound has two really major ideas. I mean he's got dozens and dozens and thousands of ideas and applications of ideas, but he's got two main ones. One of them is that the work of art and the person who makes it, the artist or the artisan, is the most important and the most crucial figure in society. He's the one who determines what the society is; he's the one who influences the society and gives vitality and consequence to the society. This is the idea that runs all the way through Pound's work. And one of his greatest quarrels is with the economic, political system which mass produces inferior objects rather than the objects made with care and talent and love by the single artist or artisan. We have things made by machines which are inferior in quality and are simply objects of utility. They are copies of real works of art, plastic copies, and they are *things.* He's not interested in people who make replicas. He's interested in real works of art, authentic art, a living tradition of art, expressing the human imagination and the human creative faculties and not mass producing it by machinery. This is one of his great hatreds of modern civilization, that it has substituted fads for the true work of art, bad replicas of it, mass-produced, which has in turn created a public that can't tell fads from the real thing. The taste has gone out of the public because of this mass production. Taste has gone out of them; therefore what to Pound is the most exquisite kind of human sentiment or feeling—that is, the encounter of a superior taste, his or somebody else's, with a truly vital work of art, something from the ancient world, maybe, a great poem from the Elizabethan era, or, above all, French literature—is lost.

The Provençal, which Pound may be said to have discovered for our time —nobody read Provençal poetry before Pound discovered it—is absolutely wonderful. He begins to develop the curious idea that culture and art not only enhance and express a civilization but in a sense create it. He comes to have a serious obsession centered around the belief that if a nation has good artists and the audience for what they produce, then this somehow passes over into the political realm, into the realm of government, so that if your language is pure and the people are sensitive to it, and to the works of their best artists, there will therefore per se result from this situation good government, good economic policy, and good politicians and politics. Now, as I say, there can be few people in the whole history of human culture who can give *that* much primacy to the artist. According to Pound, the artist is responsible really to the whole of the civilization in which he appears. That's giving the artist altogether too much authority, an authority he really should not have. But Pound himself was nothing if not an authoritarian. So, this latter obsession begins to take rather dangerous forms. He persuaded himself that a planned economy, like Mussolini's before World War II, has got this connection between the artist and the political system that he lives under, an economic system. He becomes convinced that Mussolini has indeed set up this kind of regime that Pound has posited all along as being desirable. He begins to make absurd comparisons.

Other of Pound's heroes, as far as men of government are concerned, were some of the American Founding Fathers, most particularly Jefferson, and John Adams, and, oddly enough, Martin Van Buren, whom nobody has ever heard of.

But Pound knows all about Martin Van Buren and his politics, and he will tell you at great length why he's such a great man and why, if people had paid serious attention to Martin Van Buren's economic and domestic policies, we wouldn't be in the mess we're in now. Pound has always got the angle on something. He always knows something that you don't know. He's got an original interpretation, very idiosyncratic. He's always got some little piece of information that you don't have.

He writes an absurd pamphlet called "Jefferson and/or Mussolini." It has never been held against Ezra Pound that he could think consecutively. As I say, he's a great believer in the snap judgment, in laying down the law. Along with the hatred of modern economy, mass production, he begins to develop his last and deepest and greatest hatred, which is against banks, and the practice of what he calls usury. What is usury? It's all through the Bible. The lending of money and the charging of interest thereupon. Christ himself did what? Drove the moneylenders from the temple. And Pound has been trying to drive the moneylenders from the temple ever since he's begun to read up on strange economic—crackpot economic—theories. Pound doesn't know anything about economics. He doesn't have the intellectual equipment. Pound is kind of like a jackdaw picking up something here, something there, something from Confucius, something from Jefferson, something from Mussolini, something from Flaubert, something from C. H. Douglas (1874–1952) and his theory of social credit. But when he settles in on the banks and the belief that usury is the central evil of modern life—that the lending of money by banks and charging interest on it, which then goes as profit to the bank and goes into other exploitive schemes, is evil—then he enters into his final and ugliest phase, because to Pound the usurer is not just a banker but a Jew.

The Jew becomes for Ezra Pound the bête noire of modern civilization, because he is a profiteer, at least according to Pound, because he is identified with banking, the house of Rothschild, for example, and international cartels, the banking of munitions work and factories. There's not any sin that Pound does not lay at the foot of the bankers or, as he calls them in a quaint phrase, the international Jew bankers and their compatriots. And there you begin to get the Pound that appears in the newspapers all the time. He's living in Italy, issuing broadsides against the Jews, against banking. He's issuing all kinds of crackpot pamphlets about monetary reform and stamp reform. He's carrying on an enormous correspondence with people he thinks might help him in his crusade against the banks and the usurers and the Jews or even anybody who might be interested in it. I never knew Pound in that state, of course, but I did know him.

But anyway what happens earlier is that Mussolini grants him an audience, sort of takes him up, and Pound, who was the most bookish and withdrawn of men, was very flattered. Like many such men, he was flattered by the attention of men who do things and run governments. And Mussolini gets him to broadcast anti-American propaganda, which he does. I had heard about this, as anybody who even knows the name of Ezra Pound knows about it. In fact, to the layman, or one who just reads newspapers, he would probably identify Pound as the man who was a traitor during the Second World War, who broadcast anti-American propaganda and was jailed. What happened was that when the Americans came through Italy into Rapallo, they took Ezra Pound from his villa and incarcerated him at the security prison camp at Pisa. He was treated as the most dangerous criminal in the whole place, full of murderers and rapists. The old man was sixty years old at the time, and they had him in the gorilla cage, no covering; it was just a barbed-wire enclosure, a barbed-wire box. He slept on a concrete slab, no blanket, no tent. He endured it admirably, and finally they gave him a couple of blankets to sleep under but they kept him there. It really was a terrible ordeal for the old fellow. Then they brought him back to this country to stand trial for treason. Now this is what he did that was treasonable. Who was the counterpart in England who broadcast for the Nazis and was hanged as a result? You remember him? His name was William Joyce, but he made his broadcasts under the name of Lord Hawhaw. Lord Hawhaw made some very funny broadcasts. Ezra Pound did not make any funny broadcasts. When I was at the Library of Congress four or five years ago, I went down to Archives and asked to hear some of the tapes of Ezra Pound's fascist broadcasts, and, I can tell you, never has there ever been any more ineffectual propaganda than that. It's all so childish, full of puns. I remember him talking about the American press, and about Roosevelt, and all I can remember is his referring to some of the national news magazines as *Slime* and *Jewsweek*. Most of Pound's so-called fascist propaganda was on about that level. Never can there have been such ineffectual propaganda.

He was brought back over here and was going to be tried, but he was given a series of tests, and it was decided that he was not mentally competent to stand trial. So, instead of being hanged, or imprisoned for life, he was put into an insane asylum, St. Elizabeth's in Washington. The only personal contact I ever had with him myself was when I visited him five or six times out there, and it was, for what the nature of St. Elizabeth's is, rather pleasant. If I were going to be incarcerated in a nuthouse, I'd just as soon be in one like that. It was a big, rambling, pleasant place. At least it was on visiting day, which was the only time when anybody, including Pound's wife, could get in to see him. But on those

Sunday afternoons, everybody was sitting around talking, and this lady came up to our group, and she said, "Good afternoon, Mr. Pound." And he didn't say anything, and everybody else just went on talking. And she said again, "Good afternoon, Mr. Pound, real nice afternoon, isn't it?" And he still didn't say anything, so eventually she wandered on off, and cautiously, after she was out of earshot, I leaned over and said, "Mr. Pound, does that lady live here?" And he said, "No, son, I think she's the cause of somebody else living here. Last time I said 'good afternoon' to her she monologued for an hour and a half, and we're not going to give her another chance." Anyway, the impression I got was that of a garrulous old guy who knew a lot of strange facts and who had known a lot of people. He talked endlessly about Yeats and about how he taught him to fence. But I would never have known that he had these fanatical fears that led him into this very ugly anti-Semitism, at all. He was very amiable. He was jolly, as I remember him, and when I left Washington, and went back home, there were three or four letters for me from Ezra Pound, all stuffed full of things about economics, monetary reform.

At that time, while he was still in the madhouse, he was editing a monetary reform series of pamphlets called the "Square Dollar" series. They all sounded like the *Cantos* to me. And all of it *is* like the *Cantos:* all it's got is this disjointed information, quotations in Chinese, Sanskrit—and I had about forty or so of these notes before he went back to Italy. The only thing practical that came out of our meetings was that he complained of being cold, and my wife, who's a knitting fanatic, knitted him a great big wooly sweater. He sent a diagram of how he wanted it, and he said, "May I be opened down the front, please?" He meant with buttons down the front. Maybe he still has it. After he was released he went back in care of one of his daughters who lived in a castle up in the Italian Alps and lived there for a while, and then he went down to Venice where some people who admired him took care of him. He has a little house down there, and he sits there writing a few words a day, I'm told by his publisher, James Laughlin of New Directions, a few words on the *Cantos.*

The *Cantos* themselves are his major work. The last number of *Cantos* is 120. He's close to being finished, but it's very doubtful that at his advanced age he will be able to finish 120 cantos. But I don't think it will make any real difference if he doesn't. Extra *Cantos* are not going to alter the design of the whole maddening, sometimes beautiful, sometimes incomprehensible work which Ezra Pound calls the *Cantos.* They are among the most beautiful of all poems, the most baffling to run down, because of Pound's numerous references to things that nobody but Pound knows about. There are seventeen thousand references to other literary works in the *Cantos.* I could identify maybe three or four hundred. And I'm a college professor—a thing, incidentally, that Ezra Pound hates. Although a born teacher himself, he hates college professors because he says they turn living literature dead. They ossify it; they preserve it in amber. It's not a living thing after they get through with it. And I must say that in my experience with college professors, or at least some of them, he's got a valid point there. Anyway, even if I could identify three or four hundred of these quotations from other works, I could still not be sure whether I understood the use to which Pound was putting these things, or the special relationship that he had to them and the special relationship that these quotations from other sources have to the general scheme of the *Cantos*. It's very difficult. So, I would advise you to do what I do. I would not miss the *Cantos,* dull as some of them are, because quite simply they have passages that no one else but Ezra Pound could have written, and they are surpassingly beautiful. I would not do without them.

I want to talk now about some of Pound's innovations, some of his obsessions. He believes himself to be a traditionalist. And tradition to Pound is quite simply a belief in and knowledge of the best that has been in a certain genre, a certain compartment of, say, poetry like the Provençal or the Elizabethan. These are works of art which have staying power, which mean different things to different people, which never lose their effectiveness, which, as Pound would say, are not mummified works of museum art, but are things that really are factors in people's lives, helping them and enabling them to be more perceptive, and, as he also would say, to live more, to live more fully and more profoundly than if the people in question had not encountered these works of art. He has no interest in the museum quality of the works of art, of official masterpieces, of that sort of thing. He issued, when he was beginning to make his influence felt, an extremely provocative book of his explosive opinions called *The ABC of Reading.* I urge this on you as an antidote to all the deadwood and scholarship that you are likely to encounter in the halls of academia. Pound has a wonderful faculty for blowing all that stuff right out of the window and getting down to basics. He's awfully good. His snap judgments are incredibly good snap judgments. It's just uncanny how he can fasten on a central core of a literary problem, something that matters. He doesn't stay on the periphery. He goes to the center, and he manages to sum up in this kind of cantankerous, aggressive language so that it quite literally becomes something that is unforgettable. You think, oh God, all the rest of the stuff I've read about this writer, about Milton for example, doesn't mean anything. Pound says the whole thing in a few sentences. He says in one of his pronouncements that literature is "news that stays news." Which is very cleverly said, not without a certain amount of wit.

And he has an American hardheaded refusal to be fooled by reputation, which is very, very refreshing. He wants to form his own opinions of writers. He doesn't want to accept any authorities telling him what he ought to feel. He wants to go straight to the work itself. This is an individual attitude for keeping a tradition alive and for keeping an individual connection with works of art rather than having them filtered through hundreds of pages of commentary before you ever get to read the thing itself. Think of how much has been written about Shakespeare, for example, much of it very helpful. But that's not like reading Shakespeare, Pound would say. And I agree. He wants you to go right to the thing itself and relate to it yourself and get what there is in it for you, whatever it may be. This is the way he reads. He has a great belief in the magic of the work of art, that it can not only transform individuals, but it can transform governments, political systems, everything. There can be very few people who have the innate belief in the emphasis and the power, mysterious power, of a work of art that Ezra Pound has. He says somewhere in a very eloquent statement that, when you read a book that lives, you're not holding a dead object in your hand; that the right person encountering the right book has a ball of light held in the hand. Now that seems to me to be the correct attitude.

Now the books. As I say, his life and his work are so intertwined with the whole effort and endeavor of the human imagination in the twentieth century that reading Pound's life is like reading from the inside out a whole history of what has happened to human sensibility in the last seventy years. First of all, there's quite a good biography by a man named Charles Norman, a very handsomely made book, a lot of information, very readable. It's called *Ezra Pound.* Here's a thing on Ezra Pound by a guy who's done some work with him. Here's a recent picture of the old man—very old with a muffler around him—it's called *The Life of Ezra Pound,* and the author is Noel Stock. It's also quite a good biography. I don't think as good as the Norman one, but good. Another one, also by Noel Stock, called *Reading the Cantos.* I'll talk about this later on. There's another one in the Evergreen series called *Ezra Pound* by G. S. Fraser.

As I said, Pound was a great discoverer, and re-discoverer, and above all a tireless spokesman for everything that is vital, or that he thinks is vital or living or enduring in the arts, as against what is dead and official. No one could have played a more important role. He came along at just the right time, and he was the right man for the job. Nobody's perfect, and, God knows, if you speak of Ezra Pound you speak of imperfection, but the impact he had and the things he advocated were the things that should have been advocated at that time, and the impact that someone should have had at that time.

Now, one of the things a lot of people dislike about Ezra Pound is that he is so bookish. I'll go into this more thoroughly next time, but books, art, poetry, music lived for Pound more than living human beings did. He would say that they are more valuable because they are more enduring; they have more to say. More to say than real people do, for a longer period of time. Everything that is good about us has come from what was good in human creativeness and expressiveness before us. You can get most of Pound in two big books, *Personae,* which contains the wonderful translations from the Chinese, which I, myself, think are his best poems; and then the monumental *Cantos,* maddening, unforgettable in places, un-understandable and impenetrable in many other places.

I want to finish this session by giving you some information about Pound himself. Now remember he's an American, a frontier American, who has taken to Europe, has taken to the European past as no European could ever have done. He is a super-European or citizen of the world because he is so eminently American as to believe he could become a troubadour or a member of the Provençal culture, simply by walking the roads on foot where these people, these troubadour poets, Provençal poets, had their lives, and fought their wars, and exalted their women, and had, Pound would say, an altogether better time of it than we do. This is called "Provincia Deserta." It's full of Provence place-names.

PROVINCIA DESERTA

At Rochecoart,
      Where the hills part
              in three ways,
And three valleys, full of winding roads,
Fork out to south and north,
There is a place of trees. . . . gray with lichen.
I have walked there
              thinking of old days.
At Chalais
           is a pleached arbour;
Old pensioners and old protected women
Have the right there—
it is charity.
I have crept over old rafters,
           peering down
Over the Dronne,
           over a stream full of lilies.
Eastward the road lies,
           Aubeterre is eastward,

With a garrulous old man at the inn.
I know the roads in that place:
Mareuil to the north-east,
                La Tour,
There are three keeps near Mareuil,
And an old woman,
                        glad to hear Arnaut,
Glad to lend one dry clothing.

I have walked

                into Perigord,
I have seen the torch-flames, high-leaping,
Painting the front of that church;
Heard, under the dark, whirling laughter.
I have looked back over the stream
                and seen the high building,
Seen the long minarets, the white shafts.

I have gone in Ribeyrac
                and in Sarlat,
I have climbed rickety stairs, heard talk of Croy,
Walked over En Bertran's old layout,
Have seen Narbonne, and Cahors and Chalus,
Have seen Excideuil, carefully fashioned.

I have said:
                "Here such a one walked.
"Here Coeur-de-Lion was slain.
                Here was good singing.
"Here one man hastened his step.
                "Here one lay panting"
I have looked south from Hautefort,
                thinking of Montaignac, southward.
I have lain in Rocafixada,
                level with sunset,
Have seen the copper come down
                tingeing the mountains,
I have seen the fields, pale, clear as an emerald,
Sharp peaks, high spurs, distant castles.
I have said: "The old roads have lain here.
"Men have gone by such and such valleys
"Where the great halls were closer together."
I have seen Foix on its rock, seen Toulouse, and
                Arles greatly altered,
I have seen the ruined 'Dorata.'

I have said:
"Riquier! Guido!"
                    I have thought of the second Troy,
Some little prized place in Auvergnat:
Two men tossing a coin, one keeping a castle,
One set on the highway to sing.
                    He sang a woman.
Auvergne rose to the song;
                    The Dauphin backed him.
"The castle to Austors!"
                    'Pieire kept the singing—
"A fair man and a pleasant"
                    He won the lady,
Stole her away for himself, kept her against armed
                    force:
So ends that story.
That age is gone;
Pieire de Maensac is gone.
I have walked over these roads;
I have thought of them living.

As an American, I have often read that poem. I love those place names. I've
never been to any of those places, but I love them. I wish that I myself had that
much love of a tradition, my own, or somebody else's. I don't, but I'm glad that
he did, or does.

One of the things you note first about Ezra Pound is that he is interested
in all cultural manifestations in all languages and in all historical periods. They
fascinate him; he cannot have enough of them. He's a kind of inspired amateur.
He takes what he wants from people who are lifetime scholars in one field, such
as, say, Japanese poetry, Chinese poetry. But he himself doesn't stay in that posi-
tion long enough to consolidate anything. He prefers to work by intuition, so
that his translations, especially the translations from the Chinese, have set the
model for what every other translator, or at least every other translator who is
a poet, has tried to do since that time. These translations are in a book of his, a
small book, called *Cathay*. He became interested in oriental poetry, particularly
Chinese, through the work of a Japanese scholar named Ernest Fenollosa,
whose wife admired Pound's poetry and sent him some of Fenollosa's transla-
tions and transliterations of Chinese poems which had been translated into
Japanese and which Fenollosa had then translated into English, using what he
called the ideographic method. This fascinated Pound. But what Fenollosa said
in a very famous little monograph, which Pound later edited and commented

on, called "The Chinese Written Character as a Medium for Poetry," is that Chinese writing, at least some of it, is essentially pictographic. That is, they are little pictures of things which stand for words, which stand for concepts. And it fascinated Pound, with his intense dislike for the western world's abstractions and generalizations, to find a method of writing, above all a method of conceiving, in which abstract ideas were presented in concrete entities in little pictures. For example, Fenollosa says, "Suppose we look out the window and watch a man. . . . the group holds something of the quality of a continuous moving picture."

This idea fascinated Pound. He began to experiment with ways in which to get concrete entity and clusters of images standing for abstract concepts and generalizations into English. It was a guiding principle for his work, especially for the *Cantos*. Pound, as he would do, puts his own interpretation on Fenollosa, and begins to work in the *Cantos* kind of discontinuous clusters of things, liberally interlarded with actual Chinese symbols and pictographic symbols that he has both appropriated and invented. But, as soon as Fenollosa gave him what he considers to be one of the key clues to his own developing technique, he immediately wants to apply this to translation in some way, so he gets Fenollosa's widow to send him some examples of Fenollosa's transliterations of oriental poetry. Pound really wants to do Chinese poetry. He doesn't know a word of Chinese; he doesn't know a word of Japanese. Fenollosa is not a sinologist, a Chinese expert, but a Japanese expert—so what he's done is take Japanese transliterations of the Chinese and translate in the image cluster manner from those. And this is what is sent to Pound. So in Pound's translations, or free adaptations, or whatever you would want to call them, the names of the poets are the Japanese names rather than the original Chinese names. For example, the poem "The River Merchant's Wife," you'll notice at the end that the credit for it is stated as being by Rihaku. But Rihaku is a Japanese name, not a Chinese name, and this is a Chinese poem. Rihaku is the Japanese name that was given to the great Chinese lyric poet Li Po. So, this is the man that Pound chose to translate from a Japanese transliteration. This is one of the really great poems in the English language, to say nothing of one of the greatest translations of anybody. It's called in the original "Song of Chang Gan," which is a village near Nanking. It is of a woman who married at fourteen or fifteen, which was apparently the custom at the time, and has now fallen in love with her husband, and he's gone off and she wants him to come back. The original's not a bad kind of sincere little letter type of poem, but Pound does something entirely different, and what constitutes the difference is that Pound is a poet, a good poet and sometimes a great poet. Although he does not know the original, he

knows something better, and he brings in with these *Cathay* poems, and partic-
ularly with this one, something to the translation that hasn't been there before.
I can only characterize it as Pound does, as an attempt to get into a second lan-
guage something like the feeling or the spirit that the poet senses in the orig-
inal.

Pound says over and over again, "I do not translate words." It has been
thought up till the time of Pound that was all the excuse there was for a trans-
lator: translate words. Pound says, "no"; he had Fenollosa's words, but he just
kind of got the gist of it and took off, used his own intuition and his own feel-
ing about what Chinese poetry must be like, and if it wasn't like that then it
ought to be. And he just went right ahead, didn't know the languages, or just a
smattering of them; but he had a sense of what Chinese poetry should convey
and does convey in the original. And he set out to get that into English. So this
is the way it came out.

THE RIVER-MERCHANT'S WIFE: A LETTER

While my hair was still cut straight across my forehead
I played about the front gate, pulling flowers.
You came by on bamboo stilts, playing horse,
You walked about my seat, playing with blue plums.
And we went on living in the village of Chōkan:
Two small people, without dislike or suspicion.

At fourteen I married My Lord you.
I never laughed, being bashful.
Lowering my head, I looked at the wall.
Called to, a thousand times, I never looked back.

At fifteen I stopped scowling,
I desired my dust to be mingled with yours
Forever and forever and forever.
Why should I climb the look out?

At sixteen you departed,
You went into far Ku-tō-yen, by the river of swirling eddies,
And you have been gone five months.
The monkeys make sorrowful noise overhead.

You dragged your feet when you went out.
By the gate now, the moss is grown, the different mosses,
Too deep to clear them away!
The leaves fall early this autumn, in wind.
The paired butterflies are already yellow with August
Over the grass in the West garden;

They hurt me. I grow older.
If you are coming down through the narrows of the river Kiang,
Please let me know beforehand,
And I will come out to meet you
        As far as Chō-fū-Sa.

Now, Pound has this curious thing: his translations contain a good many factual errors, but I have never seen or heard or read about a native Chinese scholar who did not think Pound was the finest thing that ever happened to Chinese culture as far as getting it into English was concerned. All the translations of the oriental language that have ever been any good have stemmed from Pound's. He really opened it up. As Eliot said, he might be said to have invented it, as far as English-speaking peoples are concerned. It's a curious fact that there were two things that Pound stuck with over the years; they were the study, in his typical hit-or-miss but very long-lived fashion, of government or economics; and the other was Chinese. He had lots of Chinese grammars with him at St. Elizabeth's, and he did, through this process of self-miseducation, get to the point where he could read it pretty well. After thirty years of this he undertook to translate the Confucian *Book of Odes.* I read through those, and it struck me that they are not in the same class as those he did at the very first of his interest in Chinese, when he didn't even know the language at all. Pound is odd in that way: he's much more trustworthy when he just knows a little bit about something and intuits the rest than when he takes the time to learn it more or less thoroughly, at least thoroughly for him. The more he knows about it and the less he intuits, the more the stuff falls off, the less good it is.

Now, that brings us to the poem that ushers in what we have come to think of as modern poetry. His method made possible *The Waste Land;* it made possible the *Cantos;* it made possible not dozens but hundreds of other poems by poets who began to use the discoveries or the techniques or the approaches that Pound brought in with this poem, *Hugh Selwyn Mauberley.* This poem has lots of allusions usually employed in an ironic way, the kind of thing that has turned multitudes off. This is the kind of poetry in which notes are not only desirable but essential, and this is one of the reasons we use this textbook, because you have notes at the back. And in reading *Mauberley* and *The Waste Land* I want you to lean on the notes, I mean *lean,* because Pound and Eliot write using this analogical method which quite literally cannot be understood at all unless you know what the allusions are to. The broad outlines of *Mauberley* are these: Mauberley is a half-fictional, half-factual character. He is in part Ezra Pound in his preoccupation for refurbishing culture, especially English culture, and making culture a living thing in the lives of people; he's a poet himself. He's partly Pound, but partly someone who isn't Pound. Mauberley is a minor poet, a real poet, a genuine poet, but a minor poet. He knows he's minor. He knows he can do small, exquisite, perfect poems. He's nonetheless a real poet, a dedicated poet, thrown up against the mass-producing, commercial type of civilization that we have. He's young; he's a believer. He believes in art, generally; he believes in culture; he believes in the interaction of the human sensibility with the great monuments of the human imagination of the past, whether painting, sculpture, music, poetry, drama. He believes that these are living things, and he knows that it's given to him to create in his small way authentic works of art, which have this energy charge, and which the succeeding generations, if they'll just pay attention to them, will not willingly let die. This is a poem which is written in a kind of a loose sequence of related poems, all having to do with Mauberley's career in London for three years. Let me just take a few lines to illustrate Pound's approach, which, as far as I know, is entirely original with him. The poem is about a man who fought the good fight for art against an indifferent, commercial society, where mass production, money making, banking, and usury are the orders of the day; and any living contact of the human sensibility with art, any contact with the life-quickening, life-enhancing force that true art is has been leached out of people. They either can't rise to it, or they have no occasion to want to try. Their preoccupations are with money making, doing the things that we all know so well from our own daily lives.

HUGH SELWYN MAUBERLEY
Life and Contacts
—*E. P. Ode pour l'Election de Son Sépulchre*

For three years, out of key with his time,
He strove to resuscitate the dead art
Of poetry; to maintain "the sublime"
In the old sense. Wrong from the start—

No, hardly, but seeing he had been born
In a half savage country, out of date;
Bent resolutely on wringing lilies from the acorn;
Capaneus; trout for factitious bait;

Ἴδμεν γάρ Τοι πάνθ' ὄσ'ἐνίTρο ίη
Caught in the unstopped ear;
Giving the rocks small lee-way
The chopped seas held him, therefore, that year.

His true Penelope was Flaubert,
He fished by obstinate isles;

Observed the elegance of Circe's hair
Rather than the mottoes on sun-dials.

Unaffected by "the march of events,"
He passed from men's memory in *l'an trentuniesme*
De son eage; the case presents
No adjunct to the Muses' diadem.

If you don't know who Capaneus was, you miss the reference, you miss what Pound is getting at. Well, without the notes at the back of the book, you probably didn't know. Who was Capaneus? Have you ever read *Seven Against Thebes*? Well, these seven heroes set out against Thebes from Argos. Capaneus was one of the seven who defied Zeus and was struck by lightning. With this reference, this one reference, Pound brings into poetry, especially poetry in English but also in other languages, a new kind of reference. He is using a figure from Aeschylus's play, *Seven Against Thebes,* in his own poem, and has brought in a technique that you might call the ironic out-of-context quotation. Here is a minor poet in London, trying for three years to resuscitate the dead art of poetry, who likens himself to Capaneus, a Greek tragic hero, who was struck by lightning by Zeus, or struck by what the Greeks used to call "the fire that falls from heaven." But he isn't a Greek hero. He's only an unlistened-to minor modern poet, so the context turns ironic. You get a kind of double per-spective on it. He isn't struck by lightning from the gods; he's simply done in by indifference of the society. He's no hero, and it's ironic that he should liken himself to one of the seven against Thebes. But they got to him anyway. He calls himself a "trout for factitious bait." That is, he's baited. He rises to illusory lures, will-o'-the-wisps. It doesn't do any good. He can't get through to them; he just exhausts himself. This is a quotation from the song the sirens sang to Odysseus, and you may remember enough of your Homer to remember the story of the sirens, who sang so sweetly of home, and you'll remember that Mauberley himself is an exile; he's an American in England. The whole poem is really the story of an exile, not exiled only from his own country but exiled from his true cultural milieu. The song of the sirens, Pound says, caught in "the unstopped ear," and you remember that the sailors didn't have enough wax to stop Odysseus's ears and so they had to tie him to the mast so he couldn't take the boat over to where the sirens were singing and wreck it. But Mauberley did hear the song. These are not the heroic seas of the Mediterranean or the old Greek world, just the small, commercial, petty, journalistic enmities and cross-currents of London literary society.

"Observed the elegance of Circe's hair / Rather than the mottos on sun-dials." That's always been kind of a difficult passage for me. I don't agree with

The poet as reader, mid-1980s. *Courtesy of James Dickey Collection, Department of Rare Books & Special Collections, Thomas Cooper Library, University of South Carolina*

what they say in the notes at the back, that he would rather observe beauty than live by rules. I always took that line to mean that that was a kind of ironic thing turned against Mauberley himself by himself—that he couldn't have been such a pure esthete as all that as to spend all his time observing the elegance of Circe's hair, that he could probably have paid more attention to mottos on sundials. The only motto I've ever seen on sundials—of course, I've only seen three or four with inscriptions, but it's always a Latin inscription—says, "It's later than you think." It's probable that Mauberley felt that he should not have been such a pure esthete, that he probably should have paid a little more attention to the motto on the sundial.

Now, these are products, the difference between products made by craftsmen in which the craftsman himself has a hand in the whole process by which they are made, as against mass production, say, where the craftsman has no relation whatever to the product. Pound thinks this is wrong. It destroys the instinct of workmanship, which is one of the most valuable things that people can have in regards to the work that they do, their relationship to it, the whole product. "The tea-rose tea-gown, etc. / Supplants the mousseline of Cos," which was fabulous stuff, apparently. "The pianola (or we would say, the jukebox) 'replaces' / Sappho's barbitos." The barbitos is kind of a little lyre, a musical instrument. Sappho, again, you may know, was an almost legendary Greek lady poet who lived on the island of Lesbos. She survives only in fragments, and is said to be a lover of women as well as of men, hence the word "lesbian." But this is the age were songs were sung from one person to another person. They were not blared out to an unseen audience of fifty million. We have the pianola or the jukebox instead of the legacy of one human being playing or singing to another.

Now, these two sections have to do with war, some of the people who went to it and their reasons for going. The fifth section generalizes on what all the sacrifice was for, generalizing, bringing another Poundian obsession, that is, what is worth dying for, what kind of country, what kind of culture, is worth dying for. They died for this mechanistic, antihuman, inhuman, money-mad, dishonest civilization, which produced nothing of permanent value. They died, Pound says, but they shouldn't have died for that. They died for civilization in which culture was something in a museum. It's usually copies of copies. "For two gross of broken statues." They're hidden away in a museum. They have no living relationship to our lives at all, except as something in a museum. Nobody goes to see it anyway. Or a "few thousand battered books." They're hidden away in a library. They're probably the wrong books anyway. They're not the books that Pound reads. That's what all this courage and this self-sacrifice were for.

Notice, by the way, one little point of technique. Notice all the "B's," the letter "B's," that begin words in [Section V]. It gives the passage a kind of explosive quality. Pound's good with that, and he doesn't overdo it, either. Just enough. Now, suddenly, Section VI takes a wholly different tack. We'll look at it next time. Section VI goes back into the last era in which art was accorded a certain position that people recognized, albeit an inferior position. He goes back to the 1890s, the time of Oscar Wilde, when people paid some attention to art and artists.

JOE LANGLAND

Now, let's take a very, very brief look at Joe Langland. Joe Langland is an American poet, very selective. He's almost as selective as Mauberley. In twelve or fourteen years he's only published two books. One of them was in a series that Scribners published called Poets of Today. My own first book appeared in this same series in 1960. Joe's appeared about 1958. This was a great idea of Scribners publishing company, to publish three first books of poems in one rather handsome volume. Nobody read them, so they discontinued the series after eight books and twenty-four poets. It was not really a very successful series, but it did publish the first books of some good writers, and Joe Langland was one of the good ones. Joe Langland is a midwestern country boy, born in Minnesota and raised in Iowa and educated at the University of Iowa and at Harvard. He's a very bright fellow; he teaches at Amherst, now. One of his books is the third book in Poets of Today, third series, called *The Green Town.* Mostly apprentice work, but very striking. He has a sense of complicated stanza form, a good many of which he invents himself, which are akin to the seventeenth-century poets like [George] Herbert and [John] Donne, who delighted in making poetry, as far as the stanzaic structures are concerned, as complicated as they could. Joe Langland does that very well. I think of all the American poets he's the one who does it best. *The Green Town,* and then the only book he's published by himself, called *The Wheel of Summer,* which came out about nine or ten years ago. He hasn't published anything else, as far as I know. But it's a very distinguished book, very good. The whole first section is about death, different kinds of death, and they're all about the deaths of animals and people that have to do with his growing up and working on a midwestern farm. The death of a child and a lamb and an old gentleman and a gunnysack of cats, a rattlesnake, a cousin, Uncle Hans, a red squirrel, a hill of ants, Aunt Marie, relatives, and so on, animals, all because of sacrifices. He shoots the squirrels and the rabbits; he sets the ant hill on fire. He sees these things die.

The Georgian Poets

The dominant group on the British scene came to be called and are called the Georgian Poets, mostly forgotten now. I'll name five names and see if you ever heard of them. I'm not naming the obscure ones, but the prominent members of the group: John Drinkwater, Lascelles Abercrombie, Wilfred Gibson, Ralph Hodson, Rupert Brooke. Rupert Brooke is the only one of that bunch that has survived at all, partly because of his Bryonic attractiveness, partly because he was killed or died of fever in World War I and was buried in a spectacularly beautiful island setting on the island of Skiros. Rupert Brooke was looked on as the great savior and hope of English poetry at this time because he is so insufferably English.

The Georgian poets had a naive and sentimental bucolic attitude; that is, someone characterized Georgian poets as musings in the hedgerows by a well-dressed dormouse. And a lot of Georgian poetry is like that. They sentimental-ized over farm lands and over picturesque brooks and rivers and over country life and gypsies and farmers and milkmaids, and it was all very comfy. This is one of the most famous Georgian poems; it's Rupert Brooke. All this is totally lost on an American, not only on an American of now, but would have been on an American of then. But this is the end of a poem of Rupert Brooke's called "The Old Vicarage."

The Old Vicarage, Grantchester

(*Café des Westens, Berlin. May, 1912*)
God! I will pack, and take a train,
And get me to England once again!
For England's the one land, I know,
Where men with Splendid Hearts may go;
And Cambridgeshire, of all England,
The shire for Men who Understand;
And of *that* district I prefer
The lovely hamlet Grantchester.
For Cambridge people rarely smile,
Being urban, squat, and packed with guile;

And Royston men in the far South
Are black and fierce and strange of mouth;
At Over they fling oaths at one,
And worse than oaths at Trumpington,
And Ditton girls are mean and dirty,
And there's none in Harston under thirty,
And folks in Shelford and those parts
Have twisted lips and twisted hearts,
And Barton men make Cockney rhymes,
And Coton's full of nameless crimes,
And things are done you'd not believe
At Madingley on Christmas Eve.
Strong men have run for miles and miles,
When one from Cherry Hinton smiles,
Strong men have blanched, and shot their wives,
Rather than send them to St. Ives;
Strong men have cried like babes, bydam,
To hear what happened in Babraham.
But Grantchester! ah, Grantchester!
There's peace and holy quiet there,
Great clouds along pacific skies,
And men and women with straight eyes,
Lithe children lovelier than a dream,
A bosky wood, a slumb'rous stream,
And little kindly winds that creep
Round twilight corners, half sleep.
In Grantchester their skins are white;
They bathe by day, they bathe by night;
The women there do all they ought;
The men observe the Rules of Thought;
They love the Good; they worship Truth;
They laugh uproariously in youth;
(And when they get to feeling old,
They up and shoot themselves, I'm told) . . .

Ah God! To see the branches stir
Across the moon at Grantchester!

There was, for example, against the Georgian poets, a rowdy, foul-mouthed South African whom they snubbed, and who took revenge in long-forgotten verse satires against the Georgians, against that sentimental, bucolic attitude. They all came from the city; they were all intellectuals; they wore glasses, and they went self-consciously about the country lanes looking for subject matter. So the big cowboy, kind of the John Wayne type from South

Africa, Roy Campbell, comes in and takes one look at the scene, and he says: [poem unidentified].

Now if Georgian poetry was going to be opposed, it would have been better opposed and was better opposed by someone who had a hard intellectual substructure, and ideas about what poetry should be, rather than just firing off shotgun blasts indiscriminately as Roy Campbell did, in all different directions. This man English poetry found in a Staffordshire man, a great big powerful guy, at least in those circles, 6'4", 225, an argumentative guy who had been kicked out of St. John's College, Cambridge, for participating in a brawl. I'd like to say that he was drunk when he was kicked out, but he wasn't. He had some strong ideas about these things, and he was not drunk. He was a teetotaler. He was killed in World War I by a blast from a German battery, and he said in a letter the week before he died that someone asked him if he had ever tasted any alcoholic beverage, and he said, "Yes, along about my thirtieth year I tasted it to see if I'd like it. I didn't." His name was T. E. Hulme. T. E. Hulme was an extremely irascible, erratic, fascinating, repellent person, but a very great deal, and perhaps the essential part, of Ezra Pound—as far as ideas, both political and ideas having to do with the practice of poetry, the theory and practice of poetry, in Ezra Pound's case—came from Hulme.

Now, Hulme's own work is extremely fragmentary. Let me present him as attractively as I can, although some things about him are not very attractive. First of all, he was essentially interested in philosophy. Pound is only incidentally interested in philosophy. Hulme is the kind of guy who would get money from his friends, and mistresses, of which there were a good many, not to go and have a party or get drunk, or anything of that sort, but to make a down payment on a philosophical book at a bookstore. We all ought to know somebody like that. He was intensely interested in ideas, and he had, in addition to this, a Johnsonian interest in the common-sense approach to esthetic problems. He believed that common sense, carried far enough, would pass over from common sense and become prophetic. But again, he's not a systematic philosopher, Hulme. A great deal of his influence was disseminated through talk. He was an incessant, compulsive talker. He organized groups; he organized clubs. He was quite willing to take the opposite side of an argument against the side he did believe rather than that there be no argument. A great deal of his influence disseminated through talk; but luckily for us, not all. He carried notebooks around with him. He was a great womanizer; he was always trying to pick up women and cohabit with them in the most unlikely places, like the staircases of elevated trains. But the thing was that the man had tremendous energy. He walked all the way across Canada and back. And his notions that were the foundation of the imagist school we'll talk about a little later came from his notion that no idea or theory of English poetry had ever yielded him the key to the way to write about the feeling of space he had as he walked across the Alberta wheatfields.

As I say, he was completely dedicated to the things he believed in. Now, he believed in poetry, and he believed in a new era of poetry. He was violently antiromantic. He did not believe in talking about abstractions. He believed that poetry should be pure presentation without moralistic overtone. It should allow the reader to develop his own conclusions. It should be the most cogent possible presentation of a moment of time. He believed in throwing off all the shackles of English versification and English rhyme. He says that even if you are born and bred in the English language, you don't hear things in this artificial metronome. You don't hear and experience the language that way. You hear and experience any language in what he called a cadence rather than this artificial iambic pentameter kind of business. He wanted poetry to be written in phrases that are meaningful in that way, rather than what he considered the mechanical way, of the old English prosody, which is much too codified. Again, as I say, he was full of theories and ideas, and he talked about them excessively, and T. E. Hulme's influence is mostly disseminated through talk, but there are two volumes and endless commentaries about him, which you can read if you get interested in him. He's a fascinating guy.

He was also, on the other side of the coin, a militant militarist. He believed in World War I. He never complained against its brutalities and cruelties, and he even engaged in a series of letters—and they were hot too—against the foremost British intellectual opposer of the war and pacifist during World War I, Bertrand Russell. And to read the exchange of correspondence between Hulme and Russell is to feel yourself at an intellectual standoff. Hulme does not get any of the worst of it. Almost, you're persuaded. Except that we know we're going to side with Russell; we're all pacifists now. And yet, to have the other side of the argument presented with such forcefulness: he was a born leader and a born swayer of men's minds. And that was why such a swayer of men's minds as Ezra Pound was completely under Hulme's domination while Hulme lived. He was killed at the age of thirty-four in the war that he believed in. He was, I'm sure, even more dangerously protofascist than Pound. Pound's fascism, as he presents it, looks silly; if Hulme had lived long enough, he would have made a presentation that would have been dangerously believable. He was a dangerous man, a repellent man, a fascinating man. And what you get of Hulme, what exists of him on the page, is in two books, one of them, or both of them, edited from his posthumous papers. He made a few lectures on poetry around London because he liked to get on the podium and hold forth. One of these, the most important, is called *Speculations*. It has all his formal philosophical works, and there's one of them that has the title of a philosophical work or a work in a learned journal that seems to me to be the ultimate in titles for philosophical papers, and that is "The Philosophy of Intensive Manifolds." I read through, in preparation for this class, "The Philosophy of Intensive Manifolds." Although I haven't done very much formal reading of philosophy since I was in college, this strikes me as an extraordinarily good article, very, very good. It takes off from [Henri] Bergson's theories of instinct. It seems to me to display an extraordinary mind, very original, very unorthodox, but very exciting.

Now, what is his importance to us? It's just this, that Hulme is a violent antiromantic, which is to say that he's a violent anti-Georgian. He believes in what [Alfred North] Whitehead, one of his favorite philosophers, calls presentational immediacy: no moralizing. Furthermore, in his most famous essay, "Romanticism and Classicism," he draws brilliantly, although with very broad strokes, unsystematically, slightly impatiently, a connection between romanticism in literature and decadence and religiosity and a whole ethical-social complex of differences between two kinds of human minds, two kinds of ways of apprehending and ordering the world. *Order* was a big word with Hulme. His feeling was this: there were two views of men, and two only. One is that man is unlimited, with unlimited horizons and unlimited possibilities. This is the romantic attitude, which he was dead set against. The other is the exact antithesis of that, which is that he is limited and he had damn well better recognize his limitations and act within those and not be a limited creature pretending to be unlimited. Hulme says romanticism—romantic poetry, romantic politics, romantic philosophy—says of man that he's unlimited, he's just scratched the surface, he's capable of anything he wants to do. The other, the classical, says of him that he's a chaotic, erratic creature, and only by the utmost self-discipline or discipline applied from the outside can anything halfway decent be got out of him. He says a romantic laissez-faire kind of a eco-political system is going to say, "Do as thou wilst." A classical system is going to say, "You can do this, this, and this, but do this at your own peril because it imperils the others." It's really a variation on [Jean-Jacques] Rousseau: that man is born free but everywhere we find him in chains. Hulme would put a certain discreet number of chains on people to discourage their bad tendencies. We don't like that idea. It's unpopular now, especially since Hitler, and even worse, Stalin. I don't know what Hulme would think of Red China, but he did believe that certain restrictions by the state were necessary to force people to be decent with each other.

The Rousseauistic or romantic attitude would assume that they were automatically going to be decent.

His theories of poetry are very close allied. He says essentially that the romantic attitude is always talking about the infinite and the absolute, whereas the classical attitude is always talking about things. The classical is presenting things, things with hard edges, things that can be responded to—images, in other words. Classical doesn't mean all this romantic talk about golden youth and merging with the absolute, the kind of thing that Shelley does. What we need now, says Hulme, is to see our world, and to have hard-edged, small, sharp, and what they called dry poems that show things and don't moralize, that make you see and make you experience. And this has been an invariably good doctrine. It led to a small group—the imagist movement—very, very small. There have been unkind people who said that the imagist movement died because none of the people could write poetry. Not so, quite. It is true that this doctrine of Hulme's was taken up by Ezra Pound and, in keeping with Pound's usual practice, was made into a manifesto, and various works were being presented to the public as a result of the manifesto. This created a stir at that time, just before World War I. What it did create was a small, kind of a vignette type of poem, almost static, kind of like a verbal snapshot where something was frozen, some little moment of human time was frozen. It's strangely static. It's kind of like a verbal still life. There's a good book in case you want to go into this further, a good Dutton paperback, called *The Imagist Poets* [by William Pratt], with a very fine introduction.

What did happen was that these people, Pound, and Hulme, and the rest had this terrific thing about delivering English poetry and the English imagination from the bondage of the past, going into new forms, new ways of seeing, new ways of existing, new ways of being, but about the time they got it going good, World War I comes in. They're all scattered to the four winds, and what happened as a result of imagism was what happened as a result of its influence on larger poems and larger poets. The imagist poets were small poets: Hulme, who only wrote a few poems himself; Pound, who went through that phase with a couple of things; Richard Aldington, who's one of the better of those people and the movement's best chronicler, were in a small, but probably irreducible way, real poets.

I recommend William Pratt's book. Let me give you an H.D. poem that is not in our book. It's only six lines. This is what Hulme would have approved of as pure presentation of one thing, say, in terms of another, where the sea coming in is presented in terms of pine and fir trees, the color of pine trees and fir trees, and it's written in cadence, rather than in regular meter, which is to say sometimes perilously close to prose. "Oread." And yet it isn't prose.

OREAD

Whirl up, sea—
Whirl your pointed pines.
Splash your great pines
On our rocks.
Hurl your green over us—
Cover us with your pools of fir.

Small, but very striking, at least to me; even after all those years it strikes you. This is another one, called "Heat." You see, according to Hulme's doctrine, which they stuck to very closely, the poem has no business dealing with abstractions; the poem is to present, and then let the reader draw his own conclusions thereby. It isn't to moralize; it is not to present and moralize about—simply to present. Here it is; this is what it's like physically. This is what it looks like, feels like, smells like, and sounds like. This is called "Heat."

HEAT

O wind, rend open the heat,
cut apart the heat,
rend it to tatters.

Fruit cannot drop
through this thick air—
fruit cannot fall into heat
that presses up and blunts
the points of pears
and rounds the grapes.

Cut through the heat—
plow through it,
turning it on either side
of your path.

The heat is essentially presented as something more solid than what it actually is, more physical.

We are a restless people, Americans. We like to move. This business of the intense contemplation of a kind of still life or snapshot in depth makes us think, "That's real good; that's very well said, but I sure am glad it doesn't go on any longer than this." The imagists, especially H.D., had that exquisite kind of tact in knowing when *not* to stretch it out, to make the image come as much from what is not said as from what is said. There are few of her poems that are more than a dozen, and some of them two dozen, lines, but the better ones are the short ones. They have this intense provocativeness and just leave you with it.

The three principles of the imagist poets are these, and they are very good principles, if you can both use them and go beyond them: "(1) Direct treatment of the 'thing,' whether subjective or objective. (2) To use absolutely no word that does not contribute to the presentation. (3) As regarding rhythm, to compose in the sequence of the musical phrase, not in the sequence of the metronome." Which, as I say, in some cases is going to bring it very close to prose. Now, Hulme said, who is the master of all this, that it is infinitely harder to write like this, because you cannot fall back on the old mechanical gestures of the English poetic line. This is a way of attempting to use imagery and thought and rhythm in an intimate and organic way, and for that you don't have the sonnet; you don't have blank verse. You only have the musing of your own thinkability, what feels right to you, which may feel right today and feel wrong tomorrow. You have only this intensely subjective thing, so it's infinitely more difficult to keep it varied and interesting than if you had the whole background of English poetic form to fall back on and help you do it. You're way out there alone by yourself, and you have nothing but your sensibility and your own ear to go on. And that makes it infinitely more difficult to do. Other people have thought otherwise, and certainly there has been a great deal of abuse of this approach. Nonetheless, certain small triumphs come from the imagist group itself, most of them gained by H.D., the best of them.

An American poet born in Bethlehem, Pennsylvania, educated at Bryn Mawr, H.D. was a girlfriend of Ezra Pound. She and Pound and William Carlos Williams and Marianne Moore used to go out walking on Sunday afternoons. Later, they all became expatriates, and H.D. married Richard Aldington, a very handsome fellow with looks like a matinee idol of the 1930s. This book, *Life for Life's Sake,* is a very good historical recreation of that time when Ezra Pound used to take them all to a tea shop and H.D. had written these poems, and Ezra Pound says, "By God, we're all Imagists, that's what we're going to call ourselves." Aldington is okay, and he writes some imagist poems, and they all get a theory together and then they write poems to illustrate the theory. But H.D. was writing them anyway. She was the instigation of the plot, and she's the only one that as an imagist really survived. Nevertheless, the important thing about imagist poets is that they gave rise to certain new concepts about poetry and certain approaches to poetry that in the hands of much larger poets became elements in a style and an approach to poetry that was infinitely more important than the relatively small doctrinaire imagist group ever conceived of.

The two most important examples, of course, are the *Cantos* and the supreme example of the intelligently applied use of imagism and the concepts of T. E. Hulme in *The Waste Land*. When we go through that, I can show you exactly how Eliot used it, but *The Waste Land*—the most important poem, probably, from the standpoint of influence, that has ever existed—without the elements that were made possible to Eliot would never have existed. Aldington was a full-blooded, womanizing, hell-raising type of guy, and H.D. was a fastidious person who lived only for art. He lived for art plus other things; she lived only for art. It was a most touching thing; they both died within the last ten years. Aldington was kind of in exile in the south of France, his royalties cut off because of his debunking biography of T. E. Lawrence, the Lawrence of Arabia, his royalties gone, his books out of print. He spent the last of his money (he himself was dying of heart failure) trying to get H.D. treated for some kind of debilitating disease in a Zurich hospital. They had been divorced for a matter of about thirty years, but he was always devoted to her, and he always held her as an example of the most pure and dedicated spirit. That is essentially what you get in H.D., very static, very imagistic, but if there's anything that can be said to last from the world of the imagist turmoil around the time of World War I, it is H.D.

Again, it's not for all readers. To some people it may seem excessively cold and excessively distant, excessively static, excessively idealistic; and yet, it's hard to read it without being disturbed by thoughts of what life could be and maybe has been at one instance of historical time, that maybe on one or two of these Greek islands there has been this intimate junction among flowers and wind and the seasons, a conjunction between that and the utmost possible creativity of their own hands and imagination, an unselfconscious sexuality and concourse and intercourse among human beings. H.D.'s is essentially an island world, almost platonist, an island world held by an utmost effort of the will in a kind of equilibrium. That's essentially H.D.'s world, very small, very intense, very static, and in the best of it, very, very beautiful. I can take a lot of H.D. The only trouble is, there's not a lot of her. If you want to pursue her further, there's a *Selected Poems* issued by Grove Press, in paperback, which you can get. I love to read her when I'm about half drunk. It's a wonderful antidote to easy sentimentality: all of this stuff about marble and being tempered in fiery crucibles to bring forth a perfect shape.

MORE EZRA POUND

You don't just study Ezra Pound. That's almost impossible to do. You study everybody he's known and the interpretations he puts on them. You study everything that has ever preoccupied him, or anybody that's ever made any impression on him, or that he's ever heard about or had opinions about and has therefore seen fit to relate to the person or to the historical event, or whatever it may be in a certain way and use in his writings. So somebody said, with quite a great deal of truth, if you try to read the *Cantos,* if you expect really to understand the *Cantos* in their entirety, you not only have to know what Ezra Pound's preoccupations have been for eighty-seven years, but you have to have been him. And none of us are Ezra Pound. So if you go through a poem, *Mauberley,* the one that we're reading now, you'll see it is relatively easy to understand compared to long sections of the *Cantos.* But the way the *Cantos* is put together—that is, with all these out-of-context quotations and references to historical matters, to *The Divine Comedy,* to Greek quotations, to Roman elegiac poets, pastoral poets, to historical events in the 1890s, writers, literary movements—makes you realize one thing about Pound's particular method, that Pound more or less invented and then Eliot perfected: you come to know one thing about the business of picking up quotations from one context and putting them into your own work in another context that is ultimately, or usually, ironic.

If you read "Yeux Glauques" as a title for a section of a poem, you read that in four lines there are references to five things that went on in the late Victorian era. Now, if you don't know what these references are to, you're stopped right there. So it follows that what you realize about poetry written according to this principle is that you've either got to look up the references, or somebody has got to look up the references. Therefore, you get a poetry that you study in college, and there's no doubt that *Mauberley* and the *Cantos* and *The Waste Land* are by far the most influential poems that have been done in English in our time. So we do read them. So, we have a poetry that depends on outside sources, secondary sources. Now, setting aside the question of whether this is the way poetry should have happened or not, we can with all truth say that this is in fact what *did* happen. Poetry has been dominated by this attitude from that day to this. People are getting sick of all these references. I know I am, but it made a poetry that became not something more or less accessible to the man on the street who likes to read poetry but a game for scholars. And this is yet another paradox about Ezra Pound, who has always spoken against the professors. He himself, you could probably say, is the biggest professor of them all. He leans on learning, on secondary references, on foreign languages, and on a lot of specialized knowledge that only he happens to know. Some people would know *what* Ezra Pound knows, and some people would know *that* Ezra Pound knows, but nobody but Ezra Pound himself knows all these things at the same time as he does.

Section six is really one of the more difficult ones. The argument would run something like this: Hugh Mauberley, an American, goes, as Pound did, to London to resuscitate "the dead art of poetry" and by implication to show people what there is in poetry that is life-enhancing. He has had very little success with this so far, and has even less in the rest of the poem. This is why he can't resuscitate the dead art of poetry; people simply don't care anything about it. Their eyes are on business, on making money, on manufacturing goods. They don't care for "monuments of enduring intellect," as Yeats says. So, he comes to realize the general background of this thing that he's trying to do. "The age demanded an image / Of its accelerated grimace." So, all of this ends up in the First World War where Pound says, in effect, "You were good young fellows, you were good and young, enthusiastic, athletic when you went, you boys that went were talked into it by the liars in public places, by the defenders of the status quo. The people—the capitalists and statesmen—they sent you over there, and for what? You didn't even have a culture worth dying for. Look, boys, it's too late to say that now, but if you're going to die for a culture, don't die for this one. It ain't worth it. We don't have anything that bespeaks us. We don't have anything to call a culture except stuff in museums, probably brought over from Greece. We don't have any living contact with any kind of culture that we've produced. All we've produced is little plastic Jesuses. What you died for, fellows, all this bravery went for two gross of broken statues, two thousand battered books."

Mauberley doesn't give up. He thinks there's some kind of spark, of feeling, a vital relationship where you don't have to be told that a work of art is good because you like it, because it affects you so strongly, and it affects you so strongly because you have the capacity to be affected strongly. But the sensibility is dying out now, and Pound is right at the tag end of the time this is happening, and he, or Mauberley, is trying to go around and do something about it. So he tries to find out something about the last time there was any real artistic movement in England. It was in the 1890s, he learns, with a bunch of doomed poets and painters who called themselves the Pre-Raphaelite Brotherhood, rather pretentiously, I might add. There were some good second-raters in that group, and there were some good first-raters that were kind of on the periphery of the Pre-Raphaelite Brotherhood. What happened with them was that they pledged themselves to an art—they started out mostly painters like [John Everett] Millais and [Edward Coley] Burne-Jones and [Dante] Gabriel Rossetti, a curious Italian, who was also a poet, probably a better one than he was a painter—but they dedicated themselves to the ideas of Raphael (1483–1520), or what they conceived to be the ideas of Raphael and the people before him.

I don't know if you've ever seen any Pre-Raphaelite paintings, but they aren't in the style of the real Pre-Raphaelites at all, which were mostly religious paintings and portraiture. The English Pre-Raphaelites are kind of literary painters; they are painters of stories. I know you've seen a lot of Pre-Raphaelite pictures, because the museums are profusely full of them. They all feature ornate, patterned clothing on people and a kind of hypnotized-looking mongoosey girl, with great staring, mesmerized eyes. They did literary and historical pictures. They were kind of illustrators, really. But they had some very good ideas, and they were very dear to Pound because they were so intensely dedicated to the arts. They sacrificed so much for art, to be able to do their paintings and write their poems. They were all extremely licentious fellows, and part of this section six here has to do with the girl who was mistress of them all, a seamstress that Ford Madox Brown found somewhere, named Elizabeth Siddal.

This is a fascinating story. I'm digressing a little bit. She was a tubercular girl, but as soon as they saw Elizabeth Siddal's long neck and yellow-green eyes and mongoosey entranced expression, they knew she was going to be every woman in their pictures. If you go to the Tate Gallery, it's full of Elizabeth Siddal. She was not only the model for all these painters but she was the mistress of all of them. She was a consumptive girl, and they liked that about her too. They passed Elizabeth Siddal, ex-seamstress, around them like a ping-pong ball. But Rossetti himself, who came eventually into the group, married her, and a bizarre thing happened as a result of this. Rossetti was an addict of chloral. It's an opium derivative. She killed herself, eventually, and Rossetti buried his love poetry with her in her casket. And chloral got to him so that he burned his talent out; he couldn't write any more, and he needed to publish the poems, so he arranged to exhume the body and get the poems. It was a long time, fifteen or twenty years, and all the hair had grown out and filled up the casket, and they had difficulty getting the book of poems, because it had hair growing through it. So he got them out and published them, and none of them were any good, either.

Anyway, this group is the last true artistic movement up to the time of Mauberley, and it was doomed. It was beginning to run full-blast into the same thing that was doing Mauberley in. Nobody cared. This was, after all, the last part of the Victorian era, when women would hold their children up to see Lord Tennyson. Huge crowds would gather to watch Lord Tennyson go by in his carriage. Can you imagine such a thing? There was still some interest in an artistic movement like the Pre-Raphaelites, and they were attacked by the Victorian guardians of propriety, who were counterattacked by critics like [John] Ruskin, who admired them, and there was a lot of public furor about it. Now this had all ended. The last large-scale public interest in art movements, in, say, the Pre-Raphaelite movement, ended with the trial of the greatest esthete of them all, Oscar Wilde. We needn't get into that fascinating or sordid and in some ways rather uplifting but also disgusting story, except to say that Wilde was the most popular or famous of these people with this art-for-art's-sake disposition. In fact, that was a phrase of his. Pound himself is a latter-day esthete. The Pre-Raphaelites were always very precious to him. He admired them and he admired some of their work. He admired the work of a man who was kind of on the fringe of the group named William Morris, who did woodcuts and engravings and tapestries, and was the finest bookbinder England probably ever had. He believed very strongly in the old handcrafted tradition and the intimate relationship of the thing that is made to the maker. William Morris was an eloquent and famous spokesman of that attitude of the time. Okay, this is kind of a retrospective of the Pre-Raphaelites. Pound, or Mauberley, wants to see what their lives are like and maybe find out what their situation as the last real artistic movement up to this time in England was like, had been like, for these people.

Who is Brennbaum? Why would Pound go to see him? I think he's either a banker or a publisher, and this is probably the first evidence of Pound's increasingly manic identification of banking with the Jews. I think this is probably the first inkling of it, although it could be read a different way. But the main point here, as it pertains to this poem, is that Brennbaum is not the inheritor of a rich and resilient tradition at all. He has either disavowed his Jewishness, or just is not aware of it, because his preoccupations, too, are elsewhere, with appearances, dressing perfectly. That's his only claim to fame. He's not Brennbaum the inheritor of x number of thousands of years of Jewish culture;

After class at the University of South Carolina, late 1980s. *Courtesy of James Dickey Collection, Department of Rare Books & Special Collections, Thomas Cooper Library, University of South Carolina*

he's only "Brennbaum 'The Impeccable.'" He's just another one of the flock of modern business people. He has no connection with his past, his culture, his heritage, and you know Mauberley's not going to get anything out of him. He's not going to get a loan or his book published, or whatever Brennbaum does.

Next, Mauberley goes to see Mr. Nixon. That's not, of course, anybody we know, but in some ways not too unlike. Mr. Nixon is the writer who has made it financially, and who has made it financially in what way? Who's made it just incidentally because he's very good and people just buy his works and have made him rich and able to buy a big yacht? Is that the way Mr. Nixon has made it? No; he's made it by deliberately setting out to make it: to take advantage of this opportunity or this person, and just figure out how to make it financially. So, here's this idealistic young poet talking to him, and Mr. Nixon kindly grants him an audience in the "cream gilded cabin of his steam yacht," which has been bought with all his ill-gotten, or at least gotten, gains from writing, novels, reviews, plays, or whatever. Mr. Nixon, Pound says, is based on a novelist named Arnold Bennett (1867–1931), who was enormously successful and quite a good novelist. Did you ever read a novel called *The Old Wives' Tale*? It's a very fine novel. *The Clayhanger* is good, too. He's not contemptible. It's just that he's very ambitious and very wily, also, as well as being good, which all helps. Dr. Dundas, in real life, was a man named William Robertson Nicoll (1851–1923), who was a Scot who disliked English writers. He was an editor of an English review, but he wanted to publish Scottish writers, so that's why he was hard for Mr. Nixon to crack, but crack him he did.

But still Mauberley goes on, and—he thinks the thing to do, as many artists and writers do—they got the hell out of the city. He's now not all that interested in changing everybody else. He sees now that the thing he's going to have to be most concerned with is in preserving himself. So he, like many another, takes off into the country. He hasn't got any money, so he gets a thatched-roof place, and it leaks, but he sits down there to work on his stuff, his poems, small poems. That to me, from my own experience and that of other writers and painters that I have known, those eight lines are the most acute and penetrating examination of this phase of the artist's existence that I know of. One does go off and try to get a place in the country and live there. That is inevitably part of it. And you do shack up with some dumb girl who can cook like hell. And there's always something good to eat, and people come to visit you, your friends, artists, other poets. The place is in disrepair, but all is not lost, because you do have a chance to practice your art.

Okay, so now he's back in London. He jumps around a great deal. The next two, sections eleven and twelve, are kind of caricatures of other people who are supposed to have something to do with culture and something to do with the arts. The first one is either a woman museum director of ancient works of art, or a private collector. You can read it any way, as you like. Why does she collect works of art or have anything to do with them? It's like tatting, or crocheting, something ladies do; it has snob value. In the next one, Mauberley shows up at a salon where women collect artists and writers, and probably their works, too, but more for snob value and just to have something to do on their Sunday afternoons.

This section ends with this sort of little songlike poem, as Mauberley/Pound sends his book out into the world, having certain wishes for it, hoping that someone will know about the existence of the book. He hopes she sees it first, or at least sees it eventually. [Henry] Lawes (1598–1662) was a madrigalist, a very fine English musician. Edmund Waller (1606–1687) wrote a wonderful lyric called "Go, Lovely Rose."

SONG

Go, lovely rose!
Tell her that wastes her time and me
That now she knows,
When I resemble her to thee,
How sweet and fair she seems to be.

Tell her that's young,
And shuns to have her graces spied,
That hadst thou sprung
In deserts, where no men abide,
Thou must have uncommended died.

Small is the worth
Of beauty from the light retired;
Bid her come forth,
Suffer herself to be desired,
And not blush so to be admired.

Then die! That she
The common fate of all things rare
May read in thee;
How small a part of time they share
That are so wondrous sweet and fair!

The next section is much shorter. In this part even Mauberley's hideout under the thatched roof has not saved him. He can't find his place now; he's beginning to get desperate. And when artists get desperate over their situation, over the society they live in, over personal things, when artists get desperate, especially the really good ones, major or minor, they usually do one of two things: commit suicide or withdraw. And the last part of *Mauberley* is the record of that, of his withdrawal. He knows that he's a small talent. His tool is not the enormous canvas or the fresco showing God creating the heavens and the earth, and earth-shaking kinds of subjects like that. No; his tool is that of the engravers—very small, a meticulous kind of art, very limited, very fastidious. This is the kind of thing he writes. And he knows that's what he ought to be doing; he ought not to be trying anything more than that. What he wants to do is *that,* if he just has a chance, if he can just survive.

The quotation to the first of the second part is a phony quotation that Pound made up, and made up the character to say it, evidently an Arab sage of some sort. "What do they know of love, and what can they comprehend? If they don't understand poetry, if they don't feel music, what is it they can understand of this passion in comparison with which the rose is crude and the perfume of violets a thundercloud?" He's beginning to drift on his reveries, living in the past, kind of daydreaming and withdrawing, becoming sufficient unto himself and feeling less and less need to try to make any effect on the world of men—the world of culture or art—or even exercise his own art. He becomes more and more subjective, more and more withdrawn. He feels now that he's spent too much time on his craft, that he's missed relationships with people, especially with women, with real flesh-and-blood beauties, instead of things carved out of porcelain or engraved in steel, that he's maybe been wrong the whole time in trying to do what he's done. Mauberley feels that he's no better than that, that he's been paralyzed into some kind of catatonic state by what he's gone through. And not only that his power to influence the culture of his time, which was nonexistent anyway—that is, as far as his power to influence it is concerned—but he really doesn't care. He has withdrawn to the extent that he has begun to dream of islands. "The Age Demanded": this is a statement that he was never suited to the age he has been in. We never know if he's gone to the South Seas, or whether he's just created them in his mind to the extent that he believes he's there. I always kind of believed he did go there, that he did end up on a raft with an oar on which he wrote one or two words. But I don't know.

"Medallion," however, is actually in a sense a reaffirmation of his life. This is actually supposed to be one of his poems. It has the hard, jewellike medallion engraving feel to it. This is one that he evidently did complete. It's like a Luini (c. 1481–1532?) in porcelain. I don't know, really, what Pound meant by it. I suppose that in this kind of hard, strict, rigid minor art he has created this durable image of a woman who, even under artificial light, has eyes that take on this unearthly glitter of things that are more permanent than actual human beings. Something like that. Even under artificial light you see something of that strange thing of the eternal which is only characteristic of a work of art.

There's Ezra Pound. I only want to say two more things. The first is that if you ever try to read the *Cantos,* understand that there are a lot of people to help you, and that it is full of very rare beauty. It's full of incidental beauties. I would read it first—you may never get back to reading it a second time—but I would read it first for the fragments and for what, given your present knowledge, you can understand of it. But the fragments themselves are so beautiful in so many places that you should be quite willing to take the rest of the things, the long, undigested segments of the political theories of Martin Van Buren and Confucius and a lot of other things that really are not interesting to anybody except him. You're willing to take those because the incidental beauties are so very beautiful. That's one thing I wanted to say. I would say that Pound's main tactical error is exactly what Randall Jarrell says it is. This is exactly what I think. His major tactical error is putting too much faith in culture and books and works of art and not enough in the ordinary, living concord and intercourse between human beings. He is so excessively bookish and so theory-ridden that there is something in the end that all his large and robust humanity cannot save him from, and that is a kind of fundamental coldness, a sense of overmanipulating things.

THE FUGITIVE POETS

I want to talk some today about an important group. I don't generally hold with talking about groups and movements because I have such a firm belief in individuality. But there have been some important groups. This is in the late 1920s. I also want to talk about the South and its relationship to cultural things generally: the relationship it has now and may have. You can't talk about the so-called Fugitive group, of which the three most famous poets are John Crowe Ransom, Allen Tate, and Robert Penn Warren—you can't talk about them and what they stood for and what they accomplished without talking about the larger social context that they represented, because they took a stand on certain social and economic issues. Their poetry and their novels, as in the case of Warren, bear a relationship to this. So you can't talk about the so-called Fugitive group, which originated in the Vanderbilt of the mid-1920s, without talking about these larger issues, issues which may well involve not only the fate of the Western world but also the fate of the earth.

Let me go back just a little bit and give you some personal background of my own in relationship to these fellows who preceded me at Vanderbilt by twenty years. I was at Vanderbilt from 1946 to 1950, and the only one of the fellows who originally formed this dynamic and very influential group of poets and political thinkers and literary critics and theorists, the only one left there was Donald Davidson, who, at the outset of the Fugitive, or what later came to be called the Agrarian movement, was the leader of it. The rest had gone: Robert Penn Warren to California and Italy and New Haven, where he now lives; John Crowe Ransom, who was the teacher of all of them, but a very modest and retiring member of the group, although some say the best poet, left to go to Kenyon College in Ohio and founded the *Kenyon Review* which he was the editor of for a number of years, and made it into an extremely distinguished magazine, probably in his time one of the most distinguished literary magazines in the world; Allen Tate to various places—to Princeton, to Italy, to wander about Europe, to live in England a while, to finally settle where he is now, about a hundred miles from Chattanooga. But at that time they were a cohesive and coordinated group with manifestos, poetic and political and economic. It's an interesting story of a group of men who opposed what they called Leviathan. They were all southerners. They were all the children or grandchildren of people who had participated in the Civil War, Reconstruction, all of the things that you hear about simply from the standpoint of taking courses in history. Ransom was born in 1888, Tate in 1899, Warren, the youngest of the group, in 1905. He was kind of the baby and the precocious genius of the bunch. They were all rural men, raised in country towns, where legends and stories that came out of the Civil War and Reconstruction were much more prevalent than they ever could be in the city, even Atlanta.

They took a stand on the South and what the South meant and what is happening to it under the onslaught of the Leviathan. Know what the Leviathan is? It's just some huge, undefined monster. It's some enormous, all-devouring beast. And to these men, and the people who associated with them and put out this very influential and very powerful magazine called *The Fugitive,* the Leviathan in our time is industry, is the encroachment of industrialism on what was originally set up as an agrarian or farming economy. They conceived that man's relationship to the land is the important thing, his rootedness in a region. His dedication to and identification with a specific locality were the most important things that he could experience, and anything outside of this would result in an unsatisfactory life situation. No matter how much wealth one accumulated, no matter how many creature comforts one acquired, one would never have this basic sense of belonging unless one had this connection with the land. This was one of the psychological interpretations of what agrarianism did mean and might mean again, but the Leviathan moved in on the South. And it has, according to these men—and I think we could see no more deadly applicability than what you see if you just walk out the door and look around at the shopping center and the concrete and chromium and plate glass, any more evidence of the deadly kind of leveling effect that this does have and will have more and more.

These fellows at Vanderbilt were on the ecology kick a long time before anybody else was. They saw what was going to happen. They saw that there was probably no way to stop it, because of the profit motive and because of technology which when applied by the profit motive does not hesitate to cut down a virgin forest to put up a factory for making plastic cigarette lighters. This is the thing that they stood against, the destruction of local customs, mores, folkways. Donald Davidson, as I say, was the head of the group. He was a less good poet than the other three more famous. He's a good poet, very good, but he's not as internationally famous as they. But he's a good poet, a real poet, and the best teacher I had in my whole entire life. He used to say, Why is it that Americans go to Europe? Do they go to Europe in fond hopes that it will be just another gigantic Rexall's? No; they go because it's different. And the differences are of different times and different places. In other words, there are places in Italy where you have to do nothing more than cross the road and the wines change, the dress changes, the cooking changes, the songs change, the landscape changes, the architecture changes. And Davidson used to say that this is the kind of thing that gives richness and variety to human life. And it does. If you have this leveling tendency, with everything exactly like everything else in different places, then you lose all that. What do you gain? Well, I suppose the industrialists would say that you gain a greater measure of progress and prosperity, and maybe you create more jobs. You have greater convenience and greater comfort. But my God, look what we've given up! This is what they would have said, and in a very large measure I would agree. I don't agree with some of the things that the Fugitives advocated. I mean, they're a little bit too far right for me, and I saw my great old teacher, Donald Davidson, destroy the part of his life that could have been and should have been the most productive in a futile and nonsensical vendetta against integration. That is not a major part of it with them, however; it just came to be something that Davidson took a stand on and became an embittered old man over.

But they are examples of poets who did take a social stand. This is popular these days; causes are popular. They had a cause that would be very unpopular now—anti-industrialist and regionalist. Davidson used to say that it is folly to assume that the quality of life is the same in Minnesota as it is in Georgia. Different factors are operating, among them being climate, things as simple as that; and we have in some ways, some localities, a rich native repository of local things, regional things. Why destroy those? Take folk music, take the blues. The blues came out of a certain kind of life, and if this life had not existed, they never would have come to be, at least not like they are. The same thing is true of bluegrass, and it's great to have them both. There's not any reason that you have to assign priorities. You might like blues better, or you might like bluegrass better. But we've got them both. Maybe this is one of the meanings of democracy, that there are local differences that can produce, and do produce all the time, or used to, before Rexall's took over, differentiated kinds of art forms, crafts, cooking. Back to why Americans go to Europe: one of [the reasons] is to eat. And it's no good to say that you'd just as soon eat pasta as sauerbraten or English ham or whatever else you want to name. They come from different regions, from different kinds of people, different cultures, and so on. And I agree very much with Davidson that it is important that these exist, that everything shouldn't come from "the home of the Whopper." I've eaten many of those, too, and maybe that's just one more incidence of cultural variety, but we don't want anything to be available to us except what comes from the home of the Whopper. This is just one little example of what local differences can mean. John Peale Bishop, who was a very eloquent writer on this and was kind of a tangential member of the Fugitives, says that as far as he was concerned, and as far as civilization was concerned, probably the only true test of native culture is whether it has developed an indigenous cookery—that is, whether it has developed an approach to eating and preparation of food.

But to get back to the poets themselves: they were a loosely organized group in Vanderbilt from 1925 to about 1930, who thought similarly, were all passionate in the interest of poetry. They were all rurally oriented from their upbringing. They were brilliant men who sensed that something was wrong with America, or that something was happening to it that they didn't like and was not good for people. They took a stand and they published a manifesto, which is quite good and very gutsy reading, even today, and it's called *I'll Take My Stand*. All of these people have essays in there: Donald Davidson, Allen Tate, John Crowe Ransom, Robert Penn Warren, Andrew Lytle. Very good, very powerful essays, and very pertinent to what's going on now.

There's a very eloquent book of Davidson's, two of them in fact. He's the spokesman for the theoretical part of the Agrarian ethos. One of them is called *The Attack on Leviathan,* which came out in the 1930s. The Agrarians attacked Leviathan and they lost. They could never have done anything else. The nature of the attack, however, is interesting, and, I think, still vital. The other one, by the old unreconstructed southerner, is called *Still Rebels, Still Yankees.* Again, it's very soundly reasoned, and, if you don't agree with Davidson's arguments about regionalism, and about the necessity for keeping differences alive, you would have to summon up some very good arguments and do some very good schol-arship to beat his, because he was a fine professional scholar in this field, and he could cite you chapter and verse on almost everything he says. He died, as I said, embittered and defeated, but his work is there and it's not anything that you would want to ignore if you're interested in the subject at all—and how could you not be?

Okay, the poetry stuff. Let me give you some books to read if you're inter-ested in the subject. First, there's *I'll Take My Stand,* which is the manifesto. Then there are Davidson's two books of essays: *The Attack on Leviathan.* He would have been backing George Wallace; there's no doubt about it. But he would have had intellectual reasons for doing this that George Wallace would never understand in a million years. The other one is *Still Rebels, Still Yankees.* I can't imagine Donald Davidson having it any other way. Then of Davidson's, if you wanted to pursue the matter of his work, there's a very fine collected poems. Let me read you one. I feel like I owe it to my old master. This is a poem called "Sanctuary," where the invaders, the militarists, are overrunning your home grounds and your farms and your house. You've got to get your stuff and your people and go to a place that the invaders don't know about, and there you can do whatever you can do to keep your family together. This is, I think, Davidson's best poem.

SANCTUARY

You must remember this when I am gone,
And tell your sons—for you will have tall sons,
And times will come when answers will not wait.
Remember this: if ever defeat is black
Upon your eyelids, go to the wilderness
In the dread last of trouble, for your foe
Tangles there, more than you, and paths are strange
To him, that are your paths, in the wilderness,
And were your fathers' paths, and once were mine.

You must remember this, and mark it well
As I have told it—what my eyes have seen
And where my feet have walked beyond forgetting.
But tell it not often, tell it only at last
When your sons know what blood runs in their veins.
And when the danger comes, as come it will,
Go as your fathers went with woodsman's eyes
Uncursed, unflinching, studying only the path.

First, what you cannot carry, burn or hide.
Leave nothing here for *him* to take or eat.
Bury, perhaps, what you can surely find
If good chance ever bring you back again.
Level the crops. Take only what you need:
A little corn for an ash-cake, a little
Side-meat for your three days' wilderness ride.
Horses for your women and your children,
And one to lead, if you should have that many.
Then go. At once. Do not wait until
You see *his* great dust rising in the valley.
Then it will be too late.
Go when you hear that he has crossed Will's Ford.

Others will know and pass the word to you—
A tap on the blinds, a hoot-owl's cry at dusk.

Do not look back. You can see your roof afire
When you reach high ground. Yet do not look.
Do not turn. Do not look back.
Go further on. Go high. Go deep.
The line of this rail-fence east across the old-fields
Leads to the cane-bottoms. Back of that,
A white-oak tree beside a spring, the one
Chopped with three blazes on the hillward side.
There pick up the trail. I think it was
A buffalo path once or an Indian road.
You follow it three days along the ridge
Until you reach the spruce woods. Then a cliff
Breaks, where the trees are thickest, and you look
Into a cove, and right across, Chilhowee
Is suddenly there, and you are home at last.
Sweet springs of mountain water in that cove
Run always. Deer and wild turkey range.
Your kin, knowing the way, long there before you
Will have good fires and kettles on to boil,
Bough-shelters reared and thick beds of balsam.
There in tall timber you will be as free
As were your fathers once when Tryon raged
In Carolina hunting Regulators,
Or Tarleton rode to hang the old-time Whigs.
Some tell how in that valley young Sam Houston
Lived long ago with his brother, Oo-loo-te-ka,
Reading Homer among the Cherokee;
And others say a Spaniard may have found it
Far from De Soto's wandering turned aside,
And left his legend on a boulder there.
And some that this was a sacred place to all
Old Indian tribes before the Cherokee
Came to our eastern mountains. Men have found
Images carved in bird-shapes there and faces
Moulded into the great kind look of gods.

These old tales are like prayers. I only know
This is the secret refuge of our race
Told only from a father to his son,
A trust laid on your lips, as though a vow
To generations past and yet to come.
There, from the bluffs above, you may at last

Look back to all you left, and trace
His dust and flame, and plan your harrying
If you would gnaw his ravaging flank, or smite
Him in his glut among the smouldering ricks.
Or else, forgetting ruin, you may lie
On sweet grass by a mountain stream, to watch
The last wild eagle soar or the last raven
Cherish his brood within their rocky nest,
Or see, when mountain shadows first grow long,
The last enchanted white deer come to drink.

That brings us to the three main boys here: John Crowe Ransom, Allen Tate, and Robert Penn Warren. The oldest of these is Ransom. His influence as a teacher of these others, his influence on the poets of his time, especially the ones younger than himself, like Warren, is absolutely inestimable. He was a mild little man. I only met him once, and I was impressed more than anything else that he talked in the Old South style. But he was a wonderful teacher to these poets, and most people think that his best work is the best work that the whole Fugitive work produced. He was certainly the most original and the most gifted technician and craftsman. First of all, one more thing about the group: there's a good little paperback that you could get started on, called *The Fugitive Poets,* edited by William Pratt, the same fellow who did *The Imagist Poets* I referred you to earlier, published by Dutton Paperback.

Ransom is an extremely subtle and for some people a rather difficult poet. His production is extremely small. His entire life work is about 140 pages. But he's got a voice in the sense that almost no other American poet has. It's very distinctive, and if you read much poetry, you can almost always tell a poem of John Crowe Ransom's without even seeing the name at the head of the poem. He's got a wry, scholarly, ironic, rueful, and kind of seriously playful style, which is not like any other that you'd know, or that I know, anyway. Let's read the one called "The Equilibrists." This is one of the really good ones of his. It's about a man and woman—southerners, surely, since their concept of honor has lasted longer than anywhere else—who love each other, but for reasons having to do with their positions in society—perhaps one of them is married, it's not made clear—cannot consummate their love for each other. And so they are impelled together by their love for each other, and they are pushed apart by these other things, and so they're just in an equilibrium, kind of like centrifugal force when you swing a bucket of water around. There are tremendous forces here, this force of attraction and this force of repulsion. This equilibrium: they can never get together, and they can never leave each other alone.

THE EQUILIBRISTS

Full of her long white arms and milky skin
He had a thousand times remembered sin.
Alone in the press of people traveled he,
Minding her jacinth, and myrrh, and ivory.

Mouth he remembered: the quaint orifice
From which came heat that flamed upon the kiss,
Till cold words came down spiral from the head,
Grey doves from the officious tower illsped.

Body: it was a white field ready for love,
On her body's field, with the gaunt tower above,
The lilies grew, beseeching him to take,
If he would pluck and wear them, bruise and break.

Eyes talking: Never mind the cruel words,
Embrace my flowers, but not embrace the swords.
But what they said, the doves came straightway flying
And unsaid: Honor, Honor, they came crying.

Importunate her doves. Too pure, too wise,
Clambering on his shoulders, saying, Arise,
Leave me now, and never let us meet,
Eternal distance now command thy feet.

Predicament indeed, which thus discovers
Honor among thieves, Honor between lovers.
O such a little word is Honor, they feel!
But the grey word is between them cold as steel.

At length I saw these lovers fully were come
Into their torture of equilibrium;
Dreadfully had forsworn each other, and yet
They were bound each to each, and they did not forget.

And rigid as two painful stars, and twirled
About the clustered night their prison world,
They burned with fierce love always to come near,
But Honor beat them back and kept them clear.

Ah, the strict lovers, they are ruined now!
I cried in anger. But with puddled brow
Devising for those gibbeted and brave
Came I descanting: Man, what would you have?

For spin your period out, and draw your breath,
A kinder saeculum begins with Death.

Would you ascend to Heaven and bodiless dwell?
Or take your bodies honorless to Hell?

In Heaven you have heard no marriage is,
No white flesh tinder to your lecheries,
Your male and female tissue sweetly shaped
Sublimed away, and furious blood escaped.

Great lovers lie in Hell, the stubborn ones
Infatuate of the flesh upon the bones;
Stuprate, they rend each other when they kiss,
The pieces kiss again, no end to this.

But still I watched them spinning, orbited nice.
Their flames were not more radiant than their ice.
I dug in the quiet earth and wrought the tomb
And made these lines to memorize their doom:—

EPITAPH

Equilibrists lie here; stranger, tread light;
Close, but untouching in each other's sight;
Mouldered the lips and ashy the tall skull.
Let them lie perilous and beautiful.

The other one that I wanted to read is based on a biblical story, "Judith of
Bethulia." This is not from the Bible; actually, it's from the Apocrypha. It's the
story of Judith of Bethulia, who was, I believe, an Israelite, whose country was
being overrun by Holofernes, a conquering chieftain, and they couldn't hold
him back, so she went to Holofernes' tent and offered her body to him. But he
went to sleep before he could do anything, whereupon Judith cut his head off.
And with that his army fell to pieces, and the Israelites came out of hiding and
slew them and ran them off. In the typical, delicate irony of Ransom, this
becomes a story with implications much different from what was intended by
the original. It was originally simply a story of patriotism. But in Ransom it
takes a completely different meaning. It's almost in some ways like *Moby-Dick*
in Melville's great chapter called "The Whiteness of the Whale." What is con-
cealed beneath the surface, how a beautiful woman, girl, can be—even in a situ-
ation where she was simply thought to be patriotic—the most terrifying,
concealing sort of a creature, who would offer herself and her charms with the
intention of murder. That's what's frightening to Ransom, that some things can
be masked under other things, motives.

JUDITH OF BETHULIA

Beautiful as the flying legend of some leopard
She had not chosen yet her captain, nor Prince

Depositary to her flesh, and our defense;
A wandering beauty is a blade out of its scabbard.
You know how dangerous, gentlemen of threescore?
May you know it yet ten more.

Nor by process of veiling she grew less fabulous.
Grey or blue veils, we were desperate to study
The invincible emanations of her white body,
And the winds at her ordered raiment were ominous.
Might she walk in the market, sit in the council of soldiers?
Only of the extreme elders.

But a rare chance was the girl's then, when the Invader
Trumpeted from the South, and rumbled from the North,
Beleaguered the city from four quarters of the earth,
Our soldiery too craven and sick to aid her—
Where were the arms could countervail this horde?
Her beauty was the sword.

She sat with the elders, and proved on their blear visage
How bright was the weapon unrusted in her keeping,
While he lay surfeiting on their harvest heaping
Wasting the husbandry of their rarest vintage—
And dreaming of the broad-breasted dames for concubine?
These floated on his wine.

He was lapped with bay-leaves, and grass and fumiter weed,
And from under the wine-film encountered his mortal vision,
For even within his tent she accomplished his derision,
Loosing one veil and another, she stood unafraid;
So he perished. Nor brushed her with even so much as a daisy?
She found his destruction easy.

The heathen have all perished. The victory was furnished.
We smote them hiding in vineyards, barns, annexes,
And now their white bones clutter the holes of foxes,
And the chieftain's head, with grinning sockets, and varnished—
Is it hung on the sky with a hideous epitaphy?
No, the woman keeps the trophy.

May God send unto our virtuous lady her Prince!
It is stated she went reluctant to that orgy,
Yet a madness fevers our young men, and not the clergy
Nor the elders have turned them unto modesty since.
Inflamed by the thought of her nakedness with desire?
Yes, and chilled with fear and despair.

There's another one by John Crowe Ransom. He doesn't, like Donald Davidson, write a great many poems about the South specifically, but there is one which is moving, and which I think is a beautiful poem, and I think an immortal poem beyond anything that Don Davidson ever wrote. It's one that I can never read without choking up. It's called "Antique Harvesters." He doesn't insist on this being the South he's talking about, but this is obviously the central implication, that men in a region, in a locality, have raised up their local gods. They can be men, gods, heroes, women. This is simply a tapestry, or a tableau, of people harvesting grain like the substance of the South. It's not good crops now. Things have happened to it. The men have to scramble for what they can get out of the earth; the land has gone sour, but it is the land and it is our land. She is the presiding deity. Maybe she's not what she once was, but she's still there, if you look.

ANTIQUE HARVESTERS

(Scene: Of the Mississippi the bank sinister,
and of the Ohio the bank sinister)

Tawny are the leaves turned, but they still hold.
It is the harvest; what shall this land produce?
A meager hill of kernels, a runnel of juice.
Declension looks from our land, it is old.
Therefore let us assemble, dry, gray, spare.
And mild as yellow air.

"I hear the creak of a raven's funeral wing."
The young men would be joying in the song
Of passionate birds; their memories are not long.
What is it thus rehearsed in sable? "Nothing."
Trust not but the old endure, and shall be older
Than the scornful beholder.

We pluck the spindling ears and gather the corn.
One spot has special yield? "On this spot stood
Heroes and drenched it with their only blood."
And talk meets talk, as echoes from the horn
Of the hunter—echoes are the old men's arts
Ample are the chambers of their hearts.

Here come the hunters, keepers of a rite.
The horn, the hounds, the lank mares coursing by
Under quaint archetypes of chivalry;
And the fox, lovely ritualist, in flight

Offering his unearthly ghost to quarry;
And the fields, themselves to harry.

Resume, harvesters. The treasure is full bronze
Which you will garner for the Lady, and the moon
Could tinge it no yellower than does this noon;
But the gray will quench it shortly—the fields, men, stones.
Pluck fast, dreamers; prove as you amble slowly
Not less than men, not wholly.

Bare the arm too, dainty youths, bend the knees
Under bronze burdens. And by an autumn tone
As by a gray, as by a green, you will have known
Your famous Lady's image; for so have these.
And if one say that easily will your hands
More prosper in other lands,

Angry as wasp-music be your cry then:
"Forsake the Proud Lady, of the heart of fire,
The look of snow, to the praise of a dwindled choir,
Song of degenerate specters that were men?
The sons of the fathers shall keep her, worthy of
What these have done in love."

True, it is said of our Lady, she ageth.
But see, if you peep shrewdly, she hath not stooped;
Take no thought of her servitors that have dropped,
For we are nothing; and if one talk of death—
Why, the ribs of the earth subsist frail as a breath
If but God wearieth.

If we give up on the things that we cherish, life will fail just as all the creation would fail if God gives up on us. His belief in us keeps us up, as our belief in the things that we have come by, that we cherish, keeps us up.

Anyway, as I say, there's not a lot of John Ransom. There's a very fine *Poems and Essays* in paperback, and there's that *Selected Poems* of Ransom. Ransom is like vintage wine. It essentially is a cultivated taste. He's not for all tastes. He's too subtle, too special, too oblique for most people. But he is the most original of all the Fugitive group, and probably will last longer in the end. He is probably their great poet, but you can't really use that term, great poet, because he's so determinedly minor. He is a small writer, but he surely is, in the general consensus of opinion, their best poet. Surely the most individual.

Allen Tate is the most prolific, or the most vociferous, and the most listened-to in the community of letters. He's an indefatigable reviewer and essayist and opinion maker. His poetry is learned and very modernist, but also very tradition-conscious. He left the South before any of the others and went to New York, and yet his roots are very firmly there in Kentucky where he comes from. It's very difficult to talk about Allen Tate because his style is such an eclectic style. He essentially is derivative from Eliot. He's not the strongly individual poet that Ransom is. In some ways he's a more powerful and direct poet than Ransom, and in his own way he's a great deal more difficult, but he never seems to have the kind of right relationship to his material that Ransom has. Ransom takes material and it becomes a Ransom poem. Tate takes material and it becomes an extremely interesting and difficult intellectual exercise that somebody else besides Tate might have done. But a head he's got. He's an enormously brilliant writer, and a great defender of the agrarian tradition, as well as a very good poet, but strangely unidentifiable. You can't say this is an Allen Tate poem as you can say this is a Ransom poem. All of his poetry is collected in *The Swimmers and Other Poems,* and it is a very distinguished volume. It's a book that, if you were reviewing it, you would talk about how distinguished it was, but you could not say that you loved it. You know those kinds of poems. But I don't want to make you think that he's not worth reading, because he is. He's very good. Extremely good. But he never has quite had it for me, although I read him all the time hoping I'll be shown the light. He's too intellectually preoccupied. This is a poem about sex, I think, and sin. I'm never quite sure what he's getting at. It's about a man and a woman, but I can never tell who is shadow and who is shade. But it's a very intriguing notion of how to write a poem about sex and sin in very strict classical form and yet be extremely tangential and modern and referential and mythical, too. One great thing about Tate; he can rise to a powerful climax, if you can make out what he's said up to that time. There's one very easy one, that is, easy for him. This is a poem, also in a sense, I think, about the South, about people who have made a culture and seen it turn into a bureaucracy, as Aeneas fleeing from burning Troy, after a long sojourn with Dido in Carthage, goes to Italy and becomes the founder of Rome. Our people did come here from Europe, and with a dream, founded a culture here. The country's turned into North and South. Our particular part is the South, the one that Tate comes from, the one he's interested in. Then he's in Washington, and he sees the enormous dome, the symbol of central government and bureaucracy and the Pentagon and Watergate, and he says, "Well, what did we think we were doing if it's all going to end up like this?" Of course we didn't know that, but we let it happen. This is called "Aeneas at Washington," that is, the founder of Rome. This is the parallel that he might have found in our situation.

AENEAS AT WASHINGTON

I myself saw furious with blood
Neoptolemus, at his side the black Atridae,
Hecuba and the hundred daughters, Priam
Cut down, his filth drenching the holy fires.
In that extremity I bore me well,
A true gentleman, valorous in arms,
Disinterested and honourable. Then fled:
That was a time when civilization
Run by the few fell to the many, and
Crashed to the shout of men, the clang of arms:
Cold victualing I seized, I hoisted up
The old man my father upon my back,
In the smoke made by sea for a new world
Saving little—a mind imperishable
If time is, a love of past things tenuous
As the hesitation of receding love.

(To the reduction of uncitied littorals
We brought chiefly the vigor of prophecy,
Our hunger breeding calculation
And fixed triumphs.)
                                        I saw the thirsty dove
In the glowing fields of Troy, hemp ripening
And tawny corn, the thickening Blue Grass
All lying rich forever in the green sun.
I see all things apart, the towers that men
Contrive I too contrived long, long ago.
Now I demand little. The singular passion
Abides its object and consumes desire
In the circling shadow of its appetite.
There was a time when the young eyes were slow,
Their flame steady beyond the firstling fire,
I stood in the rain, far from home at nightfall
By the Potomac, the great Dome lit the water,
The city my blood had built I knew no more
While the screech-owl whistled his new delight
Consecutively dark.
                                        Stuck in the wet mire
Four thousand leagues from the ninth buried city
I thought of Troy, what we had built her for.

Okay, so there's *The Swimmers and Other Poems,* and there's a very good book of essays, for he's one of the master essayists of our times, a man of letters of the modern world.

I want to take a minute or two and just talk briefly about my favorite of all these poets, Robert Penn Warren, who is an old one-eyed country guy who managed to acquire more education than anyone I've ever known in my life, but who speaks Greek and Latin with a Kentucky accent. He knows a lot. He's a very ragged, uneven poet; very, very uneven. But he has a raw primitive kind of power that Ransom with his intellectual subtleties and Tate with his learning and culture don't have. Warren has got the full power of what I call country tragedy. But he's not a good critic of his own work, so you don't in Warren get very many poems that are really finished. They're like notes for things that could be absolutely wonderful poems if he could find a way to complete them. But he never does. But the quality of power, of raw, ragged, uncompromising horrible power, nightmarish power in Warren is absolutely awesome. It really will shake you. Besides his *Selected Poems,* there's a long poem called *Brother to Dragons.* This is typical of Warren's nightmare kind of quality. It is about Charles Lewis and his family. Lewis, a cousin of Meriwether Lewis of Lewis and Clark fame, was married to Thomas Jefferson's sister, Lucy. Warren is great on genealogy. Lewis's wife's two sons, Lilburn and Isham, took a Negro slave out into the meathouse and chopped him up to pieces. Out of this episode Warren made a play for voices, *Brother to Dragons.* Jefferson, the believer in the Platonic and the good in man, and the founder of the nation on the idea that man is essentially good, has to face this terrible thing in his own family. It's about the wrestling of Jefferson with his conscience and the outcome of all these dark and horrible events, and they *are* horrible. This is the kind of thing that Warren does with death. After the event, Isham, the younger, is terrified of his brother Lilburn, and is afraid that Lilburn is going to do him in, because he's seen what Lilburn did with an ax without any hesitation. Isham helped out, but it was Lilburn's idea to do it. The slave had broken a pitcher that their dead mother had prized—a trivial pretext for this hideous deed that they perpetrated! So, they're just sitting there afterward, and Isham is a sensitive guy, and Lilburn is this great huge terrifying brute, and this is the scene where they're sitting in a cabin. A moth comes in and lights on Lilburn's hand, and Isham thinks this is a prelude to—something. He doesn't know what to expect Lilburn to do.

CONRAD AIKEN AND JOHN PEALE BISHOP

Today I'd like to talk about two poets who are remarkable poets in their ways but who, in various ways kind of unrelated to each other, missed: Conrad Aiken and John Peale Bishop. And I use the "Peale" because I can't think of any other way to say his name although I absolutely and utterly detest the use of a middle name by a writer. It's acceptable in a woman because somebody might want to know who she was before she was married, but in a man it is sheer and utter pretense. I would like to say John Bishop, except that nobody in American literary studies would know whom I was talking about if I said John Bishop, because he himself always insisted on it and always signed his name John Peale Bishop. And he was like that.

I'll talk about Aiken first. They're both southerners, Aiken from the Deep South, the coastal South, from Savannah. His father was a doctor with unstable tendencies as well as alcoholism and other unpleasant things. Until he was eleven years old, Aiken grew up in Savannah much as any other boy until one day he happened to tiptoe upstairs looking for his father and mother and found them both dead. The father in some kind of unstable frustration or rage had shot his wife and killed himself. So at this early age, Conrad was thrown on the mercy of the family. They had quite a large family. Most of the relatives who could take care of him lived in New England, so he's kind of a strange mixture of the native southerner and the administered New Englander. As it happens now, even in his eighties (he's around eighty-four or eighty-five now) he still, as some kind of Freudian explanation of his own life, spends six months in Savannah and six months in Cape Cod. I'll just go through his life briefly. He was educated at Harvard and was in the same class with T. S. Eliot, where they competed for the prestigious—I suppose it was in those days—post of class poet, for which Aiken defeated Eliot roundly, and then abdicated because he had scruples about poetic officialdom. Then he left school and went to live in Europe for a year, and then he came back and graduated somewhat belatedly. He then went back to Europe to live, mainly in England, all the time writing. He was a distinct influence on T. S. Eliot, although a year younger. He was the precocious one. Eliot was the slow and cautious one. The great poet to come out of Harvard in those days, about 1911 or 12, was not Eliot, who was just looked on as a scholarly fellow who whiled away his time writing verses. The really full-blast poet of that era, as anyone, including Eliot, would tell you, was Conrad Aiken.

Now, I think it's important to note a couple of things about him, the first and foremost of which is his fatal facility. All you have to do to know how easily Conrad Aiken writes is to take a look at this or just feel the heft of this enormous doorstop of a collected poems, which is really about half of what he published. It's just an enormous book. Nobody could write that much poetry who, if he had a selective critical consciousness about what he was doing, would have allowed that much work to appear in a collected poems. The second thing about Aiken is that with all his intelligence he is one of the two best literary critics I've ever read, the other being, oddly enough, John Peale Bishop. Both second-rate poets, or maybe not even that, though I would say surely second-rate, and both magnificent literary critics, in different ways. Aiken was in some ways seduced by the conventional in poetry. What he was expected to do in his time he did, and did better than anybody else, except that he never understood that the poet is essentially someone who works out at the edge of the periphery into what has never been done before, and not simply does again something that somebody else has done better. Now, there's an even more fatal thing about Aiken than that, and that is that he has never seen the need to experiment or to do anything in any other way as far as diction, meter are concerned than had been done before. The third thing, and perhaps the most damning thing of all about Aiken, is that he is so maddeningly indefinite and vague. He would say, as intelligent as he is, and I have heard him say, that he tried to emulate in poetry, in verse, special kinds of effects from music, such as the music of [Claude] Debussy. All of Debussy's music suggests some wavering, cloudy world, subaqueous, underwater. That's quite characteristic of Aiken; everything is seen through a kind of colored mist in a kind of conventional language.

Now, when you first read poetry, if you happen to pick up Conrad Aiken to be the first poet you read, you think the others might as well just give up. This is really *poetry*. This is the way poetry ought to be, because what little experience you've had with poetry up to that time has been with poetry like this except that Aiken is so much better than the others. This is a short example of what I mean [poem unidentified]. Ten years ago I would have said this was stuff by an inspired schoolgirl. Now, in 1972, I think it's stuff by an *unin*-spired school girl. But it's the kind of thing that schoolgirls aspire to write. The other side of the coin is that he is a musician, in verse, of extraordinary talent. There is not anything that Conrad Aiken cannot do in verse. But the whole effect of what he does in the sonnet, in blank verse, in whatever form he chooses, has that disturbing, vague kind of sleepy, distant, subaqueous, soft quality to it. Nothing is clear. There is nothing that takes precedence over anything else, and there's so much *of* it. What few themes he has are the conventional themes: love, death, time, art, loss. But his diction is so unfailingly ordinary, and this built-in vagueness is so pervasive, that you don't get any shock of recognition from any of it. This is the stuff that you like to read when you are about half drunk. It just seems absolutely wonderful then. Aiken is always talking about lovers standing in a garden.

This is one that comes off better than that. One of Aiken's few themes that does seem to have a positive coherency and power is the sense of sexual loss and the disillusionment of the love relationship. This is called "Sound of Breaking."

SOUND OF BREAKING

Why do you cry out, why do I like to hear you
Cry out, here in the dewless evening, sitting
Close, close together, so close that the heart stops beating
And the brain its thought? Wordless, worthless mortals
Stumbling, exhausted, in this wilderness
Of our conjoint destruction! Hear the grass
Raging about us! Hear the worms applaud!
Hear how the ripples make a sound of chaos!
Hear now, in these and the other sounds of evening,
The first brute step of God!

About your elbow,
Making a ring of thumb and finger, I
Slide the walled blood against the less-walled blood,
Move down your arm, surmount the wrist-bone, shut
Your long slim hand in mine. Each finger-tip
Is then saluted by a finger-tip;
The hands meet back to back, then face to face;
Then lock together. And we, with eyes averted,
Smile at the evening sky of alabaster,
See nothing, lose our souls in the maelstrom, turning
Downward in rapid circles.

Bitter woman,
Bitter of heart and brain and blood, bitter as I
Who drink your bitterness—can this be beauty?

Do you cry out because the beauty is cruel?
Terror, because we downward sweep so swiftly?
Terror of darkness?

It is a sound of breaking,
The world is breaking, the world is a sound of breaking,
Many-harmonied, diverse, profound,
A shattering beauty. See, how together we break,
Hear what a crashing of disordered chords and discords
Fills the world with falling, when we thus lean
Our two mad bodies together!

It is a sound
Of everlasting grief, the sound of weeping,
The sound of disaster and misery, the sound
Of passionate heartbreak at the centre of the world.

In this poem you can see almost everything that is good and bad about Aiken: the rhetoric, the conventionality, the vagueness; and yet—and this is what tantalizes one about the work of Conrad Aiken—in spite of all these adverse qualities, there is something that is deeply disturbing about it. I have never heard another poet talk about the "passionate heartbreak of the center of the world." Maybe that's just a rhetorical phrase. Probably, considering all the rhetoric in the thousands of pages of his *Collected Poems,* it's just another incidence of that. You don't know. I think myself that Conrad Aiken will remain a mystery forever, because he has a mixture of so many demonstrable bad qualities with such vague, tempting, tantalizing qualities of good, of something good that you can't get hold of. Yet it's there. You can't read the stuff without thinking that there's something amazing underneath all these kinds of waverings of underwater currents that his verse reminds you of, this vagueness, indefiniteness. And I'm quite sure that there'll be many generations of graduate students who will write theses showing that Aiken's indefiniteness is a more positive and evocative literary quality than the concreteness of somebody like William Carlos Williams.

He's essentially a lyric poet who's gone wrong, who tries to write long philosophical works. And you can read those with a certain amount of instruction, still, as always with Aiken, sensing an enormous sense of loss and the feeling that the poet has not known what he could do best and has not known what he should be spending all his time at, and has gone off in the wrong direction. But great gifts Conrad Aiken *has got* as a poet. He's the greatest musician of modern poetry, that kind of minor music, that kind of dim, distantly heard, haunting kind of music. This is one of his called "Annihilation," another love poem.

ANNIHILATION

While the blue noon above us arches
And the poplar sheds disconsolate leaves,
Tell me again why love bewitches
And what love gives.

Is it the trembling finger that traces
The eyebrow's curve, the curve of the cheek?
The mouth that quivers, while the hand caresses,
But cannot speak?

No, not these, not in these is hidden
The secret, more than in other things:
Not only the touch of a hand can gladden
Till the blood sings.

It is the leaf that falls between us,
The bell that murmurs, the shadows that move
The autumnal sunlight that fades upon us,
These things are love.

It is the "No, let us sit here longer,"
The "Wait till tomorrow," the "Once I knew"—
These trifles, said as you touch my finger
And the clock strikes two.

The world is intricate, and we are nothing.
It is the complex world of grass,
The twig on the path, a look of loathing,
Feelings that pass—

These are the secret; and I could hate you
When, as I lean for another kiss,
I see in your eyes that I do not meet you,
And that love is this.

Rock meeting rock can know love better
Than eyes that stare or lips that touch.
All that we know in love is bitter,
And it is not much.

I think his poetry will live, or at least some of it, if somebody can go through that enormous *Collected Poems* and make out the case for Aiken's poetry, for the best of it, that he himself has never seen fit to make, or has never been able to make.

But it also might possibly be the case that he's one of these poets who's going to be remembered more for his work in prose than for his poetry, which wouldn't be the first time, because Conrad Aiken—with this remarkable life of his, with this result of being orphaned as a result of a double suicide at age eleven, with this New England background as a sharp contrast to this lush southern coastal background, with his time at Harvard, with his friendship and association with Eliot, with the deep mover and shaker that he's been on the American literary scene for sixty years, with his criticism, his opinion making, with his enormous correspondence with people who came to him for aid with their work, which he most generously gave (he was the most generous as well as one of the most sharp and perceptive of men), with this remarkable life that he has had—has written one of the two or three remarkable autobiographies. It's a stream-of-consciousness narrative of his own life, with all kinds of time shifts and shifts and intonations of dialect. It's called *Ushant.* It's a pun. He's a great believer in puns, as in the Joycean pun. But it's a fascinating thing. Everything is in it—his theories of art, time, love. He's always spent a great deal of time around psychoanalysts and psychiatrists, and also painters. But there are accounts of himself in Paris with Eliot talking over the theory of *The Waste Land.* He's been there; he's an original witness. And down in Savannah, he showed me a whole packing case of correspondence between himself and Eliot, in which there are some very dirty poems of Eliot's which have never been published. They're very funny, too. Anyway, he's been in the forefront and the thick middle of the modern literary movement. He's been around for a long time. He was, as I say, very precocious as a young writer and he's been a very respectable figure, although somewhat neglected, for the last twenty to twenty-five years.

Whatever Conrad Aiken had to say, and the ways he's had to say it, are already said now. He says he won't write any more. And why should he? He's already written more than any poet I know has ever written, except Edwin Arlington Robinson, at least in my time. Also, let me add that he is the best literary critic, he and John Peale Bishop, that I have ever read. This is now out in paperback. It was originally called *A Reviewer's ABC's;* it's now called *Collected Criticism,* and I've stolen more from that in my own reviewing and criticism than from anybody else. And I suppose that's a tribute to him. I hope it is. But he's good. And, if you're interested in Aiken, there are three essays in the *Reviewer's ABC's* where Aiken reviews himself and assesses his own work. And nobody could be more objective. He knows what's wrong. He knows why he's not getting the most out of his talent. But he can't do anything about it. He's extraordinarily honest, and very, very well reasoned. If you had seen Aiken's review of Aiken, and if they were reviewing somebody other than Aiken, you would say, "This is eminently fair." He's also an extraordinary short-story writer and novelist. But the short stories I recommended very, very highly. They're out in a very good paperback edition, and there's a one-volume edition of all the novels, too, with an excellent, almost impenetrable introduction by R. P. Blackmur, called *Collected Novels of Conrad Aiken*. They may be a little too long for you and too introspective. I don't think there's anything he did in the novels that he didn't do better in *Ushant*, this autobiography which is a kind of autobiographical novel. But the short stories are quite different from that.

John Peale Bishop is another second-rate poet of a different kind, and, I think, of a more important order than Conrad Aiken. It's not that he's more intelligent, but he is the second of the two best literary critics I have read. He was the contemporary of F. Scott Fitzgerald at Princeton, and Fitzgerald and Bishop and Edmund Wilson formed a kind of triumvirate there of literary-minded boys before they went their separate ways for a while and then into the service in World War I. Wilson went on to become an editor and very distinguished literary critic of the *New Republic* and later the *New Yorker*, and he's now the last survivor of that bunch. Fitzgerald died, as we know, in 1940 at the age of forty-four. Bishop died a little after that. He was fifty-two. He had high blood pressure and a bad heart, and he died prematurely.

The first thing you notice about Bishop's work was characterized by somebody who reviewed him in the 1930s and who said that John Peale Bishop wears the best secondhand suit of clothes in American poetry. He lacks originality. He's derivative, terribly derivative. But he uses his derivations from Pound and Eliot with very great skill. John Peale Bishop not only could write almost as good Yeats poems as Yeats, which of course, could never have been written without the example of Yeats, but he could write almost as good Pound poems, almost as good Eliot poems, and almost as good European poems. He knew nine or ten languages, and he's one of the really good translators around. And yet, because of this derivative quality, you won't find very many critics who'll say of John Peale Bishop that he's a man of the caliber of William Carlos Williams or Wallace Stevens, or even of Aiken. Although I myself think—despite all his secondary qualities, or qualities of being a secondary artist—that he is ultimately a more memorable poet than Aiken. Let me give you four lines of Bishop that I know from memory. This is from an unnamed quatrain [poem unidentified]. That's an awful lot said about sex, about men and women and their relationship, in four lines.

Bishop was good at that. He was good at anything and everything that concerned verse forms. Now, if you want to know John Peale Bishop and read him, there's a very, very handsome double edition put out by Scribners. One is *The Collected Poems,* edited by Allen Tate, and the other *The Collected Essays,* edited by Edmund Wilson, his old friend, along with Fitzgerald, at Princeton. And I recommend these to you as being examples in the 1920s of a remarkable talent that never really found its voice because it was so good at using the effects of other voices. John Peale Bishop had a linguistic ability in understanding different poets in different languages far beyond Ezra Pound. But he did not have the intuitive ability to get to the guts of the other poetry and dig it out and use what he could for his own poetry. John Peale Bishop went along and did imitations. He did not have the transforming power as a translator that Pound did. And yet he's a wonderful translator, and far more accurate, as far as fidelity to the original text, than Pound. He just didn't have Pound's talent. But the trouble with Pound was the genius, whereas Bishop was merely a highly talented and conscientious and intelligent man. And that's where he came out.

Same with his criticism. To get cogent, closely reasoned, intelligent, perceptive essays on literary subjects, especially on poetry, you can't do better than read Bishop, or read Aiken's criticism. Compared to Bishop, with his urbanity and intelligence and ability to reason about things, Pound is nothing but a bumbling bumpkin. But yet Pound's criticism has a quality of galvanizing you and sending you back to the text in a way that Bishop's does not. The comparison between Bishop and Pound is exactly the same as that between [Honoré de] Balzac and [Gustave] Flaubert. I'm not sure of the dates, but some writer before Flaubert berated Balzac for not paying enough attention to the nuance, the right word. And Balzac turned on him impatiently and said, "My dear sir, in writing or in the novel, the important thing is not the nuance of infinite subtlety; the important thing is to possess a quality that carries all before it." I myself am of the latter opinion. Now, it could be the other way. This is not to say that one way or the other is better. In some cases force will work out over intelligence or capacity to reason, and in other cases it will work the other way. In John Peale Bishop's case, his intelligence and devotion to literature and exquisite taste were not quite enough. They were merely all he had. He never could have been a writer any other way. And it seems maybe unforgiving of me to suggest that he could have been better than he was. He was very good, and a few of his things will be around for a very, very long time. There's not very much that has been written on Bishop, but I recommend as a beginning those two volumes. Everything that you'd ever want to read of John Peale Bishop is in these two, except for two notable exceptions. One of these is his only novel, which may very well be the case as with Aiken—his one work that is going to be around for a long time. It's called *Act of Darkness*. Bishop was a border southerner. He came from Charleston, West Virginia. That's Charles Town, not Charleston. It's almost on the Virginia border. But his affiliations and sympathies were essentially southern. He wrote the best essay on the South, in connection with Ransom, Davidson, and the others, and I want to read two paragraphs of his essay on the South and tradition. I have never read anything that seemed to me to be as eloquent and as easygoing and as informed and as original as this on that subject [passage unidentified].

Now, again, you want to take issue with that. And yet, for someone as intelligent and persuasive and well-read as Bishop, you can always learn a great deal from him, even if you don't agree with him. I always come away from a Bishop essay thinking to myself, "Almost, I am persuaded." It's a great big book. You'll have a lot more education than you do now if you'll assimilate it.

I wanted to close out with the elegy on Fitzgerald. Bishop, who was looked on as the great poetic life of that generation, at least of the Princeton boys, now sees Scott Fitzgerald, a younger man, advance far beyond Bishop, who was a retiring, reclusive kind of person, someone who never tried to advance his own literary powers, who had nothing but gratitude to see Fitzgerald come out into the limelight. They were in Paris together. Hemingway was someone who always submitted his work to Bishop, and Bishop had an incalculable influence on it. Bishop used to take on his friends' work, and was very interested in that—in Fitzgerald's, in Hemingway's, in Edmund Wilson's. All the writers of that time did a lot for other writers. But none of them took much cognizance of *his* work. Most of them hadn't even read it. They thought of Bishop as some kind of gifted dilettante. He always dressed as a dandy. He was very much of an esthete, but a good esthete, a real one. Americans tend to think of all esthetes as being phony, but Bishop was real. He was really an elitist, and he would give them this fantastic criticism, and they all put it into effect, and Hemingway's work was born, and Fitzgerald's work was born.

Somebody said about Bishop and his own creative work, "Well, as a writer, John never seems to get on with it. He's like a man lying in a warm bath who hears the phone ring downstairs." Would you go? Anyway, he did write two books of remarkable poetry, that, even in their derivative way, are remarkable in a very skillful, dandified way—a very skillful, passionate work, and the emphasis on sex is surprising. You'd kind of expect esthetes to stay away from that subject. But some of the best sexual poems are by him. But let me read the elegy to Fitzgerald. This is something that really moves me, and you don't get many echoes from these other people that you're always getting in Bishop's work. You don't get that from this poem at all. He's got his skill going in it. It doesn't sound like Eliot, Pound, so much as it sounds like something that might have come to be if Bishop had survived a little longer. He might have found his voice belatedly and become the great poet that all his gifts argued that he should become. This is called "The Hours," and it's prefaced by a quotation from Fitzgerald: "In the real dark night of the soul it is always three o'clock in the morning."

THE HOURS

In the real dark night of the soul it is always
three o'clock in the morning.

—*F. Scott Fitzgerald*

I

All day, knowing you dead,
I have sat in this long-windowed room,
Looking upon the sea and, dismayed
By mortal sadness, though without thought to resume
Those hours which you and I have known—
Hours when youth like an insurgent sun
Showered ambition on an aimless air,
Hours foreboding disillusion,
Hours which now there is none to share.
Since you are dead, I leave them all alone.

II

A day like any day. Though any day now
We expect death. The sky is overcast,
And shuddering cold as snow the shoreward blast.
And in the marsh, like a sea astray, now
Waters brim. This is the moment when the sea
Being most full of motion seems motionless.
Land and sea are merged. The marsh is gone.
And my distress
Is at the flood. All but the dunes are drowned.
And brimming with memory I have found
All hours we ever knew, but have not found
The key. I cannot find the lost key
To the silver closet you as a wild child hid.

III

I think of all you did
And all you might have done, before undone
By death, but for the undoing of despair.
No promise such as yours when like the spring
You came, colors of jonquils in your hair,
Inspired as the wind, when the woods are bare
And every silence is about to sing.

None had such promise then, and none
Your scapegrace wit or your disarming grace;
For you were bold as was Danaë's son,
Conceived like Perseus in a dream of gold.
And there was none when you were young, not one,
So prompt in the reflecting shield to trace
The glittering aspect of a Gorgon age.

Despair no love, no fortune could assuage . . .
Was it a fault in your disastrous blood
That beat from no fortunate god,
The failure of all passion in mid-course?
You shrank from nothing as from solitude,
Lacking the still assurance, and pursued
Beyond the sad excitement by remorse.

Was it that having shaped you stare upon
The severed head of time, upheld and blind,
Upheld by the stained hair,
And seen the blood upon that sightless stare,
You looked and were made one
With the strained horror of those sightless eyes?
You looked, and were not turned to stone.

IV

You have outlasted the nocturnal terror,
The head hanging in the hanging mirror,
The hour haunted by a harrowing face.
Now you are drunk at last. And that disgrace
You sought in oblivious dives you have
At last, in the dissolution of the grave.

V

I have lived with you the hour of your humiliation.
I have seen you turn upon the others in the night
And of sad self-loathing
Concealing nothing
Heard you cry: I am lost. But you are lower!
And you had that right.
The damned do not so own their damnation.

I have lived with you some hours of the night,
The late hour
When the lights lower,
The later hour
When the lights go out,

When the dissipation of the night is past,
Hour of the outcast and the outworn whore,
That is past three and not yet four—
When the old blackmailer waits beyond the door
And from the gutter with unpitying hands
Demands the same sad guiltiness as before,
The hour of utter destitution
When the soul knows the horror of its loss
And knows the world too poor

For restitution,
                    Past three o'clock
And not yet four—
                    When not pity, pride,
Or being brave,
Fortune, friendship, forgetfulness of drudgery
Or of drug avails, for all has been tried,
And nothing avails to save
The soul from recognition of its night.

The hour of death is always four o'clock.
It is always four o'clock in the grave.

VI

Having heard the bare word that you had died,
All day I have lingered in this lofty room,
Locked in the light of sea and cloud,
And thought, at cost of sea-hours, to illume
The hours that you and I have known,
Hours death does not condemn, nor love condone.

And I have seen the sea-light set the tide
In salt succession toward the sullen shore
And while the waves lost on the losing sand
Seen shores receding and the sands succumb.

The waste retreats; glimmering shores retrieve
Unproportioned plunges; the dunes restore
Drowned confines to the disputed kingdom—
Desolate mastery, since the dark has come.

The dark has come. I cannot pluck you bays,
Though here the bay grows wild. For fugitive
As surpassed fame the leaves this sea-wind frays.
Why should I promise what I cannot give?

I cannot animate with breath
Syllables in the open mouth of death.
Dark, dark. The shore here has a habit of light.
O dark! I leave you to oblivious night!

EDWIN MUIR

There's a particular viewpoint of people who live on islands in that they seem, at least some of them, to be in tune with the ecological balance. I'm talking about somebody who has a farm in the Orkneys, up north of Scotland. There seems to be a special kind of human psychology that attaches itself to islands. It's not only this Baudelairian angelism, but that things take on this intensity of smallness, so that you deal with more than you would if you lived on the mainland. That is the hour when the tides come in on an island. And the fact that there's a prevailing wind from such and such a place is important. Now again, you may or may not like that kind of situation, the island psychology. The man we want to talk a little bit about today is an islander from the Orkneys. Have you ever been up to the north of Scotland, to the Orkney Islands? I tell you, you should never miss that. They don't have any trees on them; the wind is always passing. They have these little communities and farms. Now, one of the things that you notice about islands if you live on them for any length of time is that any perspective takes on a kind of magical significance. If you see a man and woman walking along the shore, this has infinite importance, as it's not going to have if you see a man and a woman walking down the street somewhere else. It's going to have a completely different kind of significance. That's one of the things that islands do to you, is to make you start thinking that way.

On islands, especially islands like the Orkneys, there is this continual sense of the elementals, the sea, the wind, a man and a woman alone on the beach, farming animals, a basic kind of pastoral existence that goes back five, six, seven centuries. This is the kind of atmosphere that Edwin Muir came from. His father came from one of the northern islands of the Orkneys. He settled with his mother on one of the central Orkney Islands and attempted to farm. All the time Edwin was growing up, he was a farm boy on the island. There's a difference in being a farm boy on the Orkney Islands and being a farm boy on the rice fields of Arkansas. Now, in brief what happened, and I bring it up, first of all, because it's the subject of one of the most fascinating and horrifying autobiographies that has been written in the twentieth century, which is Muir's own autobiography, called in his characteristically modest fashion, *An Autobiography*. What you get here is a large, poor, rural family, steeped in the traditions of the old Scottish ballads, which are in pure state in the Orkneys as they are not pure in the Highlands of Scotland. What you get is a large, relatively impecunious offshore Scottish family that keeps falling on hard times and falls under the sway of an extremely unscrupulous, inhuman, or antihuman, landlord so that the father eventually is forced off the land. Again you get the parallel here with a Tennessee, or South Carolina, or North Carolina, or Georgia farmer who, for some reason or other, because of financial reverses, leaves the land and goes to the city, in order to make the conversion from farming to working in industry.

Within one year the father is dead, the mother is dead, the two oldest boys are dead, one of the sisters is in a madhouse, and Edwin himself, who is second to the youngest, is so completely demoralized that it's doubted he'll ever regain his senses again. This is that basic conflict between farming and the industrial slum. It could hardly be shown more dramatically than by Edwin and his family moving from the offshore community into the most hideous kind of industrial slum, especially English. American industrial slums are bad enough, but they cannot compare to the English and the Scottish. So here was this boy, a young boy: he's sick a lot. At this stage of life, he simply cannot understand what the change has been and why it has been this way. What happens to him is that his psychological condition is so aggravated that he teeters on the edge of madness for a number of years, and begins slowly to come back because he is essentially a withdrawn kid and he finds his salvation in books and in the life of the imagination. He's a difficult, withdrawn, modest kind of a gentle soul. You think about Edwin Muir's sufferings in Glasgow, and you are automatically reminded of Eliot's great line, "The vision of some infinitely gentle, infinitely suffering thing." That's the way he was. He was an infinitely gentle, infinitely intelligent, sickly, but infinitely "suffering thing." He begins to get interested in politics, he begins to get interested in literature, but he's so self-effacing that he never thinks he could possibly be a poet himself.

All he wants to do is read Tennyson, write papers on Tennyson, get them published in *The New Age* or some of the important magazines. No luck. He gets older and older. He gets to be thirty-five years old. He falls in with another extremely withdrawn, scholarly, self-effacing, shy person named Willa Anderson. They marry. It's one of the most beautiful love stories in all literature. They got jobs with the government. They learned German together. They sat up by lamplight and taught each other German words. Know what the result of that is? [Franz] Kafka. They are the incomparable translators of Kafka. Nobody in the English-speaking world would know anything about Kafka if it had not been for Edwin and Willa Muir. They discovered him. The British consulate sent them over to Central Europe; they discovered him—not him but his works; they translated him, and anything you see about Kafka has been made possible by Edwin Muir and his wife.

He's shyly tried to write poetry from the age of thirty-five. He has no precedent; he doesn't know how to do it. He admires it, but he doesn't understand how it's done. So he says, "I can't be a modernist; I'll just have to write in the old traditional ballad form from the Orkneys and from my dreams and my psychoanalysis." He went through a terrible, harrowing, psychoanalytical period. But out of this, what gradually evolved was a kind of philosophy of poetry. He believed, or came to believe, that a person's life is lived on two planes: the actual and what he called the fabulous. He thought that one part of any human being was a reenactment of one of the ancient myths. Now, this may seem a little cracked, but don't knock it if you ain't tried it. The great thing about Edwin Muir's work as it gradually, slowly, and agonizingly evolved was his extraordinary ability to project himself into one of the ancient myths: into Odysseus, into the Trojan War, and last of all, into the Christian myth. He also began to develop during this time.

There's not an awful lot of Edwin Muir, only ninety to a hundred poems, a small book. What happens as a result of this is that he gets his time theories. He believes that time, for example, is not only stoppable at any single given moment, especially an important moment in history, say, like the time when the angel effects the annunciation to Mary. This is essentially a timeless incident. He not only believes that time stops at this particular moment, but he believes that it is also capable of going backwards, which is something that I have never seen a poet do. There's a remarkable poem of Muir's where Muir has the Crucifixion happen backwards. We'll just read it and see what he does. But his whole frame of reference is in this reenactment of the ancient myths and reinterpretation of the ancient myths as though no one had ever given them any thought before; as though Homer had never written the *Iliad;* the fall of Troy had never happened. It comes down to Edwin Muir from the Orkney Islands to tell you the true Trojan War, what it was really like at the Crucifixion.

But what you see in Muir's work, finally, is that he developed, out of his psychoanalytical troubles, out of his hideous changeover during his childhood from the Orkneys to Glasgow, his childhood on the Orkneys as his greatest myth of all. His greatest poems come from this. That is, of the expulsion from Eden. When Muir's family had to leave the Orkneys and go to industrial Glasgow, Edwin the young boy left a condition that he would try the rest of his life to get back to, and that would be transmuted, sublimated, into imagery that had to do with the Christian myth. Because Edwin Muir was never able to get back to the Orkneys, he had an extraordinary insight into the expulsion from Eden. And he would be the first to point this out: that because of our deep, unconscious, psychological drive, we, each in his own measure, reenact the ancient myths that we were intended to reenact. Let's read the one about the backwards Crucifixion. Let me warm you up on one. You remember the myth of Prometheus, the guy who stole fire from the gods and gave it to man, and they chained him to a rock and a buzzard fed on his liver. So here again is one of the extraordinary things that Muir does: he imagines that Prometheus is finally released, and Prometheus is, of course, a giant. It's called "The Grave of Prometheus."

THE GRAVE OF PROMETHEUS

No one comes here now, neither god nor man.
For long the animals have kept away,
Scared by immortal cries and the scream of vultures;
Now by this silence. The heavenly thief who stole
Heaven's dangerous treasure turned to common earth
When that great company forsook Olympus.
The fire was out, and he became his barrow.
Ten yards long there he lay outstretched, and grass
Grew over him: all else in a breath forgotten.
Yet there you still may see a tongue of stone,
Shaped like a calloused hand where no hand should be,
Extended from the sward as if for alms,
Its palm all licked and blackened as with fire.
A mineral change made cool his fiery bed,
And made his burning body a quiet mound,
And his great face a vacant ring of daisies.

. . . and "Suburban Dream":

SUBURBAN DREAM

Walking the suburbs in the afternoon
In summer when the idle doors stand open
  And the air flows through the rooms
  Fanning the curtain hems,

You wander through a cool elysium
Of women, schoolgirls, children, garden talks,
  With a schoolboy here and there
  Conning his history book.

The men are all away in offices,
Committee-rooms, laboratories, banks,
    Or pushing cotton goods
    In Wick or Ilfracombe.

The massed unanimous absence liberates
The light keys of the piano and sets free
    Chopin and everlasting youth,
    Now, with the masters gone.

And all things turn to images of peace,
The boy curled over his book, the young girl poised
    On the path as if beguiled
    By the silence of a wood.

It is a child's dream of a grown-up world.
But soon the brazen evening clocks will bring
    The tramp of feet and brisk
    Fanfare of motor horns
    And the masters come.

The thing you like about Muir: he's got a little different slant on things than you usually find. Let's do this one, which is one of his really great ones, about the seven days of creation, when animals were made, and when human beings were made. Muir writes in short, strict forms. Not lush; not Tennysonian; not Victorian; but short, curt, very strict form, where every statement he makes means something that you've got to grapple with. It's tough but uncompromising, and the integrity is awesome. This is just called "The Animals."

THE ANIMALS

They do not live in the world,
Are not in time and space.
From birth to death hurled
No word do they have, not one
To plant a foot upon,
Were never in any place.

For with names the world was called
Out of the empty air,
With names was built and walled,
Line and circle and square,
Dust and emerald;
Snatched from deceiving death
By the articulate breath.

> But these have never trod
> Twice the familiar track,
> Never never turned back
> Into the memoried day.
> All is new and near
> In the unchanging Here
> Of the fifth great day of God,
> That shall remain the same,
> Never shall pass away.
>
> On the sixth day we came.

It was all timeless, until men came and invented time, but for the animals, it is an eternal heaven, an eternal present.

This is the one about the Crucifixion going backwards. Now, when Muir took on a myth, it was not just a literary exercise. He believed sincerely that men's lives work on two levels, on the actual and on the fabulous, and that we reenact myths. But let me read "Telemachos Remembers" before we get into this one. You remember the scene in the *Odyssey* where Odysseus has been gone fighting the Trojan war for ten years. His castle in Ithaca throngs up with suitors, who are trying to make it with his wife. And she weaves, and she says that when she finishes weaving, she'll make a choice. So she weaves during the day and unravels at night. Now, Muir has imagined that dilemma in what seems to me to be a very remarkable way because what he does is to show the nature of love as being partially making and partially unmaking. It's a beautiful tapestry: warriors, horses, who remain perpetually only half made: a foot here, an arm there, a horse's eye. And Telemachos remembers that as a little boy he didn't understand what was going on.

Telemachos Remembers

> Twenty years, every day,
> The figures in the web she wove
> Came and stood and went away.
> Her fingers in their pitiless play
> Beat downward as the shuttle drove.
>
> Slowly, slowly did they come,
> With horse and chariot, spear and bow,
> Half-finished heroes sad and mum,
> Came slowly to the shuttle's hum.
> Time itself was not so slow.
>
> And what at last was there to see?
> A horse's head, a trunkless man,

Mere odds and ends about to be,
And the thin line of augury
Where through the web the shuttle ran.

How could she bear the mounting load,
Dare once again her ghosts to rouse?
Far away Odysseus trod
The treadmill of the turning road
That did not bring him to his house.

The weary loom, the weary loom,
The task grown sick from morn to night,
From year to year. The treadle's boom
Made a low thunder in the room.
The woven phantoms mazed her sight.

If she had pushed it to the end,
Followed the shuttle's cunning song
So far she had no thought to rend
In time the web from end to end,
She would have worked a matchless wrong.

Instead, that jumble of heads and spears,
Forlorn scraps of her treasure trove.
I wet them with my childish tears
Not knowing she wove into her fears
Pride and fidelity and love.

This is called "The Transfiguration," a poem about what things could really be like in heaven. It's just a momentary vision of what would happen. We see it, we hold it for a second, and then it's gone. We don't know where it's gone, or how we saw it.

THE TRANSFIGURATION

So from the ground we felt that virtue branch
Through all our veins till we were whole, our wrists
As fresh and pure as water from a well,
Our hands made new to handle holy things,
The source of all our seeing rinsed and cleansed
Till earth and light and water entering there
Gave back to us the clear unfallen world.
We would have thrown our clothes away for lightness,
But that even they, though sour and travel stained,
Seemed, like our flesh, made of immortal substance,
And the soiled flax and wool lay light upon us
Like friendly wonders, flower and flock entwined

As in a morning field. Was it a vision?
Or did we see that day the unseeable
One glory of the everlasting world
Perpetually at work, though never seen
Since Eden locked the gate that's everywhere
And nowhere? Was the change in us alone,
And the enormous earth still left forlorn,
An exile or a prisoner? Yet the world
We saw that day made this unreal, for all
Was in its place. The painted animals
Assembled there in gentle congregations,
Or sought apart their leafy oratories,

Or walked in peace, the wild and tame together,
As if, also for them, the day had come.
The Shepherds' hovels shone clean at the heart
As on the starting-day. The refuse heaps
Were grained with that fine dust that made the world;
For he had said, 'To the pure all things are pure.'
And when we went into the town, he with us,
The lurkers under doorways, murderers,
With rags tied round their feet for silence, came
Out of themselves to us and were with us,
And those who hide within the labyrinth
Of their own loneliness and greatness came,
And those tangled in their own devices,
The silent and the garrulous liars, all
Stepped out of their dungeons and were free.
Reality or vision, this we have seen.
If it had lasted but another moment
It might have held for ever! But the world
Rolled back into its place, and we are here,
And all that radiant kingdom lies forlorn,
As if it had never stirred; no human voice
Is heard among its meadows, but it speaks
To itself alone, alone it flowers and shines
And blossoms for itself while time runs on.

But he will come again, it's said, though not
Unwanted and unsummoned; for all things,
Beasts of the field, and woods, and rocks, and seas,
And all mankind from end to end of the earth
Will call him with one voice. In our own time,
Some say, or at a time when time is ripe.

Then he will come, Christ the uncrucified,
Christ the discrucified, his death undone,
His agony unmade, his cross dismantled—
Glad to be so—and the tormented wood
Will cure its hurt and grow into a tree
In a green springing corner of young Eden,
And Judas damned take his long journey backward
From darkness into light and be a child
Beside his mother's knee, and the betrayal
Be quite undone and never more be done.

The last one is an atomic bomb poem. Muir himself would have said, I'm sure, would have said, "I was taken out of Eden when I was twelve or thirteen years old. I never got back to the Orkneys where, as an imaginative child, I knew an animal like a horse was a godlike presence. He wasn't just an animal. He was something fabulous." He would likely say that this poem, called "Horses," is probably a conjunction of reading the newspapers about the atomic bomb and what is likely to happen to the human race. This is about that day, and the people are huddling together, and there is the appearance of horses.

HORSES

Those lumbering horses in the steady plough,
On the bare field—I wonder why, just now,
They seemed terrible, so wild and strange,
Like magic power on the stony grange.

Perhaps some childish hour has come again,
When I watched fearful, through the blackening rain,
Their hooves like pistons in an ancient mill
Move up and down, yet seem as standing still.

Their conquering hooves which trod the stubble down
Were ritual that turned the field to brown,
And their great hulks were seraphim of gold,
Or mute ecstatic monsters on the mould.

And oh the rapture, when, one furrow done,
They marched broad-breasted to the sinking sun!
The light flowed off their bossy sides in flakes;
The furrows rolled behind like struggling snakes.

But when at dusk with steaming nostrils home
They came, they seemed gigantic in the gloam,
And warm and glowing with mysterious fire
That lit their smouldering bodies in the mire.

The poet in the early 1990s. *Courtesy of University Publications, University of South Carolina*

Their eyes as brilliant and as wide as night
Gleamed with a cruel apocalyptic light.
Their manes the leaping ire of the wind
Lifted with rage invisible and blind.

Ah, now it fades! it fades! and I must pine
Again for that dread country crystalline,
Where the blank field and the still-standing tree
Were bright and fearful presences to me.

Every time I read that poem I love it. There are some things I would change, but I'm glad I didn't have a chance.

Let me give you the books in case you're interested in Edwin Muir. Oxford University Press is his publisher. Edwin Muir, *Collected Poems.* The Charles Eliot Norton Lectures at Harvard that he did just before he died, called *The Estate of Poetry.* Highly recommended. There's a fine little edition that T. S. Eliot did, called *Selected Poems,* that Faber and Faber, the English publisher, put out. Very good biographical things. First of all Edwin Muir's own autobiography, one of the greatest of the twentieth century, and one of the most scary and horrible, and also the most uplifting. There are a couple of very good critical books by Edwin Muir, too. One of these is *The Structure of the Novel,* which is very short, very readable, and very much to the point. The other is a kind of general survey of twentieth-century literature in English called *The Present Age.* There's been a good deal of comment on Muir, but nobody knows quite what to make of him. He's a homemade visionary. But he's a visionary compounded out of the offshore community of the Orkney Islands, out of his hideous family breakup, out of this clash between agrarianism and the worst kind of industrialism, in this case represented by Glasgow, and his wanderings over Europe as a functionary of the British government. He was in Prague, for example, and he saw the best things in Europe go under the onslaught of Hitler's totalitarianism. Again, that brought on a psychoanalytical condition that drove Muir back into the psychiatric hospital: oversensitive, very weak physically, very imaginative, very dedicated, completely a creature of integrity. At the end of his life, he sailed into his rest. He was made the warden, that is, the boss man, of a Scottish workingman's college, up in the north of Scotland. And there, he fulfilled his functions dutifully, as he would do; he was the most honest of men, and spent the last two years of his life writing a few poems, taking care of a technical school. There's not an awful lot of him, but he's a remarkable writer. He seems sometimes kind of stiff and old-timey, but even if you talk in the old-timey idiom, if you're saying such remarkable things as he is, you surely do merit being paid attention to. So, I'll leave you with that.

Philip Larkin

So now, as I promised, we can have a brief look at Philip Larkin, who is a poet kind of incomprehensible to Americans. He is one of these poets who is beloved by intellectuals of the British welfare state. His vision is so British and so confined to England that he seems to have almost nothing to say to anybody outside of England. This is why he is so greatly beloved in England and so difficult for an American to comprehend. Philip Larkin is a very good writer, and he represents, as near as I can tell, the reaction to romanticism in England. He represents the reaction against the kind that we were talking about in connection with T. E. Hulme the other day. He's the guy who's against reading too much stuff. He'd say, kind of like Amis, who's a good friend of his, who says, "All right, we all read Yeats and D. H. Lawrence, and we're trying to be superhuman. I submit that we're not superhuman. We're ordinary fellows; our pleasures are ordinary and we can speak of them with a certain elegance, but they are ordinary. We're ordinary men, living in an orderly society. We're not Blake, we're not Yeats, we're not Michelangelo; so let's face it, and let's get down and write the kind of practical stuff that means something, that's truthful, that people can understand and feel a rapport with. For Chrissake, let's get off all this superhuman business. We don't need it. We've had too much of that already." Philip Larkin is the great spokesman of that viewpoint.

He comes from Coventry, and when he rides on a train, he'll just be riding in a day coach, and he looks out and he'll see a kind of a nondescript English town, and he'll see the sign on the station, and he'll say, "Well, Coventry, I'll be damned. I was born here." It's that attitude. And he's very good. First of all, the books, if you want to read Larkin. The first is called *The North Ship*. It's not bad. But the slender volume that made Larkin's reputation is called *The Less Deceived*. These are all issued by St. Martin's Press, which is a subsidiary of Macmillan. And then there's the one about going through Coventry on the train and all the middle-class pleasures he describes, *The Whitsun Weddings*. There's also a novel, not bad either, called *A Girl in Winter*. Let's read the one called "Deceptions," which is quite a good example of his. All the girls were taken advantage of by rich or even midly well-to-do gentlemen, drugged, gotten drunk, compromised. And you must reflect that being compromised as a girl 115 years ago was a lot worse than being compromised as a girl now. For example, there was the concept then of being "ruined." That's what this poem is about.

DECEPTIONS

"Of course I was drugged, and so heavily I did not regain my consciousness till the next morning. I was horrified to discover that I had been ruined, and for some days I was inconsolable, and cried like a child to be killed or sent back to my aunt."
—Mayhew, London Labour and the London Poor.

Even so distant, I can taste the grief,
Bitter and sharp with stalks, he made you gulp.
The sun's occasional print, the brisk brief
Worry of wheels along the street outside
Where bridal London bows the other way,
And light, unanswerable and tall and wide,
Forbids the scar to heal, and drives
Shame out of hiding. All the unhurried day
Your mind lay open like a drawer of knives.

Slums, years, have buried you. I would not dare
Console you if I could. What can be said,
Except that suffering is exact, but where
Desire takes charge, readings will grow erratic?
For you would hardly care
That you were less deceived, out on that bed,
Than he was, stumbling up the breathless stair
To burst into fulfillment's desolate attic.

She was betrayed; she was deceived; but she was less deceived than he was. To be the person who had to be reduced to doing something like this, he's the one that the judgment is on. That's a Larkin poem, a quiet poem. It's nice. One of the things that anthologies don't usually get into about Larkin is that he has humor. There's one about old photographs where you look at your girl's pictures with other fellows. This is called "Lines on a Young Lady's Photograph Album."

LINES ON A YOUNG LADY'S PHOTOGRAPH ALBUM

At last you yielded up the album, which,
Once open, sent me distracted. All your ages
Matt and glossy on the thick black pages!

Too much confectionary, too rich:
I choke on such nutritious images.

My swivel eye hungers from pose to pose—
In pigtails, clutching a reluctant cat;
Or furred yourself, a sweet girl-graduate;
Or lifting a heavy-headed rose
Beneath a trellis, or in a trilby hat

(Faintly disturbing, that, in several ways)—
From every side you strike at my control,
Not least through these disquieting chaps who loll
At ease about your earlier days:
Not quite your class, I'd say, dear, on the whole.

But o, photography! As no art is,
Faithful and disappointing! that records
Dull days as dull, and hold-it smiles as frauds,
And will not censor blemishes
Like washing-lines, and Hall's-Distemper boards,

But shows the cat as disinclined, and shades
A chin as doubled when it is, what grace
Your candor thus confers upon her face!
How overwhelmingly persuades
That this is a real girl in a real place,

In every sense empirically true!
Or is it just *the past?* Those flowers, that gate,
These misty parks and motors, lacerate
Simply by being over; you
Contract my heart by looking out of date.

Yes, true; but in the end, surely, we cry
Not only at exclusion, but because
It leaves us free to cry. We know *what was*
Won't call on us to justify
Our grief, however hard we yowl across

The gap from eye to page. So I am left
To mourn (without a chance of consequence)
You, balanced on a bike against a fence;
To wonder if you'd spot the theft
Of this one of you bathing; to condense,

In short, a past that no one now can share,
No matter whose your future; calm and dry,

Philip Larkin

It holds you like a heaven, and you lie
Unvariably lovely there,
Smaller and clearer as the years go by.

Archibald MacLeish

Archibald MacLeish came from a midwestern family, and published his first book in 1915, was in World War I, and came back to a very distinguished career as a poet. He and Robinson Jeffers were thought to be the rising American poets in the 1920s, aside from people like Pound and Eliot who were expatriates. MacLeish then began to dabble in politics in an odd way, and during the latter part of Roosevelt's administration was undersecretary of state, which is an exalted position for a lyric poet. There were lots of parodies of MacLeish, and a good deal of questioning of his motives. Edmund Wilson had a famous parody of MacLeish which showed him as an enterprising, wide-eyed young fellow, now middle-aged, who was just trying to figure out a way to make it and get on in the world, name drop, and become the acquaintance of the rich and famous. And I'm afraid there is a certain amount of that about MacLeish. He has lent his name to some very dubious enterprises. If you see a Hallmark spectacular on television about the meaning of America, and if you look for the credit of the writer, it's quite likely Archibald MacLeish. He has a slender but very genuine lyric talent, but he also has, or has had, a right-wing rhetorical stance, which makes him less and less popular. I don't know exactly what to think about MacLeish.

Still, I go back and read some of the early poems. There's a very good *Collected Poems.* But let me tell you the worst thing that MacLeish did. He'll never live this down if he lives to be two hundred. During World War II he attacked what was the main creative tradition of American letters—that is, Hemingway, Faulkner, Eliot, Pound, Aiken. He attacked them and he invented a name for them, for these people who were singers of doom and were getting in the way of the war effort. They were not helping with their writing to win the war. He called them "The Irresponsibles." But the trouble was that the Irresponsibles were all more talented than MacLeish, no matter what form of doom they sang, and they turned on him. Everybody who was interested in the free expression of the human imagination turned on MacLeish, who wanted to turn literature and the talents of the best writers of his time into the channels of propaganda to win the war. None of them did. His stuff was pathetic, about the young dead soldiers, and so on. It's nothing like the kind of thing that MacLeish *can* write. That's all the bad side, and if you investigate Archibald MacLeish, you're going to run up against a lot of this somewhere or other along the line, so you might as well be prepared for it. There is this stigma of propagandistic poetry. There is this stigma of calling down his betters for not being nationalistic enough in a time of crisis. There are his connections with New Deal politics. There is all that that will essentially cloud the issue. Now, this is not anybody's fault but MacLeish's. It seems to me, from what little I know of him personally, that he acted honorably in all these things, according to his beliefs at the time; nevertheless, as a poet, he has done nothing but suffer from all these public stances that he has taken, one after the other.

So what has MacLeish got going for him? He has got an exquisite, small, lyric talent, which is inimitable, which is immediately recognizable. I would say, from my own reading of MacLeish's work, that MacLeish writes the kind of poetry that Hemingway would have written if Hemingway had been able to write good poetry. Because there's that sinewy, spare, very masculine kind of idiom, that masculine kind of sound. And the sound is essentially that of nostalgia and loss. MacLeish is one of the few Americans, or poets in any language, that I would truly characterize as haunting. He is hard to shake off. He really has an ear. And he has a quality of infinite loss, of longing, this kind of masculine longing. Once you encounter it, you acknowledge him as a real poet. You forget the politics: Archibald MacLeish, with all these honors, his librarianship of Congress. Not poetry consultant, but the librarian of Congress, which is an enormously prestigious position, and if you go to the Library of Congress, you will see, chiseled out in solid marble, the name Archibald MacLeish. And he was a fine librarian. The librarian who was there when I was, L. Quincey Mumford, said that MacLeish set the standard in modern times for librarians. So there's no question that he's a man of enormous ability. And I myself, if I leave you with any one idea today, it's that no matter the references to MacLeish's political views and stances, you don't let that keep you away from the poems because the poems are good.

MacLeish is essentially a lyric poet, and it is another irony in his career that all his honors, the Pulitzer Prize, and god knows what else, came to him as the result of a long poem about the conquest of Mexico, called "Conquistadors," which came out in the 1930s. It's a fantastic technical tour de force. It's a long, long poem in something like twenty-eight books about the conquest of Mexico, and it's written in terza rima. You know what that is? To be very brief, it's a three-line stanza form in which the first and the third lines rhyme and the middle line of that rhymes with the first of the next three, and so on. *The Divine Comedy* is written in this form. But what is the difference in doing what Dante did and in what MacLeish did—what is the essential difficulty? Italian is a rhyme-rich language and English is a rhyme-poor language. So it's far, far more difficult for MacLeish to do what he did than for Dante to do what he did. It's a real tour de force of English prosody and stanzaic construction. And it's a very powerful poem of the conquest of an indigenous population by so-called civilized people with guns and horses. I recommend it to you. It's good, and very, very readable. And very powerful, and very beautifully written. Nevertheless, it's the impulse of someone who is essentially a lyric poet, who had a characteristic personalized tone in the short poem. It's that lyric impulse extended over the epic length. MacLeish's talent is really not geared up to the long flight, although it is remarkable how he keeps the long flight going with his lyric talent, which is essentially a short-poem kind of talent. It's remarkable how he does it. But there is a definite sense of strain about it, so that *Conquistadors* is best read as a series of related lyrics rather than as a long narrative.

He's an old man now, all the honors have come to him; almost every honor that the American literary establishment can bestow has come to Archibald MacLeish. He's coming up on eighty years old. But he had, in his seventies, a remarkable success on the stage, oddly enough. *J. B.* I don't know whether you've seen *J. B.* You might not like it. But it's a good evening in the theatre. I detest the theatre myself, but I did see that and was crazy about it, so it must be good. It's a modern-day variation on the Job stories. He's since done one on the Hercules legends, which is very good, but didn't have *J. B.*'s popular success. So, if you're interested in Archibald MacLeish, there's the *Collected Poems* and a new one which just came out last year whose title I like called *The Wild Old Wicked Man*. But what it all comes down to and what his contribution is, what his literary claim to fame as a poet is, is in the short pieces, the lyric poems. And there again, he is one of the few that deserves to be called haunting. But he has a real cadence, a sound. There's one of his called "An Epistle to Be Left in the Earth." It's the time capsule idea, and in it he employs a device which he popularized and which everybody else stole, which is this business of running the lines of poetry across the page like this, a suspended line. This is an epistle to be left in the earth by people who have a poet tell what is happening. We don't understand our situation. Nature has changed, and something doomful is coming upon us. Our change is essentially psychological, but we write this, and it will tell you in later generations what it was like, how this thing came upon us. And we finished the poem and put it in a time capsule and buried it.

This is one of the most beautiful poems that the English tongue has ever conceived of. It's called "You, Andrew Marvell." You know who Andrew Marvell was? He's a poet roughly of the time of John Donne and Milton whose obsession was with death. "The grave's a fine and private place / But none I think do there embrace." But what MacLeish does is to take the shadow of the earth as it revolves, and tell how it crosses various countries coming toward England where Andrew Marvell is lying in the sun, thinking of the coming of the shadow. The coming of the shadow is really death, night. I have never seen such a marvelous, evocative use of place-names in a poem.

You, Andrew Marvell

And here face down beneath the sun
And here upon earth's noonward height
To feel the always coming on
The always rising of the night

To feel creep up the curving east
The earthy chill of dusk and slow
Upon those under lands the vast
And ever climbing shadow grow

And strange at Ecbatan the trees
Take leaf by leaf the evening strange
The flooding dark about their knees
The mountains over Persia change

And now at Kermanshah the gate
Dark empty and the withered grass
And through the twilight now the late
Few travelers in the westward pass

And Baghdad darken and the bridge
Across the silent river gone
And through Arabia the edge
Of evening widen and steal on

And deepen on Palmyra's street
The wheel rut in the ruined stone
And Lebanon fade out and Crete
High through the clouds and overblown

And over Sicily the air
Still flashing with the landward gulls
And loom and slowly disappear
The sails above the shadowy hulls

And Spain go under and the shore
Of Africa the gilded sand
And evening vanish and no more
The low pale light across that land

Nor now the long light on the sea

And here face downward in the sun
To feel how swift how secretly
The shadow of the night comes on . . .

There's another, much less typical, but one that I like. It's one of the few poems I have ever read about the underwater world. And it's in that exquisite MacLeishian cadence, too, very rhythmical. It's called "The Reef Fisher."

THE REEF FISHER

For K. MacL.

Plunge beneath the ledge of coral
    Where the silt of sunlight drifts
    Like dust that settles toward a floor—
    As slow as that: feel the lifting
Surge that rustles white above
    But here is only movement deep
    As breathing: watch the reef fish hover
    Dancing in their silver sleep
Around their stone, enchanted tree:
    Stoop through the wavering cave of blue:
    Look down, look down until you see,
    Far, far beneath in the translucent
Lightlessness, the huge, the fabulous
    Fish of fishes in his profound gulf:
    Grip your stickled spear to stab
    And sink below the shadowy shelf—

But fear that weed, as though alive,
    That lifts and follows with the wave:
    The Moray lurks for all who dive
    Too deep within the coral cave.
Once tooth of his has touched the bone
Men turn among those stones to stone.

MARK VAN DOREN

Mark Van Doren, an old friend of MacLeish's, is almost the exact opposite kind of figure. Where MacLeish has been public, Van Doren has been private, although a teacher at Columbia University for a number of years, something like thirty years, and very greatly revered. So great is Van Doren's magnanimity and so great the breadth of his enormous humanism and enormous sympathy that there's no sincere person who's interested in literature or who even thinks he's interested in literature that Mark Van Doren would not sit down and talk with and give the benefit of his lifelong scholarly devotion to these matters.

As a poet he does not have the distinctive kind of talent that MacLeish has. He is a real poet, but he's very muted, very low-key. Someone said he was kind of a spinoff of Robert Frost. But that's not quite true. He's a vastly more intelligent man than Robert Frost was. But Van Doren as a poet never really had the distinctive sound or the idiom that a writer like Frost had. If you compare Robert Frost and Mark Van Doren as poets roughly of the same persuasion, writing about pastoral subjects, you could do worse than revert to the proverb that the fox knows many things, but the hedgehog knows one big thing. Robert Frost is the hedgehog. He knows one big thing. Van Doren is the fox; he knows many, many things, but none of the things either singly or together add up to Frost's big thing. You can say of Mark Van Doren as a poet that he's a distinguished poet, a good poet, but strangely muted and diffuse. He's definitely worth reading. There's one list-poem of his that I want to read to you. As he gets to be an old man, he lists things that he likes in the world, different kinds of things. What Van Doren likes is the enormous multiplicity of different kinds of things, different kinds of sensations, different kinds of things to taste, different aspects of the multifarious world. He's a modest writer, and he generally doesn't write very long—usually very short, tight, lyric—poems. And this poem is just about the things he likes [poem unidentified]. You should read the poems, and incidentally, thank God, he's written a good many of them. There's a fine, new, big, handsome *Collected and New Poems, 1924–1963,* and there's a longer one, of a more specialized taste, *Narrative Poems,* and they're very good indeed. But I would say—and about MacLeish, too—his best things are in the lyric mode rather than in the longer narrative.

Now, unlike MacLeish, whose work in prose is essentially scattered and sort of just collected by assiduous editors, including MacLeish himself, Van Doren is, in addition to his poetry, a professional scholar and an interpreter of literary work; that is to say, a critic, though of a very, very special kind. Of all the readable critics, he has, as Wordsworth said of poets, the tone of a man speaking to men. I know of no one more characteristic of this than Mark Van Doren. He has written a number of extremely well regarded critical works. I mention the John Dryden book, which is the work that caused T. S. Eliot to reevaluate the whole eighteenth century, and if you go to college and study eighteenth century, it is Eliot's judgment following Van Doren's book on Dryden that you will be influenced by inevitably. He wrote this book on Dryden when he was a graduate student at Columbia, and for a very, very young man, or for any age man, it's remarkable work. You can understand more about the eighteenth century and about the eighteenth-century approach to literature—to poetry, to the drama, to comedy, to tragedy, to the interrelation of philosophy and politics and the rest of these extra-literary disciplines—by reading Van Doren's *Dryden* than anything else that I know. That really is his main scholarly work. He's also written a book on Shakespeare that you could very profitably peruse. I read through it a week or so ago, and it has what I think would delight Van Doren most to have said about him as a critic: it makes you want to go back and read the plays. He must surely have been one of the great teachers; in fact, I'll go further than that and say he *is* one of the great teachers. He has a little incidental book of miscellaneous pieces called *The Happy Critic*. Nowadays you are supposed to be a miserable critic, and you are supposed to have a lot of sociological implications whenever you write about literature.

Mark Van Doren is very much at home with literature. He loves it. He loves the great writers. He knows them. He knows ten or twelve languages. He reads all the time. His life is literature, and in that mansion of many windows, nobody has ever been more at home. You feel that Mark Van Doren and Dante could sit down and have a cup of wine, and they would understand each other in depth within five minutes—because his forbearance is so great, his sensitivity is so keen, and his sympathy with what a writer is doing, or tries to do, or even fails to do, is so human that no one could fail to enjoy Mark Van Doren's company. We had him do a lecture at the Library of Congress when I was there, and there were not many people present; but all the time I was at the Library of Congress, I never saw a larger crowd gather around a writer after he was finished, to get close to him, converse with him, and feel that kind of lovely, deep, warm, human radiance that comes off Mark Van Doren. He's exemplary. And the fact that he doesn't have the absolutely highest, greatest gifts as a creative writer seems to make him even more sympathetic. Because he's not on that mountaintop with Dante or with Shakespeare. He's someone whose great quality is accessibility. He'll sit and talk to you as long as you want to, and give you the benefit of all this enormous life-work of his devotion to literature, an intelligent devotion to literature. And it's remarkable.

The book that I have found most useful of his, because so little is written about epic poetry, is this one called *The Noble Voice.* He's better on poems that are very remote from us like the *Iliad,* which is the ultimate war poem. It would be hard to find an essay on a work of literature, in this case, the *Iliad,* which would make you want to read it more, or that would be more shrewd in its assessment in what makes the *Iliad* the great poem that it is. He says, in one instance, for example, that it can be simple because there's not a long literary tradition behind it which has said all these things before. It can say these things, like the Aegean or the Mediterranean is "wine-dark," which is the most obvious thing about it. It *is* the color of wine. If you had had a lot of people before you who said it looked like wine, then you'd have to find something else to say, but Homer had the enormous advantage of being able to say that it looked like in fact what it does look like. This is the kind of thing that Van Doren does in his criticism, which I can take an awful lot of.

All this leads up to a nice book, something that television made possible: they put on a long three-hour spectacular of Archibald MacLeish and Mark Van Doren talking things out, or rapping. And when those guys rap, it's really worth listening to. This is called *The Dialogues of Archibald MacLeish and Mark Van Doren,* and it's put out by Dutton. It's a good book, and there will probably be some reruns of the film, probably on ETV. They walk around—part of it is on MacLeish's farm, and part of it is on Van Doren's farm—and they talk about love, death, time, art, aging, Homer, Shelley, Milton. It's as easygoing as they are.

WILFRED OWEN

There can hardly be another notable English poet whose best productions, and really, in Owen's case, his only good productions, are so limited to one subject. Wilfred Owen is not a war poet; he is *the* war poet. There is nothing else that he wrote about. So, with this revulsion against war that World War I caused, and with this plain, honest voice, Wilfred Owen—all of his estheticism and all of his theories and all of his literary influences just vanished when he began to put these poems down about his experiences in the trenches. That was all changed. It was as though somebody else other than the promising, young, esthetic poet Wilfred Owen had written earlier. His experience was essentially reformed, and in a sense reborn, in the heat of the crucible of the Western Front. And when you read these Wilfred Owen war poems, you think of the words of Ishmael in the Bible and also in *Moby-Dick,* "I alone have come back to tell thee." He was the voice of the truth and the horror and, as he says himself, the pity of war. Let me read to you just a few sentences. He never lived to see this come out. He had serious doubts as to whether it would ever be published. These were the notes to his preface. The preface itself was never written, but these were notes for the preface of his book.

Owen was an extremely kindhearted man who revered the imagination, but he himself was not terribly imaginative until just the last couple of years of his life. Now, his reputation grows steadily. Even more tantalizing, the reputation grows because of the Owen legend: that here is a guy forced to fight, who could have done things for humanity, who could have been active in social issues, who would see and change them, who could make people see and change them for the better. One thing you can say about Owen: he did have enormously broad and deep sympathies, and they're not phony, as so many of the social poets are these days. You read through the letters and you see two things that are the core of Wilfred Owen's being. One of them was the love of and devotion to poetry; and the other was the devotion to men, to human beings, to the betterment of their conditions. That was why war was so hideous. Here they were killing and maiming each other when they should have been doing some good for each other.

And so, when a poet dies at the age of twenty-five and especially when he is killed like this, there are all sorts of speculations about if he did this at the age of twenty-five under these hideous conditions, what might he have gone on to do? I'm very sorry Wilfred Owen was killed, but again, as far as his reputation was concerned, it's probably the best thing in the world for us that he was killed. I do not think he would have developed beyond what he already did. In fact, there's quite a good deal of evidence to show that he would have lapsed back into the same kind of pretty-pretty stuff that he wrote before the war. He might not have. He might have gone on to engage social themes in his poetry. But none of it, no matter what he wrote, would ever have the impact of what he actually did write. So there's really no use speculating on Wilfred Owen's possible life. He did what he had to do, and he did far better than his beginning would have allowed him to suspect that he might conceivably be able to do. In other words, Wilfred Owen is one example of a writer who builded far better than he knew.

His reputation grows and grows. He begins to appear in all these anthologies. But his one detractor is William Butler Yeats, who edited the most influential anthology of the day, *The Oxford Book of Modern Verse,* and he deliberately refuses to print Owen. Now, Owen was a good guy, in addition to being a good poet. He was a lovable person, quiet and shy. Yeats was an arrogant bastard some of the time. If there were any justice in things, Wilfred Owen would be a great, great poet, and everybody would be willing to kick Yeats in the ass and forget about him. Not so. Wilfred Owen is only fragmentarily a poet at all, and William Butler Yeats is probably the greatest poet of the twentieth century. But this is the kind of thing that makes people detest Yeats. Here this guy was floundering around in the rats and the muck "over there" and desperately trying to write something before he gets blown up again and killed, and here Yeats is sitting back in his drawing room saying, "I won't have it, we can't live with him." That appears in Yeats's introduction to his *Oxford Book of Modern Verse.* But this is an even more damning and even more unforgivable statement that Yeats made in reference to Owen. This is in a private letter that he allowed to be published [letter unidentified]. That's generally cited against Yeats. How could a great poet like him have been so wrong? But yet the tantalizing thing is that he's not that wrong, either. It can be looked at that way, very easily—because there is a lot of sucked sugar stick in Wilfred Owen, and nobody says anything about it. But what happens to Owen's reputation because of this revulsion against war and because he was the only poet of any stature of all who had these kinds of opinions in World War I—what happens is that the politically conscious poets of the 1930s—[W. H.] Auden and [Stephen] Spender—take up

Owen as a great forerunner of them and their attitudes. And they bore him up and made a great deal out of him, and get him in more anthologies, and more and more people are interested in him, and lo and behold, here we have a great poet after all. And a great poet made great by an output of what could be called "good" of less than ten pages.

There is almost nothing of Wilfred Owen that matters. But what happens as a result of the Wilfred Owen mystique is that every scrap that had his name on it, laundry bills, and that sort of thing, has been exhumed, all this awful early stuff, and even then, with everything, all these early poems, his work is still less than a hundred pages. Everything that he ever wrote in verse is less than a hundred pages. And I'd say that fewer than ten pages of that is any good. Benjamin Britten, the British composer, writes a famous composition called *War Requiem* with words by Owen, and Owen gets to be a figure of world importance. This is obvious nonsense. Wilfred Owen is painfully bad most of the time. He has a few nice things. There is only one thing by Wilfred Owen that I think is good, that's good as a poem. There're good lines in things, or pretty good, but there's only one that I think is good all the way through. It's very good. He's gotten off his Keatsian archaisms now and has adopted a kind of plain-speaking conversational tone. This is about going off to war and coming back. It's about a train full of soldiers, and the women give them flowers, and then they come back one by one to places that they don't even remember any more. It's very short. It's called "The Send-Off."

THE SEND-OFF

Down the close, darkening lanes they sang their way
To the siding-shed,
And lined the train with faces grimly gay.
Their breasts were stuck all white with wreath and spray
As men's are, dead.

Dull porters watched them, and a casual tramp
Stood staring hard,
Sorry to miss them from the upland camp.
Then, unmoved, signals nodded, and a lamp
Winked to the guard.

So secretly, like wrongs hushed-up, they went.
They were not ours:
We never heard to which front these were sent.
Nor there if they yet mock what women meant
Who gave them flowers.

Shall they return to beatings of great bells
In wild trainloads?
A few, a few, too few for drums and yells,
May creep back, silent, to still village wells
Up half-known roads.

Another is called "Exposure," and these are two things that are really very good. I wouldn't say great. You would say Yeats is great, but [his poems] certainly are way above most of the stuff of Wilfred Owen. He just looks better than he actually is because of the circumstances. But he is a real poet; he became a real poet under these conditions and he develops respect in those who read him.

But before we go into this I should say something about his own technical innovations. He thought of himself as a devoted craftsman in poetry, and in some ways he was, and he did a good deal of experimentation with rhyming. English is a rhyme-poor language, not like Italian or Spanish. And he thought that he saw a way to increase the rhyming possibilities of English by using consonance, which is rhyming words like mystery and mastery, where the consonants rhyme but the vowels don't. You usually would try to rhyme the vowels. But he reverses that, and makes a systematic practice of rhyming the consonants instead of the vowels, and he thought that would expand the rhyming possibilities a very great deal. It was very widely adopted, mainly by Auden and his followers, who claim on this basis of one thing that Owen did that Owen was the great opener-up of new territory for poets. Well, in a way that one thing helped them, but that's all he did. Anyway, here's one in which he uses that technique, called "Exposure." It's about the uncomfortableness, the physical agony, of war, when you're out there and the rain's beating down on you and you're freezing to death, developing trench foot from not being able to change your socks, and you're slogging around in the mud all the time.

EXPOSURE

Our brains ache, in the merciless iced east winds that knive us . . .
Wearied we keep awake because the night is silent . . .
Low, drooping flares confuse our memory of the salient . . .
Worried by silence, sentries whisper, curious, nervous,
      But nothing happens.
Watching we hear the mad gusts tugging on the wire,
Like twitching agonies of men among its brambles.
Northward, incessantly, the flickering gunnery rumbles.
Far off, like a dull rumour of some other war.

What are we doing here?
The poignant misery of dawn begins to grow . . .
We only know war lasts, rain soaks, and clouds sag stormy.
Dawn massing in the east her melancholy army
Attacks once more in ranks on shivering ranks of grey,
　　　　But nothing happens.
Sudden successive flights of bullets streak the silence.
Less deathly than the air that shudders black with snow,
With sidelong flowing flakes that flock, pause, and renew;
We watch them wandering up and down the wind's nonchalance,
　　　　But nothing happens.
Pale flakes with fingering stealth come feeling for our faces—
We cringe in holes, back on forgotten dreams, and stare, snow-dazed,
Deep into the grassier ditches. So we drowse, sun-dozed,
Littered with blossoms trickling where the blackbird fusses,
　　　　—Is it that we are dying?
Slowly our ghosts drag home: glimpsing the sunk fires, glozed
With crusted dark-red jewels; crickets jingle there;
For hours the innocent mice rejoice: the house is theirs;
Shutters and doors, all closed: on us the doors are closed,—
　　　　We turn back to our dying.
Since we believe not otherwise can kind fires burn;
Nor even suns smile true on child, or field, or fruit.
For God's invincible spring our love is made afraid;
Therefore, not loath, we lie out here; therefore were born,
　　　　For love of God seems dying.
Tonight, this frost will fasten on this mud and us.
Shrivelling many hands, puckering foreheads crisp.
The burying-party, picks and shovels in shaking grasp,
Pause over half-known faces. All their eyes are ice.
　　　　But nothing happens.

Well-observed details, well-handled stanzas, and very inept, kind of amateurish writing. But these stanzas seem to me to point out to all those back home the depth of fear.

Now, let me go on a little bit more about my personal feeling about Owen. He was a guy whose poems are things that you desperately want to like. He's got all the credentials, especially for our state of mind now. He's a man who's a poet, who went to the war, who served, and served well, and he did go back when he could have stayed out, and was killed. So the poems have an authenticity from his death that they do not have on the page. They've got some authenticity and some remarkable qualities, but they do not have as much of these things as if Owen had not gone through what he went through and had not died as he did. This may be good for Owen's reputation, but ultimately it is not good for his reputation. It served to get him noticed when otherwise he might not have been, but it also tends to blow his reputation up beyond what it should be, and makes a pacifist martyr out of him instead of having the attention focused on what he really would have preferred it to be focused on, that is, his qualities as a poet. Then, in keeping with this whole Wilfred Owen mystique, this pacifist martyr, the letters are issued. I read them, and I was even more confused. I had about decided that I had to start all over again, because they were the best letters I had ever read. The evidence of a really remarkable sensibility is in them everywhere. It's in the letters far more than in the poetry. They are really good letters, and they're very funny. All the horror, and there's plenty of that, all the descriptions of burial parties and dismembered corpses and people shooting, and all the horrible things that you can think of, you encounter in Wilfred Owen's letters. But that's not all. Some of them are very funny. And you get the impression of a really remarkable personality. Maybe he did have it in him to be a great poet. But he isn't, and don't you ever let anyone tell you that he is.

RANDALL JARRELL

Rather than risk not passing him on to you, it would be better this time to talk about Randall Jarrell, who was a dear, close associate and friend and who died four years ago under peculiar circumstances. He just felt like he didn't want to go on with it any more. It took place in North Carolina, where he had already tried to slash his wrists. His motor circuits to his hands were tied up, and a hospital was trying to rehabilitate him from his wrist-slashing episode, and he jumped in front of a car and just finished it. It's indicative of something about the life of the American intellectual that this guy, who had more gifts than any of us—Randall was nine years older than I was, but in any given nine years I would never have been able to make up the differences between Randall Jarrell and me as far as intelligence, as far as intuition, as far as the amount of stuff written, amount of stuff read, and a sensitive kind of individual relationship to what had been read. No, no, he was way out of sight for me. He didn't know the big thing as Theodore Roethke knew the big thing, but he knew many things. And in any kind of discussion, whether literary or political, nobody could go up against him. He just knew too much; he was too smart; he thought on his feet too fast. And yet, he killed himself. He knocked all this out by jumping in front of the nearest available automobile, because at the age of fifty-two he had arrived at a point where he could not bear the burden of his own insights and his own intelligence. Maybe this says something about American writers.

As a poet, he's deliberately low-key and extremely witty and very learned and almost desperately sincere. You have the feeling that with Randall Jarrell you have finally encountered a poet who is leveling with you absolutely. Nothing is done for literary effect. It's as though it were a voice speaking from the grave, to say, "Listen, you've got to listen because I've got it; I know it." He wrote a lot, maybe too much. But like any good poet—you can't use the word "great" in relation to Jarrell—but what you do say about Jarrell is that he's a minor poet who's better than the major poets. He doesn't attempt world-shaking themes. He goes to the small, intimate moment. He doesn't go wide, but

250

he does go in, deep and quiet. But the thing that should not be left out of account is that his wit is absolutely devastating. He's a good hater. I have a theory that you can't love anything greatly unless you can also hate greatly. And he had that. He was devastating! There's this big *Complete Poems*. There's this novel about university life that you must read [*Pictures from an Institution*]. It's not about a big schlock state university like this; it's about a small, exclusive girls' school where the girls get all the best advantages. It's just terribly funny, all the pretensions of those kinds of places. There are a couple of books of criticism. The best book on poetry that I know: it's funny, very funny in a learned way that makes you want to be learned so you can be so devastatingly funny yourself, in such a learned way. So, *Poetry and the Age*. And then a follow-up book of criticism about American culture called *A Sad Heart at the Supermarket*. And then there's a posthumous book called *The Third Book of Criticism*.

Randall Jarrell was a curious guy, a terrific guy. When you were in his presence for five minutes, you knew you were privileged. He was a man of obsessions. Sports car racing was one, of all things for a college professor. Tennis was another. But mainly his obsession was literature, and the ballet, and painting, and everything that pertained to the arts. He had an intense personal relationship with ballerinas. Just to watch. And he'd write about them rhapsodically, although he didn't know anything about the technical part of the dance. But he wrote about them with such enthusiasm that you just wanted to see them perform. When he wrote about Frost, you wanted to read Frost. You feel that you've never read him before. He's that kind of critic. He's got that kind of human enthusiasm, that tremendous ecstatic drive, that very human thing. Randall Jarrell ought to be looking mighty good to people now, because the kinds of questions he asked fifteen years ago are exactly the kinds of things people are talking about now.

The poetry we should look at. Jarrell was born in Nashville. He's a southerner, and his name in the South is usually pronounced *Jarr*-el, but he insisted, because of his first name, that it be pronounced Jar*rell*. So that's what you should call him, that lovely, eccentric, mad guy, of the kind of intelligence that you would attribute not to a human being but to an angel. The one we should read is "90 North," which is one that he wrote while he was at Vanderbilt. The central metaphor is of polar exploration where the person is dreaming of being someone like [Admiral Robert E.] Peary or one of the polar explorers. But it's really not a metaphor for physical travail; it's a metaphor for the human condition generally: That I dreamed I went to the north polar cap and I saw everything frozen around me, and my breath was congealing in the air, but I knew I had arrived at the zero point, where everything is south, and I knew then what the human condition means. That it's like this, after all this work and all this sacrifice, it's not anything. And what they told us in the schools is wrong, and now I am in a position to know the truth. I'm here at "90 North," and they are not, even in the dream.

90 NORTH

At home, in my flannel gown, like a bear to its floe,
I clambered to bed; up the globe's impossible sides
I sailed all night—till at last, with my black beard,
My furs and my dogs, I stood at the northern pole.

There in the childish night my companions lay frozen,
The stiff furs knocked at my starveling throat,
And I gave my great sigh: the flakes came huddling,
Were they really my end? In the darkness I turned to my rest.

—Here, the flag snaps in the glare and silence
Of the unbroken ice. I stand here,
The dogs bark, my beard is black, and I stare
At the North Pole . . .
                    And now what? Why, go back.

Turn as I please, my step is to the south.
The world—my world spins on this final point
Of cold and wretchedness: all lines, all winds
End in this whirlpool I at last discover.

And it is meaningless. In the child's bed
After the night's voyage, in that warm world
Where people work and suffer for the end
That crowns the pain—in that Cloud-Cuckoo-Land

I reached my North and it had meaning.
Here at the actual pole of my existence,
Where all that I have done is meaningless,
Where I die or live by accident alone—

Where, living or dying, I am still alone;
Here where North, the night, the berg of death
Crowd me out of the ignorant darkness,
I see at last that all the knowledge

I wrung from the darkness—that the darkness flung me—
Is worthless as ignorance: nothing comes from nothing,
The darkness from the darkness. Pain comes from the darkness
And we call it wisdom. It is pain.

It is the desperate honesty of an intelligent man, a superintelligent man, who has nothing to lose, and who is going to try to tell you what he thinks. It's not the intelligence of the ordinary man, although Jarrell had his roots in ordinariness. It's the intelligence of the ordinary man who has become far more intelligent, but who still maintains himself among the average.

Jarrell is very low-key. He doesn't use any rhetorical tricks, and some of his stuff is very close to prose. But you can't read anything of Jarrell's without having to cope with it.

Something about Jarrell's life. He was born in Nashville, and was a precocious high school student in the public high school. He was a scholarship student at Vanderbilt, where he attracted immediate attention. He went into the Air Force, washed out as a pilot, became a gunnery instructor. He never saw combat, but identified intensely and very physically with the fellows in combat, and especially, although he was an Air Force guy, with the Navy pilots. And his best war poems, which are among the best we have, are about shot-down Navy pilots. He came back and became one of the great teachers of our time, until the age of fifty-two.

This one is "The Death of the Ball Turret Gunner." It's very short.

THE DEATH OF THE BALL TURRET GUNNER

From my mother's sleep I fell into the State,
And I hunched in its belly till my wet fur froze.
Six miles from earth, loosed from its dream of life,
I woke to black flak and the nightmare fighters.
When I died they washed me out of the turret with a hose.

The great thing about Jarrell is that he really instinctively identifies with the soldiers' not knowing why they're asked to do this, why?

Let me read to you a translation. He had a marvelous instinctive feeling for poets who were like him in other languages. And [Rainer Maria] Rilke, the German poet, was foremost among all of these. This is a free adaptation of Jarrell's from Rilke's second book, called "Washing the Corpse."

WASHING THE CORPSE
(Rainer Maria Rilke)

They had got used to him. But when they brought
The kitchen lamp in, and it was burning
Uneasily in the dark air, the stranger
Was altogether strange. They washed his neck,

And since they had no knowledge of his fate
They lied till they had put together one,

Always washing. One of them had to cough,
And while she was coughing she left the heavy

Sponge of vinegar on his face. The other
Stopped a minute too, and the drops knocked
From the hard brush, while his dreadful
Cramped hand wanted to demonstrate
To the whole household that he no longer thirsted.

And he did demonstrate it. Coughing shortly,
As if embarrassed, they went back to work
More hurriedly now, so that across the dumb
Pattern of the wallpaper their contorted shadows

Writhed and wallowed as though in a net
Until the washing reached its end.
The night, in the uncurtained window-frame,
Was relentless. And one without a name
Lay clean and naked there, and gave commandments.

He wrote fine children's books, so when you have children of your own, you can get books of his called *The Animal Family* and *The Bat-poet*. *The Bat-poet* is a sweet little book about a bat who is a poet and who goes around intoning his poems to other animals. And the bat poems in Randall Jarrell's *Bat-poet* book are not bad poems for a bat to have written.

This one has a special poignancy for me. His last letters were to me, and he sent me this poem, which I think is his best poem. It's a combination of sex and harvest in California where this woman is an old woman who is remembering picking lima beans. Okay, this is the one that Randall sent to me while I was in California. It meant a great deal to him to have lived in California in the Depression, and, as he said, to walk outside your door, and the smog in the 1930s was already beginning, and your eyes began to water. He said then, "I couldn't imagine what it was, but I know now." This is one of the things that Randall did best, going into the personality of another person, usually a woman or a little girl who doesn't understand. He's very good at understanding how women feel, what it must have been like for them. This is a working-class girl from California remembering, as an old woman, how it was in the fields.

GLEANING

When I was a girl in Los Angeles we'd go gleaning.
Coming home from Sunday picnics in the canyons,
Driving through orange groves, we would stop at fields
Of lima beans, already harvested, and glean.
We children would pick a few lima beans in play,

But the old ones, bending to them, gleaned seriously
Like a picture in my Bible story book.

So, now, I glean seriously,
Bending to pick the beans that are left.
I am resigned to gleaning. If my heart is heavy,
It is with the weight of all it's held.
How many times I've lain
At midnight with the young men in the field!
At noon the lord of the field has spread his shirt
over me, his handmaid. "What else do you want?"
I ask myself, exasperated at myself.
But inside me something hopeful and insatiable—
A girl, a grown-up, giggling, gray-haired girl—
Gasps: "More, more!" I can't help hoping,
I can't help *expecting*
A last man, black, gleaning,
To come to me, at sunset, in the field.
In the last light we lie there alone:
My hands spill the last things they hold,
The days crushed beneath my dying body
By the body crushing me. As I bend
To my soup spoon, here at the fireside, I can feel
And not feel the body crushing me, as I go gleaning.

SIDNEY KEYES AND ALUN LEWIS

Today we'll talk about World War II and a couple of British guys. Sidney Keyes was killed in the African campaign when he was twenty, and his body was never recovered. He's the less interesting of the two, Sidney Keyes and Alun Lewis, but perhaps the more potentially interesting. You can't tell that from what actual work we do have. He's one of these lonely, precocious British boys, largely self-educated. He won all kinds of scholarships to the big, established universities. He wrote his only two books while he was in college. One of them was called *The Iron Laurel,* and the other one was called *The Cruel Solstice.* They've been collected along with a few posthumous things in one tiny little book called *Collected Poems of Sidney Keyes.* I read through this just to see what I thought, and my opinion is bewildered, indeed. Here is obviously a young guy who's tremendously talented and tremendously informed. He's given to long, elegiac poems about the discovery of the self, about war, about the evolution of European history; and you would think it would take someone older than twenty years old to know anything significant at all. But he has two long poems that are fascinating, even though extremely literary. One of them is called "The Wilderness," which is a poem about the evolution of the self, especially the English self, in terms of modern European historical evolution. And the other is called "The Foreign Gate," which is much more private and much more personal to Sidney Keyes himself. He was supposed to have had some extraordinary new poems on his person when he was killed. He was in a line outfit in the African war, and he showed somebody a sheaf of manuscripts, put it back in his tunic, and that's all there was of that, because it was never found. And that is the kind of thing to make you speculate about what might have been, because the trouble with his work, as brilliant as it is, it does not have the touch or the feel of something personally experienced.

He can write, and writes marvelously, about European history as it comes true as a prophecy of [Georg Wilhelm Friedrich] Hegel. Hegel said it was going to be like this, and here it is. But in something Sidney Keyes the poet had experienced, you don't have that feeling. You have the feeling of its being essentially read-up-on and bookish, and you feel like that last sheaf of poems that Keyes was supposed to have had with him might have bridged that gap. He might have gotten over there and had this personal feeling of body-to-body experience that his poetry lacks, the *only* thing that his poetry lacks.

I'll read to you a couple of Keyes poems. This is one which has a certain amount of personal feeling in it. The long, ambitious things do not. They are just kind of icy landscapes of modern war devastating Europe, beautifully described. But it's like looking on the history of Europe from a spaceship, looking down on it from a great height without having to be involved with it. But there are some nice little things that he did that do have a sense of personal involvement, and I'll read to you a couple of them. This is called "Elegy." It's for a relative of his. I'm not sure whether it was a brother or a grandfather. [Keyes wrote the elegy for his grandfather.]

ELEGY

(*In memoriam S.K.K.*)

April again, and it is a year again
Since you walked out and slammed the door
Leaving us tangled in your words. Your brain
Lives in the bank-book, and your eyes look up
Laughing from the carpet on the floor:
And we still drink from your silver cup.

It is a year again since they poured
The dumb ground into your mouth:
And yet we know, by some recurring word
Or look caught unawares, that you still drive
Our thoughts like the smart cobs of your youth—
When you and the world were alive.

A year again, and we have fallen on bad times
Since they gave you to the worms.
I am ashamed to take delight in these rhymes
Without grief; but you need no tears.
We shall never forget nor escape you, nor make terms
With your enemies, the swift departing years.

Parts of it are good, such as the thing about drinking from your silver cup. That's a nice reminiscence of a person. One feels that. One has that feeling about objects that someone dead has left, and that ritual ceremony. It has good things like that in it, and it has a lot of cliché stuff too. The thing about this relationship to Keyes's work generally is that it's very good, but not quite good enough.

This is one that I read while I was overseas in the service, called "Remember Your Lovers." It meant an awful lot to me, because this was exactly the kind of thing that I was trying to write. Here was somebody exactly the same age that I was, who was killed the previous six months to the time that I was reading the poem. I read this in an anthology. It was quickly collected, became a famous World War II poem. But it was exactly the same thing that I was trying to write, that many young men in the same condition, in the service, undergoing the ordeal of war—he in North Africa and I in New Guinea at that time—were trying to write. And the main thing about it is that it's very romantic stuff. It's very heavily influenced by Tennyson and the late romantic writers in England. Now, why we, myself and Keyes and these other young men, were trying to write like that, when we were looking down the machine gun barrel every day, is something that I will never know. But this is just the kind of thing that I was trying to do, and Keyes did so much better than I did. Now listen to this. Some of it is very affecting in the way that heavy, lush, romantic verse is affecting some of the time. When he's not trying to be classical, he's openly indulging in emotions, using some of the stock paraphernalia of the English romantic verse. And yet by damn, it lacks sentimentality. It gets to you anyway.

REMEMBER YOUR LOVERS

Young men walking the open streets
Of death's republic, remember your lovers.

When you foresaw with vision prescient
The planet pain rising across your sky
We fused your sight in our soft burning beauty:
We laid you down in meadows drunk with cowslips
And led you in the ways of our bright city.
Young men who wander death's vague meadows,
Remember your lovers who gave you more than flowers.

When truth came prying like a surgeon's knife
Among the delicate movements of your brain
We called your spirit from its narrow den
And kissed your courage back to meet the blade—
Our anaesthetic beauty saved you then.
Young men whose sickness death has cured at last,
Remember your lovers and covet their disease.

When you woke grave-chilled at midnight
To pace the pavement of your bitter dream
We brought you back to bed and brought you home
From the dark antechamber of desire

Into our lust as warm as candle-flame.
Young men who lie in the carven beds of death,
Remember your lovers who gave you more than dreams.

From the sun sheltering your careless head
Or from the painted devil your quick eye,
We led you out of terror tenderly
And fooled you into peace with our soft words
And gave you all we had and let you die.
Young men drunk with death's unquenchable wisdom,
Remember your lovers who gave you more than love.

When Sidney Keyes wrote that, he was such a bright, precocious boy in languages and comparative literature. Again, precocity: this is one thing he had, more than any other poet of his generation, but is it enough? He never got a chance to find out. But let me read to you one poem. You remember who Marshal [Semyon Konstantinovich] Timoshenko was? He was the Russian peasant general who stood against the German army and defeated them and began to force them back. He stood against them, and stood with everything they had in Russia in those snowfields to keep the Germans from going on further. This was written in 1942, when Keyes had just gone on active service. This is called "Timoshenko."

TIMOSHENKO

Hour ten he rose, ten-sworded, every finger
A weighted blade, and strapping round his loins
The courage of attack, he threw the window
Open to look on his appointed night.

Where lay, beneath the winds and creaking flares
Tangled like lovers or alone assuming
The wanton postures of the drunk with sleep,
An army of twisted limbs and hollow faces
Thrown to and fro between the winds and shadows.
O hear the wind, the wind that shakes the dawn.
And there before the night, he was aware
Of the flayed fields of home, and black with ruin
The helpful earth under the tracks of tanks.
His bladed hand, in pity falling, mimicked
The crumpled hand lamenting the broken plow;
And the oracular metal lips in anger
Squared to the shape of the raped girl's yelling mouth.
He heard the wind explaining nature's sorrow
And humming in the wire hair of the dead.

He turned, and his great shadow on the wall
Swayed like a tree. His eyes grew cold as lead.
Then, in a rage of love and grief and pity,
He made the pencilled map alive with war.

So Keyes had two books, *The Iron Laurel* and *The Cruel Solstice,* and they are collected in this small, small book with a preface by Herbert Read. Keyes will survive, I think, in some way. Maybe in a small way, a minor way. But he's good in that he began to transcend the literariness of his precocious upbringing and his precocious education, and began to get into some of the deep stuff. He was just beginning to when he was killed.

Alun Lewis was an entirely different case. He did live six, seven, eight more years than Sidney Keyes, but he was an entirely different type of human being. He was the son of a man in South Wales who taught school in a coal mining village, and Alun Lewis himself was raised to be a teacher, because being a teacher and winning scholarships is one of the few ways out of the coal mines in Wales or in north central England. D. H. Lawrence was another such example. He became a great winner of examinations, scholarships. Alun Lewis didn't come from as poor a people as Lawrence. His father himself was a schoolmaster, but he was trained and raised to be a schoolteacher, and he became a teacher, not only a secondary-school teacher, but a university teacher, and he taught at the University of Wales. He was from a very early age much concerned with social problems. He saw the desperate plight of the miners. He was the kind of person, very much like John Keats in some ways, who simply could not see another person in a situation which was degrading or painful or humiliating without identifying with him and wanting to do something about it. Therefore, in all of Lewis's work, there is a strong thread of social concern, pity, and outrage.

Well, what happened to him chiefly is this. He was a university teacher. He married a working-class woman who was one of these big earth-mother type gals, named Gweno. They never had any children because he went on active duty almost immediately after they were married. He was an intelligence officer, and he went into war with very, very strong misgivings. He had very powerful pacifist leanings because he didn't believe that men should fight, but England was in danger and he thought he should try to do something. So, Alun Lewis goes into the service. His position there is kind of ambiguous, because he tries hard to be a good officer, but it's obvious that he really isn't of the officer class and he really doesn't want to be doing what he's doing. So he's shunted around in different places in the service, and then he becomes a good officer because he steels himself. He's getting ready to be sent into combat, and he knows that if he doesn't do what he's supposed to do, then his men will die. So he makes of himself as good an officer as he can. He's sent to India, where he spends some time kicking his heels in a base camp, making out official reports, and supervising the men's soccer teams, and requests transfer to the Burma front where he's sent. He goes into combat and becomes one of the better jungle-fighting commanding officers in his division. He's cited for bravery a couple of times. And then what happens? Nobody knows. He goes out on patrol and he's guarding the rear section. He's armed with a carbine and a service revolver. And his men go around a turn in the trail. There's a shot. They go back, and Alun Lewis is lying in the trail with his brains blown out. Now, people have a way of covering these things up, but what it seems like to me from the evidence I've read is that he killed himself. What they say is that he was killed by an accident with his service revolver. But there was no reason for him to have his revolver out. He had his carbine as well, and that would have been the weapon he would have used. But something happened with his revolver, and he was killed.

His letters to his wife, Gweno, are among the most moving and eloquent that I have ever read from any man to any woman: not mushy and not senti-mental, just strong steady affection, and news about what he was doing. They're real letters. They're not letters written for posterity. He was becoming increas-ingly discouraged about the world, about society, about what would be the issue of the war, about the same old conditions of the privileged and the under-privileged coming right back after all the sacrifice of blood and the kind of his-torical upheaval that he himself was participating in in Burma, which I'm sure was very much like New Guinea, with the most hideous conditions to put men into to fight a war. He was becoming increasingly discouraged, and he felt that all the hope he had for humankind and everything he'd worked for through his poetry and prose was hopeless now. Now, I'm just guessing, but as far as I can tell, that's what happened to him.

But if you want to read the work of the finest British poet that came out of World War II, you've got to go to him. He is more satisfactory, for example, than Sidney Keyes was, as good as he is. Keyes is fragmentary and very much in the first stages of things. Keith Douglas and Alun Lewis were the two best ones they had, and, of the two, I prefer Lewis. Douglas is a shade too knowing, a lit-tle too cynical, a little too distant, but when you read Alun Lewis you feel like you're reading somebody who's talking to you in an intimate, imaginative, con-cerned way that matters. It's not "literature"; it's that human communication in depth that the best poetry is. There's a lot of Alun Lewis that's not that good. But a poet has a right to be judged by his own best work, and the best of his *is* that good. If you want to read him, there are a couple of small books. One is the poems before he died, called *Raiders' Dawn*. And one with the curious title from the book of Job, *Ha! Ha! Among the Trumpets.* That's what the marvelous horse in the book of Job neighs going into battle. There's a book of combined letters, which I really do urge you to get from the Gotham Book Mart, if you're interested in Alun Lewis. It's called *In the Green Tree*. And those are the letters to Gweno and the best of the last short stories. There was a book of short stories published while he was alive, called *The Last Inspection,* which are also very good. And then recently there's a *Selected Poetry and Prose.* It has the best of the poems and it has "The Last Inspection" and "Ward O-3B," and a couple of the other short stories. But you should read those letters.

Now, let's read one of Alun Lewis's, and I'll show you some of the things we've talked about [poem unidentified]. This is a very good example of the kind of thing that Lewis does in that he's with a platoon of men in the jungle, like in Burma, and he said in one of the letters to Gweno, "I just finished a poem I liked. I think it's about the best thing I've done. I think it's about the jungle, but when I read it, I found that it was a commentary on Western civilization." Nothing that Alun Lewis writes about is very far from some kind of central concern with men and what concerns them and what their future is likely to be. He was a great worrier about the future because he had seen so much of the past, not only in the war, but also in the coal mines where he came from: men in bread lines and unemployment and underprivilege and overprivilege and the rest of the things that have concerned men almost from the beginning; that is, men like him who have this capacity and this pity and this rage to change all this. Alun Lewis, unlike Sidney Keyes—it's possible to predict what he would have done. Now, I'm not saying that he'd be one of these poets of social protest. He was too much of a poet and too little of an actual propagandist for that, but the poems would be concerned about the things that he was already concerned with. In the books of Lewis that we have, there are poems about the coal mines and poems about the soldiers and poems about the Indian peasants. But what the subjects would have been had he lived beyond his immediate landscape in Burma and his immediate childhood memories of the coal mines, there's no way to know. But you can be sure that it would have something to do with the plight of men and his own rage to change it.

Let me show you what kind of war this Burma war was, and let me recommend a remarkable novel called *Look Down in Mercy,* by a man named Walter Baxter, and it's the most horrible thing I've ever read in my life. It's about the war in Burma and about a weak upper-class British commanding officer who has no business being a commanding officer because he's unable to make the right decisions and unable to save his men. It has the same kind of atmosphere of Alun Lewis's poems: that hypnotic power of a strange place, of the jungle, that results in this poem where the poet, who is one of the men, begins, under the hypnotic power of the jungle atmosphere, to think about things in a different way, things like the future of Europe, the future of the poor, and the future of society. He, lulled under this hypnotic trance, is social daydreaming. This is a combination of his social daydreaming and the strangeness of the jungle. [poem unidentified]

He's a fine writer. I won't say of Alun Lewis as I will say of Sidney Keyes, "He's good but he would have been better." Alun Lewis, I believe, has already told us what he wanted us to know.

W. H. Auden

A very brief background on Auden is that he came from engineering and mining people. His ancestry is Icelandic, but his people come from the middle part of England. And he had never had any interest in poetry until he was around twenty years old. He went to Oxford, where he met Stephen Spender and some of the other people who since have come to be associated with him, and began to turn on as far as poetry was concerned. He's a brilliant guy; he would have done well in anything. He could have been a doctor, a mining engineer, which he wanted to be, or a chemist. He could have done anything. He just had that dazzling, retentive, jackdaw type intelligence that could pick up things from various areas of experience and put them to his own use. And his eclecticism is part of his poetry. It might be the good part, but it might be the part that will keep him from being, in the eyes of history, a great poet. But he went to public school, and was a confirmed and overt and aggressive homosexual from his very early days. He associated with other brilliant guys of the same persuasion. They were people like Christopher Isherwood, who wrote *I Am a Camera,* which has been revived about twenty times and is called now *Cabaret,* and Stephen Spender, and others. And they turned in the 1930s to social themes even when they were just in college.

When they were in college, Auden was the intellectual leader of his generation. Nobody would deny that. He had such gifts. He was so persuasive that quite literally nobody could stand against him. They acknowledged his leadership easily and readily and were glad that it was there. They turned to social themes in the belief that the writer, especially the poet, who has his fingertip on the pulse of his time, should be *in* the conflict, should have something to do with the shaping of the future of mankind. So, consequently, after Eliot and this elegant, religious withdrawal that Eliot stood for, the pendulum swung all the way to the other extreme of Auden and Spender and Cecil Day Lewis and Louis MacNiece and Allen Upward. And they began to talk very persuasively, especially Auden did, very disturbingly in their poems about what's wrong. People were very, very much involved in the social issues. But the concern of the artist and especially the poet was similar, so Auden and his group were left-ists. They were Marxists. All of them, at one time or another, belonged to the official English version of the Marxist Party. They were card-carrying Com-munists, and they did espouse the cause of revolution, the collapse and decay of bourgeois-financed capitalism, and were in favor of a new kind of eco-nomically fairer society.

Spender did this very naively. He thought of it as an enormous Boy Scout camp. Auden had no such illusions as that, but he did think that economic con-ditions could be better and there could be a more equitable division of goods. Day Lewis, who is now the poet laureate in England, was really the best of them politically. The most lucid and persuasive and cogent explanation of that par-ticular position of these particular poets at that time you'll find in C. Day Lewis. Auden's all went into his poetry, and so did Spender's. Spender's now reads like something written by a gifted but naive schoolboy who believed, in theory, in companionship and brotherhood, not having known very much of it. Auden's is much more disturbing. Auden's early poems, the ones that made him famous, are not about the millennium of brotherhood and walking in the sunlight together and tearing down the old images of the past and building a brave new world, a new heaven and a new earth where all men are brothers. That's Spender's. But Auden's are not like that. He was not on the positive side at all. Auden's early poems were about what the trouble is, not what to do about it, or what it's going to be like when we solve it, but what it is. They're full of images of broken-down factories and polluted canals and railways that don't work and rusty hinges and torn-up automobiles in vacant lots. You can't read, even today, these early poems of Auden's without being disturbed about the course of civilization generally. Because although we have plush times now in the United States, and generally in the Western world, still there's enough residue of what might happen that you can get from Auden's early poems for them to be almost as disturbing now as they must have been when there were broken-down pylons and terribly run-down apartment houses and everything looked shabby and hopeless. Well, that was the climate where Auden started out.

Now, how he did this, the actual tone that Auden took, is fascinating and characteristic of him. He didn't write simply descriptive poems of, say, a run-down factory or an abandoned factory. He wrote poems which brought his great ability, which is a single ability which takes a million forms, into play, and that is the ability to generalize creatively. We all generalize, but nobody in the whole human race has ever generalized as Auden can generalize. Because he's able to draw the most surprising conclusions from things that the rest of us thought we had the answer to pretty well. He'll say just one little thing. I remember an interview I heard somebody do with him just after I came back from the Second World War. Someone who was interviewing him mentioned the atrocities that were committed by the Germans and the atrocities committed against the American troops in the Pacific. And he said, "That is always a characteristic attributed to the other side." Well, it is. It might have happened, and it did happen, but the Audenistic generalization is that it's something you put on the other fellow. You don't generally think of it that way. But it's true.

Whenever Auden makes one of these fantastic statements, you've got to listen, because he's a lot smarter than you, and he's thought about it more, and he's taken that kind of daring logical leap that will land him in a generalization that you couldn't have believed, but which just may very well be exactly the case. And this is the kind of thing that Auden brings to bear in his poems, this fantastic ability to generalize creatively and most of the time rightly.

Now I'll give you an example of an Audenism in which he's completely wrong. Or at least I think I've caught him out at least once. He says that parody in literature is possible only in the case of a brilliantly original writer. In other words, if you don't have an original writer to parody, which is to say, as he does say, someone who is markedly good and original, unless you have that, you don't have anything to parody. In other words you can parody Dylan Thomas, you can parody T. S. Eliot, you can parody James Joyce, but you cannot parody anyone who does not have that creative brilliance. There's something wrong with that, because you can parody a bad style just as well as you can a good style—Edgar Guest or Edith Sitwell. The fact that someone is unmistakably idiosyncratic in his style does not necessarily make him good. But I think if I told that to Auden he would destroy me in two seconds. He knows so much.

After Oxford, he leads the neo-Marxist in literature mainly by writing, not getting up and making speeches as Day Lewis did. He did go to fight in Spain, but it was just a token gesture. He never saw any combat; neither did any of the rest of them. He comes back just after the Spanish Civil War and just before Hitler's invasion of Poland and decides that the place to be is not England. So, he gets the hell out of there, and he comes over here and he marries Erica Mann, who's [the German novelist] Thomas Mann's daughter. He quickly takes out citizenship papers and becomes an American citizen. Everybody's perfectly glad to have him, the great post-Eliot English poet. So he comes over here and marries Erica Mann to be sure that she gets a passport. They never lived together. Technically, I believe they're still married, but they never had anything to do with each other except officially. He settles almost immediate into what he calls the homosexual mafia in New York. And he lives down there in shabby digs in the East Village. He's a night man. He likes the night. He pulls the curtains down in the daytime. He says the view distracts him. And he sits there and writes poems and hundreds of brilliant introductions to books that he likes. He writes literary criticism. He's a man of letters, a night person who is completely and absolutely and utterly devoted to the mind and to creativity and to thought and to the activities of his small group.

Out of this has come some of the most provocative, intelligent poetry of our times. What people can't understand about Auden, and I don't believe that time will ever solve it, is how Auden can have so many gifts. He is unquestionably the most skillful versifier that's ever handled the English language. There's nothing he can't do. He can use any form, from a simple folk ballad, usually in his case with lots of Freudian overtones, to the most complicated Italian form or the form of the Norse sagas or the Icelandic sagas, adapted in his own way to English. But what is disturbing about Auden is that he can do everything but the one thing. Let's look at one poem that gives you this fantastic generalizing power. This is an Audenesque description of a Brueghel picture in a museum—I believe it's in Brussels—but the generalization is not about painting at all. It's about human suffering and how the old masters showed you what human suffering really is. Maybe they didn't even know that's what they were doing. But Auden knew that's what they were doing. This one is about Icarus, who tried to escape from Crete and flew too close to the sun and melted the wax on his wings. In [Pieter] Brueghel's (1525–1569) picture in the foreground there's a farmer plowing the land at the edge of this cliff, and off in the horizon there's one of those stylish, square-rigged ships, and in the right-hand corner there are these tiny little legs that are just going into the ocean. If you didn't look, if you didn't know that's what was happening, you would miss it. So, this Auden takes for his text. The great thing about Auden is that anything is fair game to him. He can turn the Auden poetry-making machine on anything and come up with something that sometimes is just tremendous, that nobody without his ability to generalize creatively would have thought about even. He thinks about it. He's great at opening a poem: "About suffering they were never wrong, / The Old Masters. . . ."

MUSÉE DES BEAUX ARTS

About suffering they were never wrong,
The Old Masters: how well they understood
Its human position; how it takes place
While someone else is eating or opening a window
    or just walking dully along;

How, when the aged are reverently, passionately waiting
For the miraculous birth, there always must be
Children who did not specially want it to happen, skating
On a pond at the edge of the wood:
They never forgot
That even the dreadful martyrdom must run its course
Anyhow in a corner, some untidy spot
Where the dogs go on with their doggy life and the torturer's horse
Scratches its innocent behind on a tree.

In Breughel's *Icarus,* for instance: how everything turns away
Quite leisurely from the disaster; the ploughman may
Have heard the splash, the forsaken cry,
But for him it was not an important failure; the sun shone
As it had to on the white legs disappearing into the green
Water; and the expensive delicate ship that must have seen
Something amazing, a boy falling out of the sky,
Had somewhere to get to and sailed calmly on.

Auden's concerns have become, with the years, increasingly religious. He has become a convert to Anglo-Catholicism, and he's become increasingly intolerant of and antagonistic towards any kind of secularism. He can tell you exactly why God exists. Of course it's all intellectual. And that characterizes everything that Auden does. And that may be the thing that militates against him in the final estimate, that he has too many things going, that his position is not central enough. He'd just as easily do this thing as that thing. There's not any sense of necessity about most of Auden. So much of it seems to be an intellectual trickery, and intellectual playing, superbly, with ideas. He'll use a little [Søren] Kierkegaard here, a little [Marcel] Proust there, a little Matthew Arnold there, a little [Charles] Baudelaire here. And he'll make them all into this enormous figure of a poet called Auden who can do anything, borrow anything from anybody, and make it into something that that poet would never have recognized because he's been through the Auden mill. He's an amazing magician, and he gives you plenty to think about, but he doesn't touch you. He's too impersonal, finally. But boy, what a show!

This is about gambling, and he takes gambling as nobody but him would have done, as a secularized form of churchgoing. In other words, this is what we have instead of churches. But people go for the same reasons, only they don't know it. They have no mythology, and yet the instinct that causes people to see the bull dancers in Crete and Gothic cathedrals takes them, in their religious quest, into temples, sometimes into labyrinths and sometimes into casinos. But the instinct is basically religious. It is what has always brought people into places of worship, but with us and our materialistic culture, it's into gambling houses. There's much more personal commitment in this one than in the others. And maybe this is why I like it of the three or four of Auden's that I like the best. The touchstone is the genre of the creative generalizing power, without which there wouldn't be any Auden.

Let me read to you this one about college and about teachers. It was the Phi Beta Kappa poem at Harvard in 1946 after all the veterans had gotten out of the army, and everybody was trying to get the university experience back together. It's called "Under Which Lyre." He takes mythological figures and again, as Auden would do, uses them in a different way. Ares, of course, the god of war. But the two main antagonists here stand for two different ways of taking human life: Hermes or Mercury is the unpredictable, flighty, imaginative, disorganized, creative type; Apollo, the official sun god, who drives the chariot of the sun across the sky, is the guy who organizes and sets up courses in education in colleges and puts in computer systems and all the superorganizational things in college life and in modern life generally. So Apollo is the organizer and Hermes is the scapegrace, quicksilver, capricious, hard-to-hold, crazy kind of influence. With somebody whose mind is as organized and as well-stocked as Auden's, you would think that he would be on the side of Apollo. No; no way! So this is about the veterans coming back to school and what happens to them. Apollo is wrong, although he gets things done. Hermes is right, but you can't depend on him.

Now, on the other side of things, there is an awful lot of Auden. This is a *Collected Shorter Poems,* and, as you might imagine, there's a *Collected Longer Poems.* The prose I recommend as absolutely fascinating and wonderful and completely diverting. To encounter Auden's essays: he's throwing stuff off so fast that you're exhilarated when you finish with an essay by Auden. But it's also as if you've been run over by a truck. You just can't stand up against all that barrage of information and intelligence interpreted in so many new ways. But exhilarating it is. It's just tremendous fun. He's the one guy, the foremost guy in our time, who makes the intellect and the play and dance of ideas almost physically exhilarating. It's disturbing, and sometimes it's kind of hard to follow, but it's just tremendous fun. If so much of his stuff were not so doomful and depressing, you would retain the idea of a guy who for sixty-five years has had a good time out of his mind. I think about all his prose that you would want to read, although there's a great deal of it, is in this book called *The Dyer's Hand.* Some of it is kind of personal for him, whom you think of being the impersonal poet par excellence. He hardly ever says *I,* and when he does it's a kind of impersonal

I like the editorial *we*. You don't get to know anything about Auden's personal life. He's the farthest possible thing from being a so-called "confessional poet." Auden's work is a public poetry; it's pronouncing on events; it's drawing conclusions about historical movements and social and economic and psychoanalytical movements and using everything that comes to Auden in whatever form. He just transfuses it in this fantastic cauldron of a brain of his, and it emerges as something that it would never recognize itself. He's made it into something very, very thought-provoking and disturbing, and also some of the time very funny.

I wish I could talk some more on Auden, but I could talk a whole year on Auden and hardly scratch the surface. There's so much he can do and so much he is doing. There is a tremendous excitement in the play of the mind on ideas, a great concerted mastery of poetic form, a great ability to surprise you about small things and large things like historical issues and movements, about anything from psychoanalysis to the naming of the cat. Every time I see a new poem by Auden I read it, because he's just got so many guns. He's so good. But there's always, to me, something about him that's a little bit unsatisfactory. He gives you plenty to think about, infinite amounts of stuff to think about, but he goes to the reader's head a shade too easily. He doesn't get you in the heart. But you must read him. Read the prose, too.

DYLAN THOMAS

Dylan Thomas was a Welsh boy from Swansea who had a prodigious verbal gift as a young guy. Very unstable, began drinking heavily as a teenager, worked briefly as a newspaper reporter in Wales, drifted to London into the BBC scene, into the Sunday *Times Literary Supplement* scene, into the various reviewing jobs, always poor, but saw early in life that he could make it as a *character*. Allen Ginsberg tries to make it as a character, with social implications. But unlike Allen Ginsberg, Dylan Thomas had an enormous gift and was a dedicated poet, tremendously dedicated in his early years. He'd go through 250 drafts of a poem to get the sound he wanted. He was no charlatan like Ginsberg. The pity of it is that he allowed himself to be made, for money and for fame, for whiskey and for sex, into a charlatan. So now, when people listen to Dylan Thomas read his poems on records, they are not cognizant of Dylan Thomas because this is the man that wrote these poems; no, they are cognizant of the poems because Dylan Thomas, the famous, raffish, drunken character, happened to be the guy who wrote the poems. They are more interested in him than in anything he wrote, and they're interested in what he wrote because it was he that wrote it, and that's a shame, because he's a magnificent poet. And all the couples who are hanging out together now, stoned on marijuana in Greenwich Village listening to the records of Dylan Thomas, don't really know how good he is, nor do they care.

I would say, of the great original users of the English language, who have brought something truly original to the use of English in poetry, the two finest, the two most original in the whole canon of English poetry, are Gerard Manley Hopkins and Dylan Thomas. But of the two, the more original is Dylan Thomas. Now, if that's what you're looking for, if that's your criterion, Dylan Thomas is the better, the greater. Hopkins has essentially a "made" style as John Berryman had a "made" style; it's very labored; although very exciting, it's very labored, very artificial. Dylan Thomas's style seems natural to him. If you had not heard these words said in just this order, you would never have comprehended how such a situation could have existed. He's wonderful, original—but he is deadly as an influence. Hopkins: you can use him in a limited way as an influence on your work; but Thomas, no. I have never known a single writer that he's had a good influence on. Because he is so idiosyncratic and so original and so of a piece with his own sort of thing, that anybody who borrows from Dylan Thomas does not end up borrowing from Dylan Thomas to use it for his own purposes; he merely ends up sounding like a poor imitation of Dylan Thomas. He has no progeny; he had very few predecessors. I don't know whether this is good or bad. Auden, with his much more public style, has given birth to thousands of poets who learned from him, but nobody has learned from Dylan Thomas except "go thou and do otherwise." There's almost nothing that Dylan Thomas can bequeath another poet, and this may be both a sign of his worth and a sign of his limitation.

The story is this. Here is this preternaturally brilliant South Wales boy whose father is a schoolmaster, and he has a very close kind of family feeling, but no one could quite figure him out. He's not that much different from the other kids around Swansea, where he grew up in South Wales, but he has this great gift of gab. He's a congenital liar, but what he said later in life is that the lies gave rise to the poems. And there's something to ponder about that. As Picasso said, art is the lie that enables us to see the truth. Dylan Thomas knew that in the beginning. He would go to a movie when he knew perfectly well that he had been to that movie, and he would come in and say that he'd been to another movie. And he would develop the theme of the movie that he had *not* seen as an intellectual exercise.

He drifted out of Wales, into London, into the bohemia of the BBC and broadcasting and the early days of telecasting, and was an actor. He had a magnificent voice, like Richard Burton. He's that sort of rhetorical speaker. He had that kind of superb BBC voice. They thought, when they heard Dylan Thomas read his own work, he could read the telephone directory and it would be exactly the same. He bummed around, he whored around, he drank himself into a very low state. He married a strange, powerful enigmatic earth mother of a figure, an Irish girl. And he just was generally a mess around England. He turned himself from a kind of angelic-looking, ethereal, great big-eyed boy with curly hair into a fat little pig. But the thing that happens is that a well-meaning guy who's an editor of an anthology, John Malcolm Brinnin—he's head of the YMHA Poetry Reading Series in New York—figures that Dylan Thomas would be great to bring over to America. And there the trouble began. Because Dylan Thomas in this country was not only liked or loved, he was adored. He was taken up by every university, every coed, every host eagerly dispensing free whiskey, which Thomas lapped up at a great rate. He made three tours over here from enormous fees from universities, and he figured that he didn't have to write anything more. All this scrupulous attention and the 250 draft things that he had done before: in the last six years of his life he wrote no poetry. He read poetry that he had previously written as a young guy who loved poetry. And he came over here, and slopped around, and traded on what he had already done with his beautiful and powerful Welsh voice, and he made records. And in the end he died in a New York hospital with people competing for his favors. Other poets, women, anthologists were crowding in the corridors to see how our marvelous Welsh bard was doing. But he died of a sickening complaint, a combination of diabetes and what the doctors call a massive alcoholic insult to the brain.

So where does that leave us? It leaves us with three things. It leaves us with Thomas's original work, which is fantastically good, some of it, but not as good as it would have been without the Dylan Thomas legend. He would have been accounted an original, a fine minor poet. But with the life, and with the stories told about him, and all the publicity, it has been ballooned up out of all proportion to what it really was. So, the work is one thing. The next thing is the life. And there can be very few lives of poets in which the two have been intermingled to such an extent. But it seems to me that it's the task of my generation and your generation to disentangle what Dylan Thomas wrote, actually put on the page, from all the rest of the publicity stuff that attended him while he lived and while he died, and has attended him after he died. Those are two things: what he actually did write and what he came to exist as a legend. The third thing is what his example means: the poet killed by commercial society, the fine British poet who was murdered by America, who was murdered by *Mademoiselle* magazine, who was murdered by too many cocktail parties, who was murdered by commercial exploitation.

What does one answer to this? Of course, someone who was as colorful as Dylan Thomas—and he worked hard at it—is going to be taken up by *Mademoiselle* and *Cosmopolitan,* just like a former-day version of Burt Reynolds. That's going to happen. What we have to do, to recognize now, is that nobody forced this on Dylan Thomas. In other words, if you ever go to a cocktail party as a visiting poet and drink five straight double martinis and speak in obscenities loudly and attempt to pick up anybody from a coed to the president's wife, then you've got to be prepared for what? And that's exactly what happened to him. Not at one place, but at every place.

Let me read a couple of more things about Thomas's last days, and then we'll get to his work. This is quite a good article by Elizabeth Hardwick, who's Robert Lowell's wife that he just deserted, if that matters. But she's an uncommonly fine essayist. This is in a book called *A View of My Own.* This is Dylan Thomas's death in a New York hospital, contested over by mistresses, wives, poets, editors, organizers of his tours, sightseers [passage unidentified]. Now, nobody could conduct his life like that and expect to last very much longer. And Thomas himself surely sensed something of the same thing. I think that in the end, since he couldn't write poetry anymore, or at least didn't write it anymore, he felt himself being done to death by his admirers, but was too weak to pull out of it, to go to an isolated place and try to work out some new poems. Since he couldn't pull out of it financially, and above all, emotionally, he just chose to finish it off, to drink himself to death, to give that massive insult of alcohol to the brain and get it over with because he was in a corner from which he could not extricate himself. He was too weak. He did not have the resources of will such as Yeats had. Yeats was another roaring boy in a different way. But Yeats opted for the long life. Dylan Thomas opted for the short, happy life, which turned into a hell, and he died at the age of thirty-eight or thirty-nine.

What lessons are in this? I think the lessons that we need to learn from Dylan Thomas are not so much from the life, although you can learn plenty from that, too, but from the work. Let me give you the work, what it is, where you can get it, and where, in a sense, you can encounter Dylan Thomas, because he is damn well worth it. He is a remarkable writer. First of all, there is a *Collected Poems*. I would say that about ninety poems, and maybe about one hundred ten, with the variants of the early drafts, and that's all the poetry that exists of Dylan Thomas. The rest of the stuff is fragmentary and is trading on his being a poet and on his being able to read what he wrote with a magnificent voice. It's a very operatic kind of thing. I listened to some of his records when I first started to give readings, and they said to me, do it any other way, because it's so actorish. It's embarrassing to me to listen to Dylan Thomas. Other people like him, but to me he's embarrassing. It's not exactly insincere—though maybe that, too—but actorish. And you can't forget when you hear this that Dylan Thomas was an actor, and a very well paid one, on the BBC, that he cultivated this aspect of his being. He traded on it.

There are a couple of posthumous books of prose. There's an unfinished novel called *Adventures in the Skin Trade and Other Stories*. Then there's a play he did, a play for voices. He called it *Under Milk Wood;* everybody knows about that. There are the letters to Vernon Watkins, which are among the best ever written from one poet to another, explaining what he's trying to do. Fantastic stuff. I would recommend this to any young poet or old poet or anybody who's interested in poetry and the imagination and the fire that one can take when one realizes that one's own gift is really capable of something extraordinary. He talks about this to Watkins. *Letters to Vernon Watkins.* And that's about all there is of Dylan Thomas. The rest of the books you'll find pertaining to Dylan Thomas are books *about* Dylan Thomas. The life is absorbing. You can't set the life against the work. There's no point in that. What you need to do is define their relationship to one another. But there are plenty of people who *will* set the life against the work and say that the life is more fascinating than the work. The *poems* are what Dylan Thomas is going to have to be judged by in the final analysis. There's a very good, long, although I expect a definitive life, by Constantine FitzGibbon simply called *The Life of Dylan Thomas,* and all the hideousness of what the guy did to himself, and did to anybody else that was ever connected with him, is in that. I've been absorbed in this book all morning, and I must say that I don't think that I'm going to teach Dylan Thomas in any more courses. I hope that this is my last time to encounter and retrace this melancholy story of a very great talent harnessed to a very weak guy, a weak charming guy, a crazy fun guy. I don't want to go through this again.

The poems themselves are talked about very learnedly in a University of Chicago Press publication called *The Poetry of Dylan Thomas* by Elder Olson. If you want to go into the more symbolic meanings and the Freudianism and the rest of it, he will help you. But again, only graduate students want to encounter Dylan Thomas in that way. They want to encounter Dylan Thomas through the records and the legend of the roaring boy and the ass-pincher, the drunkard who said wonderful, crazy things and got up and read his poems and the poems of other people, such as Yeats, in this magnificent voice. And the last, most melancholy of all is Brinnin's account of what actually happened on the American tours: *Dylan Thomas in America.* Okay. I'll read to you a page of this [passage unidentified]. This is toward the end when his diabetes is really getting to him and when he's really socking the stuff down, when he's drinking two or three quarts of whiskey a day. And Brinnin and the other people who are with him all feel this sense of guilt because they got him into this, because he wanted to come over here and make a lot of American money. Now this is a fearsome, harrowing document about a guy going downhill fast, a guy of enormous talent, who was loved to death, and partied to death, and misunderstood to death. You must read John Malcolm Brinnin's *Dylan Thomas in America.* That is what must *not* happen, but to him, the most extraordinary, different one of all, it did, and it finished him. But it wasn't America. It was a combination of himself, his needs, his own anxieties, and his own alcoholic tendencies, and also coupled with the terrible thirst that diabetes gives a guy. This is part of it, though I don't think it's been sufficiently recognized.

Now, two or three more things. Let's read a Dylan Thomas poem. You'll notice, if you just look at the poem on the page, how scrupulous he was about balancing the poem on the page. This is what you would call an invented form. You must understand the excitement a poet can get out of inventing a form and following the whole form all the way through to the end, just to see what he can do with it. What is it William James says, something like, genius is the ability to act according to laws of one's own invention? And this is a poem in which Thomas acted according to the laws of his own invention. But listen to the guy's ear. It's so fantastically beautiful. It's a poem simply about childhood on a farm. His aunt had a place called Fern Hill—and he went out as a little boy to play there. And it's about childhood and about your feelings for the locality, the hay barns, the foxes that you hear barking at night when you're tucked in, and the chickens and all these things, and the sudden realization, as an older man, of what this really meant, what it meant to be a child on a farm with a hay barn and the foxes and the chickens and a simple life. And that you can never go back there.

FERN HILL

Now as I was young and easy under the apple boughs
About the lilting house and happy as the grass was green,
The night above the dingle starry,
            Time let me hail and climb
Golden in the heydays of his eyes,
And honoured among wagons I was prince of the apple towns
And once below a time I lordly had the trees and leaves
            Trail with daisies and barley
Down the rivers of the windfall light.

And as I was green and carefree, famous among the barns
About the happy yard and singing as the farm was home,
In the sun that is young once only,
            Time let me play and be
Golden in the mercy of his means,
And green and golden I was huntsman and herdsman, the calves
Sang to my horn, the foxes on the hills barked clear and cold,
            And the sabbath rang slowly
In the pebbles of the holy streams.

All the sun long it was running, it was lovely, the hay
Fields high as the house, the tunes from the chimneys, it was air
And playing, lovely and watery
            And fire green as grass.
And nightly under the simple stars
As I rode to sleep the owls were bearing the farm away,
All the moon long I heard, blessed among stables, the night-jars

Dylan Thomas

Signing books at the University of South Carolina World War II symposium, 1995. *Photograph by J. T. Wagenheim*

Flying with the ricks, and the horses
                    Flashing into the dark.

And then to awake, and the farm, like a wanderer white
With the dew, come back, the cock on his shoulder: it was all
Shining, it was Adam and maiden,
                    The sky gathered again
And the sun grew round that very day.
So it must have been after the birth of the simple light
In the first, spinning place, the spellbound horses walking warm
Out of the whinnying green stable
                    On to the fields of praise.

And honored among foxes and pheasants by the gay house
Under the new made clouds and happy as the heart was long,
In the sun born over and over,
                    I ran my heedless ways,
My wishes raced through the house high hay
And nothing I cared, at my sky blue trades, that time allows
In all his tuneful turning so few and such morning songs

Before the children green and golden
  Follow him out of grace,

Nothing I cared, in the lamb white days, that time would take me
Up to the swallow thronged loft by the shadow of my hand,
In the moon that is always rising,
  Nor that riding to sleep
I should hear him fly with the high fields
And wake to the farm forever fled from the childless land.
Oh as I was young and easy in the mercy of his means,
  Time held me green and dying
  Though I sang in my chains like the sea.

If it weren't for the verbal magic about it, I would say it is sentimental, some-
thing like Tennyson. And yet, there's an undeniable beauty and power about it.

But the main thing I have always felt about Dylan Thomas—and nobody
has paid more homage to him, or loved his work more than I do—is that there
was something at the heart and core of Dylan Thomas that was essentially
phony and that he covers up with his enormous verbal magic. In the journals
of Winfield Scott, who was another suicide—died in 1968—he says that there
are two kinds of writing: this verbal magic, like Thomas, and the writing that
comes from actual human experience. The greatest poets combine the two:
Shakespeare frequently, Robinson now and then. If I had to choose, Scott said,
I'd choose the second. He'd go with the human thing rather than the verbal
legerdemain, for Wordsworth or Hardy, for example, rather than Poe or [Arthur]
Rimbaud. This is all an oversimplification, I know, but I think the flat assertion
of the two kinds indicates two very great touchstones, two very different
approaches to the writing of poetry. Now, as Scott says, sometimes they can be
combined; nevertheless, the dichotomy is essential. There are some poets who
reside completely in one or in the other. I don't know what posterity will say
about Thomas, but if you like the sound of words in combinations that you
would never think could have been so melodious and so appealing, even if you
don't know what the denotations of the words are, you're bound to go with him,
because he can *do* it. He is extremely seductive and very, very appealing.

Let me read to you one more by Dylan Thomas. This is the best of all of
his, the most characteristic. It's called "The Hunchback in the Park."

THE HUNCHBACK IN THE PARK

The hunchback in the park
A solitary mister
Propped between trees and water

Dylan Thomas

From the opening of the garden lock
That lets the trees and water enter
Until the Sunday somber bell at dark

Eating bread from a newspaper
Drinking water from the chained cup
That the children filled with gravel
In the fountain basin where I sailed my ship
Slept at night in a dog kennel
But nobody chained him up.

Like the park birds he came early
Like the water he sat down
And Mister they called Hey mister
The truant boys from the town
Running when he had heard them clearly
On out of sound

Past lake and rockery
Laughing when he shook his paper
Hunchbacked in mockery
Through the loud zoo of the willow groves
Dodging the park keeper
With his stick that picked up leaves.

And the old dog sleeper
Alone between nurses and swans
While the boys among willows
Made the tigers jump out of their eyes
To roar on the rockery stones
And the groves were blue with sailors

Made all day until bell time
A woman figure without fault
Straight as a young elm
Straight and tall from his crooked bones
That she might stand in the night
After the locks and chains

All night in the unmade park
After the railings and shrubberies
The birds the grass the trees the lake
And the wild boys innocent as strawberries
Had followed the hunchback
To his kennel in the dark.

279

This was a great theme of Thomas's, the theme of metamorphosis. You have a hunchback, and he's a figure of pity in the park. But when the gates are closed, and the children have gone home, and everybody has fed the animals and played games on the rockeries, out of the hunchback's body rises a magnificently straight and beautiful woman, who stands in the dark all night, unseen. It's because of the extreme deformity that the extreme straightness and beauty come to be. But it's never seen, except by the poet, who imagines it.

CODA

From James Dickey's final class session, 14 January 1997, University of South Carolina

Invent. Invent is the guts of it. To invent. You can say as much as you like with stuff you know. But don't be confined to it. Don't think about—honestly—don't think about telling the truth. Because poets are not trying to tell the truth, are they?

They are trying to show God a few things he maybe didn't think of. It takes us to supply that. We are not trying to tell the truth. We are trying to make it so that when we sit down to write we are absolute lords over our material. We can say anything we want to, any way we want to. The question is to find the right way, the best way to do it. This is what we are going to be looking for.

This is going to take us through some very strange fields, across a lot of rivers, oceans, mountains, forests. God knows where it will take us. That is part of the excitement of it, and the sense of deep adventure. Which is what we want more than anything. Discovery. Everything is in that. Everything *is* that.

We have to fight for it. We have to fight through to it. We have to cut the angel out of the marble, out of the rock, the form of the angel. Michelangelo used to say the angel is already in the stone; all I got to do is chip the rock from around it and set it free. Well, the shape is already in there. It takes a lot of chipping to get that angel to stand up, much less to fly. Sort of heavy for that. So, as I say, this is a strange and long journey that we are undertaking.

With my current physical shape this will almost undoubtedly be my last class forever.

But what we start here I would like you to continue on your own. When we get started, I want you to fight this thing through, with your own unconscious, with your own dreams, and see where it comes out. That is the excitement and the fun of it—deep discovery, deep adventure. It is the most dangerous game, and the best.

Flaubert says somewhere that the life of a poet is a hell of a life; it is a dog's life, but it is the only one worth living. You suffer more. You are frustrated more by things that don't bother other people. But you also live so much more. You live so much more intensely and so much more vitally. And with so much more of a sense of meaning, of consequentiality, instead of nothing mattering. This is what is driving our whole civilization into suicide. The feeling that we are living existences in which nothing matters very much, or at all. That is what is behind all the drugs and the alcoholism and suicide—insanity, wars, every-thing—a sense of nonconsequence. A sense that nothing, nothing matters. No matter which way we turn it is the same thing. But the poet is free of that. He is free of that.

For the poet, everything matters, and it matters a lot. That is the realm where we work. Once you are there, you are hooked. If you are a real poet, you are hooked more deeply than any narcotics addict could possibly be on heroin. You are hooked on something that is life-giving instead of destructive. Some-thing that is a process that cannot be too far from the process that created everything. God's process. You can say what you can of God. I don't know what your religion might be. You can say what you want as to whether this is a chemist's universe or a physicist's universe or an Old Testament, New Testa-ment, God's universe—whatever kind of universe you might want to attribute the cosmos to. You can attribute it any way you want. To an engineer, as I say, to a physicist or an astronomer. Or whatever you might want the deity to be.

Those are things that he *might* be. What this universe indubitably *is* is a poet's universe. Nothing but a poetic kind of consciousness could have con-ceived of anything like this. That is where the truth of the matter lies. You are in some way in line with the creative genesis of the universe. In some way—in a much lesser way, of course. We can't create those trees or that water or any-thing that is out there. We can't do it. But we can re-create it. We are second-ary creators. We take God's universe and make it over our way. And it is different from his. It is similar in some ways, but it is different in some ways. And the difference lies in the slant, in the slant that we individually put on it and that *only* we can put on it. That is the difference. That is where our value lies. Not only for ourselves, but for the other people who read us. There is some increment there that we make possible that would not otherwise be there.

I don't mean to sell the poet so long or at such great length, but I do this principally because the world doesn't esteem the poet very much. They don't understand where we are coming from. They don't understand the use for us. They don't understand if there is any use. They don't really value us very much. We are the masters of the superior secret, not they. Not they. Remember that when you write. You are at the top level, and they are down there with Elvis and Marilyn Monroe and the general idols of the schlock culture we live in. We are the elitists. I don't mind saying that at all. Quality is what we strive for, best standards.

James Dickey died five days later: 19 January 1997.

SOURCES

It cannot be determined which editions of the books James Dickey used when reading poems to the class. The following list of sources identifies wherever possible the first editions of the books. For the convenience of the readers outside of the United States, both the first American and first British editions are cited.

Aiken, Conrad. *Collected Criticism*. New York and London: Oxford University Press, 1968.

———. *Collected Novels of Conrad Aiken*. Ed. R. P. Blackmur. New York: Holt, Rinehart and Winston, 1964.

———. *Collected Poems*. New York: Oxford University Press, 1953.

———. *A Reviewer's ABC's: Collected Criticism of Conrad Aiken from 1916 to the Present*. Ed. Rufus A. Blanshard. New York: Greenwich/Meridian, 1958; London: Allen, 1961.

———. *Ushant: An Essay*. Boston: Little, Brown, 1952; London: Allen, 1963.

Aldington, Richard. *Lawrence of Arabia: A Biographical Enquiry*. Chicago: Regnery, 1955; London: Collins, 1955.

———. *Life for Life's Sake: A Book of Reminiscences*. New York: Viking, 1941; London: Cassell, 1968.

Amis, Kingsley. *A Case of Samples: Poems 1946–1956*. London: Gollancz, 1956; New York: Harcourt, Brace, 1956.

———. *A Look Round the Estate: Poems 1957–1967*. London: Cape, 1967; New York: Harcourt, Brace, 1968.

———. *Lucky Jim: A Novel*. London: Gollancz, 1954; New York: Doubleday, 1954.

———. *Take a Girl Like You*. London: Gollancz, 1960; New York: Harcourt, Brace, 1961.

———. *That Uncertain Feeling*. London: Gollancz, 1955; New York: Harcourt, Brace, 1956.

Auden, W. H. *Collected Longer Poems*. London: Faber and Faber, 1968; New York: Random House, 1969.

———. *Collected Shorter Poems, 1930–1944*. London: Faber and Faber, 1950.

———. *The Dyer's Hand and Other Essays*. New York: Random House, 1962; London: Faber and Faber, 1963.

————. "A Knight of the Infinite." Review of *Gerard Manley Hopkins: A Life,* by Eleanor Ruggles. *New Republic,* 21 August 1944, 223–24.

Barbellion, W. N. P. *A Last Diary: The Journal of a Disappointed Man.* New York: Doran, 1920; London: Chatto and Windus, 1920.

Baxter, Walter. *Look Down in Mercy.* London: Heinemann, 1951; New York: Putnam, 1952.

Bell, William. *Travel Poems and Others.* San Antonio, Tex.: Trinity University Press, 1972.

Bennett, Arnold. *Clayhanger.* London: Methuen, 1910; New York: Doubleday, Doran, 1910.

————. *The Old Wives' Tale.* London: Chapman and Hall, 1908; New York: Hodder and Stoughton, 1909.

Bishop, John Peale. *Act of Darkness.* New York: Scribner, 1935; London: Cape, 1935.

————. *The Collected Essays of John Peale Bishop.* Ed. Edmund Wilson. New York: Scribner, 1948.

————. *The Collected Poems of John Peale Bishop.* Ed. Allen Tate. New York: Charles Scribner's Sons, 1948.

Bowers, Edgar. *The Form of Loss.* [Denver, Colo.]: Swallow, 1956.

Bridges, Robert. *The Shorter Poems of Robert Bridges.* Oxford, U.K.: Clarendon Press, 1931; Westport, Conn.: Hyperion Press, 1979.

Brinnin, John Malcolm. *Dylan Thomas in America: An Intimate Journal.* Boston: Little, Brown, 1955; London: Dent, 1956.

Britten, Benjamin. *War Requiem.* Op. 66. London and New York: Boosey and Hawkes, 1962.

Brooke, Rupert. *The Collected Poems of Rupert Brooke.* New York: John Lane, 1915; London: Sidgwick and Jackson, 1918.

Brower, Reuben. *The Poetry of Robert Frost: Constellations of Intention.* New York: Oxford University Press, 1963.

Causley, Charles. *Union Street.* London: R. Hart-Davis, 1957; Boston: Houghton Mifflin, 1958.

Cecil, David. *Hardy, the Novelist: An Essay in Criticism.* London: Constable, 1943; Indianapolis, Ind., and New York: Bobbs-Merrill, 1946.

Chase, Richard. *Emily Dickinson.* New York: Sloane, 1951; London: Methuen, 1952.

Davidson, Donald. *The Attack on Leviathan: Regionalism and Nationalism in the United States.* Chapel Hill: University of North Carolina Press, 1938.

————. *Poems: 1922–1961.* Minneapolis: University of Minnesota Press, 1966.

————. *Still Rebels, Still Yankees and Other Essays.* Baton Rouge: Louisiana State University Press, 1957.

Davie, Donald. *Articulate Energy: An Inquiry into the Syntax of English Poetry.* London: Routledge and Paul, 1955; New York: Harcourt, Brace, 1958.

————. *Ezra Pound: Poet as Sculptor.* New York: Oxford University Press, 1964; London: Routledge and Paul, 1965.

————. *New and Selected Poems.* Middletown: Wesleyan University Press, 1961.

De la Mare, Walter. *Behold, This Dreamer! Of Reverie, Night, Sleep. . . .* London: Faber and Faber, 1939; New York: Knopf, 1939.

————. *Collected Poems.* New York: Holt, 1941; London: Faber and Faber, 1942.

————. *Come Hither: A Collection of Rhymes and Poems for the Young of All Ages.* London: Constable, 1923; New York: Knopf, 1923.

————. *Love.* London: Faber and Faber, 1943; New York: Morrow, 1946.

————. *Memoirs of a Midget.* London: Collins, 1921; New York: Knopf, 1922.

————. *The Return.* London: Arnold, 1910; New York: Putnam, 1911.

Dickey, James. *Deliverance.* Boston: Houghton Mifflin, 1970; London: Hamish Hamilton, 1970.

————. "The Poet of Secret Lives and Misspent Opportunities." *New York Times Book Review,* 18 May 1969, pp. 1, 10.

Dickinson, Emily. *Emily Dickinson.* Ed. John Malcolm Brinnin. New York: Dell, 1960.

————. *The Letters of Emily Dickinson.* Ed. Thomas H. Johnson. Cambridge, Mass.: Belknap Press of Harvard University Press, 1958.

————. *The Poems of Emily Dickinson.* Ed. Thomas H. Johnson. Cambridge, Mass.: Belknap Press of Harvard University Press, 1955.

————. *Selected Poems of Emily Dickinson.* Ed. Conrad Aiken. London: Cape, 1924; New York: Modern Library, 1948.

Douglas, Keith. *Alamein to Zem Zem.* London: Editions Poetry London, 1946; New York: Chilmark, 1966.

————. *Collected Poems.* London: Editions Poetry London, 1951; New York: Chilmark, 1967.

Ellmann, Richard. *Yeats: The Man and the Masks.* New York: Macmillan, 1948; London: Macmillan, 1949.

Fenollosa, Ernest. *The Chinese Written Character As a Medium for Poetry.* New York: Arrow, 1936; London: Nott, 1936.

FitzGibbon, Constantine. *The Life of Dylan Thomas.* Boston: Little, Brown, 1965; London: Dent, 1965.

Fraser, G. S. *Ezra Pound.* Edinburgh: Oliver and Boyd, 1960; New York: Grove, 1961.

Frost, Robert. *The Poetry of Robert Frost.* New York: Holt, Rinehart and Winston, 1969; London: Cape, 1972.

————. *Selected Prose of Robert Frost.* New York: Holt, Rinehart and Winston, 1969.

Graham, W. S. *Cage without Grievance: Poems.* Glasgow: Parton Press, 1942.

————. *Malcolm Mooney's Land.* London: Faber and Faber, 1970.

————. *The Nightfishing.* London: Faber and Faber, 1970; New York: Grove, 1970.

———. *The Seven Journeys: Poems.* Glasgow: MacLellan, 1944.

Gregory, Horace. *The Dying Gladiators and Other Essays.* New York: Grove, 1961.

Grigson, Geoffrey. *Gerard Manley Hopkins.* London and New York: The British Council by Longmans, Green, 1955.

H.D. *Selected Poems.* New York: Grove, 1957; London: Deutsch, 1957.

Hagedorn, Hermann. *Edwin Arlington Robinson: A Biography.* New York: Macmillan, 1938.

Hall, James, and Martha Steinmann, eds. *The Permanence of Yeats: Selected Criticism.* New York: Macmillan, 1950.

Hamburger, Michael. *Travelling I–V.* London: Agenda Editions, 1972.

Hardwick, Elizabeth. *A View of My Own: Essays in Literature and Society.* New York: Farrar, Straus and Cudahy, 1962; London: Heinemann, 1964.

Hardy, Thomas. *The Dynasts. Part First.* London: Macmillan, 1904; New York: Macmillan, 1904.

———. *The Dynasts. Part Second.* London: Macmillan, 1906; New York: Macmillan, 1906.

———. *The Dynasts. Part Third.* London: Macmillan, 1908; New York: Macmillan, 1908.

———. *Jude the Obscure.* London: Osgood, McIllvaine, 1895; New York: Harper, 1895.

Hecht, Anthony. *The Hard Hours: Poems.* New York: Atheneum, 1967; London: Oxford University Press, 1967.

———. *A Summoning of Stones.* New York: Macmillan, 1954.

Hill, Geoffrey. *For the Unfallen: Poems, 1952–1958.* London: Deutsch, 1959; Chester Springs, Pa.: Dufour, 1960.

———. *King Log.* London: Deutsch, 1968; Chester Springs, Pa.: Dufour, 1968.

———. *Mercian Hymns.* London: Deutsch, 1971.

Hopkins, Gerard Manley. *The Poems of Gerard Manley Hopkins.* Ed. W. H. Gardner and Norman MacKenzie. New York and London: Oxford University Press, 1948.

Housman, A. E. *The Collected Poems of A. E. Housman.* London: Cape, 1939; New York: Holt, 1940.

———. *The Name and Nature of Poetry.* Cambridge: Cambridge University Press, 1933; New York: Macmillan, 1933.

———. *A Shropshire Lad.* London: Paul, Trench, Trübner, 1896; New York: John Lane, 1897.

Howard, Richard. *Alone with America: Essays on the Art of Poetry in the United States since 1950.* New York: Atheneum, 1969; London: Thames and Hudson, 1970.

Howe, Irving. *Thomas Hardy.* New York: Macmillan, 1967; London: Weidenfeld and Nicholson, 1968.

Hulme, T. E. "The Philosophy of Intensive Manifolds." In *Speculations.* London: Paul, Trench, Trübner, 1924; New York: Harcourt, Brace, 1924.

———. "Romanticism and Classicism." In *Speculations*. London: Paul, Trench, Trübner, 1924; New York: Harcourt, Brace, 1924.

———. *Speculations: Essays on Humanism and the Philosophy of Art*. London: Paul, Trench, Trübner, 1924; New York: Harcourt, Brace, 1924.

Hyman, Stanley Edgar. *The Armed Vision: A Study in the Methods of Modern Literary Criticism*. New York: Knopf, 1948. 2d rev. ed. New York: Vintage Books, 1955.

I'll Take My Stand: The South and the Agrarian Tradition, by Twelve Southerners. New York and London: Harper, 1930.

Jarrell, Randall. *The Animal Family*. New York: Pantheon, 1965; London: Hart-Davis, 1967.

———. *The Bat-poet*. New York: Macmillan, 1964; London: Macmillan, 1966.

———. *The Complete Poems*. New York: Farrar, Straus and Giroux, 1969; London: Faber and Faber, 1971.

———. *Poetry and the Age*. New York: Knopf, 1953; London: Faber and Faber, 1955.

———. *A Sad Heart at the Supermarket: Essays and Fables*. New York: Atheneum, 1962; London: Eyre and Spottiswoode, 1965.

———. *The Third Book of Criticism*. New York: Farrar, Straus & Giroux, 1969; London : Faber, 1975.

Johnson, Thomas H. *Emily Dickinson: An Interpretive Biography*. Cambridge, Mass.: Belknap Press of Harvard University Press, 1955.

Keyes, Sidney. *The Collected Poems of Sidney Keyes*. London: Routledge, 1945; New York: Holt, 1947.

———. *The Cruel Solstice*. London: Routledge, 1943.

———. *The Iron Laurel*. London: Routledge, 1942.

Kingsmill, Hugh. *The Table of Truth*. London: Jarrods, 1933.

Langland, Joseph. *The Green Town: Poems*. Vol. 3 of *Poets of Today*. New York: Scribner's, 1956.

———. *The Wheel of Summer*. New York: Dial, 1963.

Larkin, Philip. *A Girl in Winter*. London: Faber and Faber, 1947; New York: St. Martin's, 1963.

———. *The Less Deceived*. Hessle, U.K.: Marvell, 1955; New York: St. Martin's, 1960.

———. *The North Ship*. London: Fortune, 1945. Enlarged ed., London: Faber and Faber, 1966.

———. *The Whitsun Weddings: Poems*. London: Faber and Faber, 1964; New York: Random House, 1964.

Lattimore, Richmond, ed. and trans. *The Iliad*. Chicago: University of Chicago Press, 1951; London: Routledge, Paul, 1951.

Lewis, Alun. *Ha! Ha! Among the Trumpets: Poems in Transit*. London: Allen and Unwin, 1945; New York: Macmillan, 1945.

———. *In the Green Tree*. London: Allen and Unwin, 1948.

————. *The Last Inspection.* London: Allen and Unwin, 1942; New York: Macmillan, 1943.

————. *Raider's Dawn and Other Poems.* London: Allen and Unwin, 1942; New York: Macmillan, 1942.

————. *Selected Poetry and Prose.* London: Allen and Unwin, 1966.

Lindsay, Vachel. *Collected Poems.* London and New York: Macmillian, 1923.

————. *The Golden Whales of California and Other Rhymes in the American Language.* New York: Macmillan, 1920.

Linscott, Robert, ed. *Selected Poems and Letters of Emily Dickinson.* New York: Anchor/Doubleday, 1959.

Logue, Christopher. *Patrocleia: Book 16 of Homer's Iliad Freely Adapted into English.* Lowestoft, U.K.: Scorpion Press, 1962. Published in the U.S. as *Patrocleia: A New Version.* Ann Arbor: University of Michigan Press, 1963.

————. *War Music: An Account of Books 16 to 19 of Homer's Iliad.* London: Cape, 1981; New York: Farrar, Straus, Giroux, 1987.

————, trans. *Pax: From Book 29 of the Iliad.* London: Turret Books, 1967.

MacLeish, Archibald. *Collected Poems.* Boston: Houghton Mifflin, 1963.

————. *Conquistador.* Boston: Houghton Mifflin, 1932; London: Gollancz, 1933.

————. *The Dialogues of Archibald MacLeish and Mark Van Doren.* Ed. Warren V. Bush. New York: Dutton, 1964.

————. *J. B.: A Play in Verse.* Boston: Houghton Mifflin, 1958; London: Secker and Warburg, 1969.

————. *The Wild Old Wicked Man and Other Poems.* Boston: Houghton Mifflin, 1968; London: Allen, 1969.

Masefield, John. *Dauber: A Poem.* London, William Heinemann, 1913; New York: Macmillan, 1913.

————. *Gallipoli.* London: Heinemann, 1916; New York: Macmillan, 1916.

————. *The Nine Days Wonder (The Operation Dynamo).* London: Heinemann, 1941; New York: Macmillan, 1941.

Muir, Edwin. *An Autobiography.* London: Hogarth Press, 1954; New York: Sloane, 1954.

————. *Collected Poems, 1921–1951.* London: Faber and Faber, 1952; New York: Grove, 1953.

————. *The Estate of Poetry.* London: Hogarth Press, 1962; Cambridge: Harvard University Press, 1962.

————. *The Present Age from 1914.* London: Cresset, 1939; New York: McBride, 1940.

————. *Selected Poems.* With preface by T. S. Eliot. London: Faber and Faber, 1965.

————. *The Structure of the Novel.* London: Hogarth Press, 1928; New York: Harcourt, Brace, 1929.

Norman, Charles. *Ezra Pound.* New York: Macmillan, 1960; London: McDonald, 1969.

Olson, Elder. *The Poetry of Dylan Thomas.* Chicago: University of Chicago Press, 1954.

Owen, Wilfred. *Collected Letters.* London and New York: Oxford University Press, 1967.

———. *Poems.* London: Chatto and Windus, 1920; New York: B. W. Huebsch, 1921.

Pick, John. *A Hopkins Reader.* New York and London: Oxford University Press, 1953.

Pope, Alexander, trans. *The Iliad of Homer.* London: W. Boyer for Bernard Lintott, 1715–1720.

Pound, Ezra. *ABC of Reading.* London: Routledge, 1934; New Haven, Conn.: Yale University Press, 1934.

———. *The Cantos of Ezra Pound.* Comp. John Hamilton and William W. Vasse. [New York]: New Directions, 1948; London: Faber and Faber, 1954.

———. *Cathay: Translations by Ezra Pound for the Most Part from the Chinese of Rihaku.* London: Matthews, 1915.

———. *Hugh Selwyn Mauberley, by E. P.* [London]: Ovid Press, 1920.

———. *Jefferson and/or Mussolini: L'idea statale; Fascism As I Have Seen It.* London: Nott, 1935; New York: Liveright, 1936.

———, trans. *The Classic Anthology Defined by Confucius.* Cambridge, Mass.: Harvard University Press, 1954; London: Faber and Faber, 1955.

Pratt, William. *The Fugitive Poets: Modern Southern Poetry in Perspective.* New York: Dutton, 1965.

———. *The Imagist Poem: Modern Poetry in Miniature.* New York: Dutton, 1963.

Priestley, J. B. *Literature and Western Man.* London: Heinemann, 1960; New York: Harper, 1960.

Ransom, John Crowe. *Poems and Essays.* New York: Vintage, 1955.

———. *Selected Poems.* New York: Knopf, 1945; London: Eyre and Spottiswoode, 1947.

Read, Herbert. Preface to *The Collected Poems of Sidney Keyes.* New York: Holt, 1947.

Robinson, Edwin Arlington. *Captain Craig: A Book of Poems.* Boston: Houghton Mifflin, 1902; London: Watt, 1902.

———. *The Children of the Night: A Book of Poems.* Boston: Badger, 1897.

———. *Collected Poems.* New York: Macmillan, 1921; London: Palmer, 1922.

———. *Selected Poems.* Ed. Morton Dauwen Zabel; intro. by James Dickey. New York: Macmillan, 1965.

———. *The Torrent and the Night Before.* [Cambridge, Mass.: Riverside Press] privately printed, 1896.

———. *The Town Down the River: A Book of Poems.* New York: Scribner, 1910.

———. *Tristram.* New York: Macmillan, 1927; London: Gollancz, 1928.

Ruggles, Eleanor. *Gerard Manley Hopkins: A Life.* New York: Norton, 1944; London: John Lane, 1947.

Russell, Bertrand. *History of Western Philosophy.* New York: Simon and Schuster, 1945; London: Allen and Unwin, 1946.

Scott, Winfield Townley. *Exiles and Fabrications.* New York: Doubleday, 1961.

Smith, Chard Powers. *Where the Light Falls: A Portrait of Edwin Arlington Robinson.* New York: Macmillan, 1965; London: Collier-Macmillan, 1965.

Spengler, Oswald. *The Decline of the West.* Ed. and trans. Charles Francis Atkinson. London: Allen and Unwin, 1922; New York: Knopf, 1926.

Squires, Radcliffe. *The Major Themes of Robert Frost.* Ann Arbor: University of Michigan Press, 1963.

Stock, Noel. *The Life of Ezra Pound.* New York: Pantheon, 1970; London: Routledge and Paul, 1970.

———. *Reading the Cantos: A Study of Meaning in Ezra Pound.* New York: Pantheon, 1967; London: Routledge and K. Paul, 1967.

Swift, Jonathan. *Prose Writings of Jonathan Swift.* Oxford: Blackwell, 1962–1968.

Tate, Allen. "Emily Dickinson." In *Collected Essays.* Denver, Colo.: Swallow, 1959.

———. *The Swimmers and Other Selected Poems.* London: Oxford University Press, 1970; New York: Scribner, 1971.

Tennyson, Alfred Tennyson, Baron. *Idylls of the King.* London: Moxon, 1859; Boston: Ticknor and Fields, 1859.

Thomas, Dylan. *Adventures in the Skin Trade and Other Stories.* Norfolk, Conn.: New Directions, 1955; London: Putnam, 1955.

———. *Collected Poems: 1934–1952.* London: Dent, 1952. Published in the U.S. as *The Collected Poems of Dylan Thomas.* Norfolk, Conn.: New Directions, 1953.

———. *Under Milk Wood: A Play for Voices.* London: Dent, 1954; [New York]: New Directions, 1954.

Thomas, Dylan, and Vernon Phillips Watkins. *Letters to Vernon Watkins.* London: Dent, 1957; New York: New Directions, 1957.

Thompson, Lawrance. *Robert Frost: The Early Years, 1874–1915.* New York: Holt, Rinehart and Winston, 1966; London: Cape, 1967.

———. *Robert Frost: The Years of Triumph, 1915–1938.* New York: Holt, Rinehart and Winston, 1970; London: Cape, 1971.

Van Doren, Mark. *Collected and New Poems, 1924–1963.* New York: Hill and Wang, 1963.

———. *The Happy Critic, and Other Essays.* New York: Hill and Wang, 1961; Edinburgh: Oliver and Boyd, 1962.

———. *John Dryden: A Study of His Poetry.* New York: Holt, 1946. Originally published as *The Poetry of John Dryden.* New York: Harcourt, Brace and Howe, 1920; Cambridge, U.K.: Fraser/The Minority Press, 1931.

———. *Narrative Poems.* New York: Hill and Wang, 1964.

———. *New Poems.* New York: Sloane, 1948.

———. *The Noble Voice: A Study of Ten Great Poems.* New York: Holt, 1946.

————. *Shakespeare.* New York: Holt, 1939.

Van Druten, John. *I Am a Camera: A Play in Three Acts.* Adapted From the Short Stories of Christopher Isherwood. New York: Random House, 1952; London: Gollancz, 1954.

Wagenknecht, Edward, ed. *Six Novels of the Supernatural.* New York: Viking, 1944.

Warren, Austin. *Rage for Order: Essays in Criticism.* Chicago: University of Chicago Press, 1948.

Warren, Robert Penn. *Selected Poems, 1923–1943.* New York: Harcourt, Brace, 1944; London: Fortune, 1952.

Whicher, George Frisbie. *This Was a Poet: A Critical Biography of Emily Dickinson.* New York and London: Scribner, 1938.

Wing, George. *Hardy.* Edinburgh: Oliver and Boyd, 1963; New York: Barnes and Noble, 1963.

Winters, Yvor. *Edwin Arlington Robinson.* Norfolk, Conn.: New Directions, 1946. Rev. ed., New York: New Directions, 1971.

————. "Robert Frost: Or, the Spiritual Drifter as Poet." *Sewanee Review* 56 (August 1948): 564–96.

Yeats, William Butler. *Collected Plays.* London: Macmillan, 1934; New York: Macmillan, 1935.

————. *Collected Poems.* London: Macmillan, 1933; New York: Macmillan, 1933.

————. *The Oxford Book of Modern Verse.* Oxford: Clarendon Press, 1936; New York: Oxford University Press, 1936.

PERMISSIONS

"The Equilibrists," "Judith of Bethulia," and "Antique Harvesters" from *Selected Poems, Third Edition, Revised and Enlarged,* by John Crowe Ransom, © 1924, 1927 by Alfred A. Knopf, Inc. and renewed 1952, 1955 by John Crowe Ransom. Used by permission of Alfred A. Knopf, a division of Random House, Inc.

"The Equilibrists," "Judith of Bethulia," and "Antique Harvesters" from *Selected Poems,* by John Crowe Ransom, © 1991. Also reprinted with the kind permission of Carcanet Press Limited.

"Aeneas at Washington" from *Collected Poems* by Allen Tate. Copyright © 1977 by Allen Tate. Reprinted by permission of Farrar, Straus and Giroux, LLC.

"Fern Hill" by Dylan Thomas, from *The Poems of Dylan Thomas,* copyright © 1945 by The Trustees for the Copyrights of Dylan Thomas. Used by permission of New Directions Publishing Corporation.

"Hunchback in the Park" by Dylan Thomas, from *The Poems of Dylan Thomas,* copyright © 1943 by New Directions Publishing Corporation. Used by permission of New Directions Publishing Corporation.

"Fern Hill" and "Hunchback in the Park" from *Collected Poems* by Dylan Thomas, Dent, with permission by David Higham Associates Limited.

"All Souls' Night," "Two Songs from a Play," and "Long-legged Fly" by William Butler Yeats. Reprinted by permission of A. P. Watt on behalf of Michael B. Yeats.

"Two Songs from a Play" and "All Souls' Night" reprinted with the permission of Scribner, an imprint of Simon & Schuster Adult Publishing Group, from *The Collected Works of W. B. Yeats, Volume 1, The Poems, Revised,* edited by Richard J. Finneran. Copyright © 1928 by The Macmillan Company; copyright renewed © 1956 by Georgie Yeats.

"Long-legged Fly" reprinted with the permission of Scribner, an imprint of Simon & Schuster Adult Publishing Group, from *The Collected Works of W. B. Yeats, Volume 1, The Poems, Revised,* edited by Richard J. Finneran. Copyright © 1940 by Georgie Yeats; copyright renewed © 1968 by Bertha Georgie Yeats, Michael Butler Yeats, and Anne Yeats.

Index

ML

SDY